STEPHEN MINISTER

CHRIST CARING • FOR PEOPLE • THROUGH PEOPLE

TRAINING MANUAL
VOLUME 1

EXECUTIVE EDITOR

Joel P. Bretscher

WRITING AND EDITING TEAM

Isaac B. Akers • Julie G. Bode • Stephen B. Glynn

Kenneth C. Haugk • Pamela Y. Montgomery • Robert A. Musser

Rachel L. Remington • Justin M. Schlueter • Janine L. Ushe

DESIGN TEAM LEADER

Kirk A. Geno

Stephen Ministries • St. Louis, Missouri

Stephen Minister Training Manual, Volume 1 (Also known as the *Stephen Ministry Training Manual* or *Stephen Series Training Manual*)

ISBN: 978-1-930445-09-3

2045 Innerbelt Business Center Drive
St. Louis, MO 63114-5765
United States of America

The Story of Stephen Ministry

Easter was a few days away. Spring had long since blown away the last traces of winter in St. Louis, Missouri, but the young pastor standing underneath the hospital awning could barely enjoy the warm breeze stirring the nearby trees. He'd just finished visiting the last of a number of congregation members in the hospital, and his mind was already racing ahead to the unfinished sermon for the next day's service waiting on his desk at home. As he made his way through the parking lot toward his car, one thought passed through his exhausted mind, before it was quickly pushed out by the hectic collection of responsibilities that made up his schedule for the rest of the week.

This is really tough. I need help caring for all these people.

Later that year as the rainy autumn swept in, the same pastor found himself sitting in a café with two seminary students who wanted to intern in his congregation because they knew he was also a clinical psychologist. As they talked about the difficulties of providing pastoral care to everyone who needed it, they came up with an idea that would eventually grow into a ministry spanning the globe: *What if we trained laypeople to do one-to-one, distinctively Christian caring ministry with those going through difficult times in life?*

That was where Stephen Ministry began.

The first class of Stephen Ministers in Dr. Kenneth Haugk's congregation had nine people in it. They were folks like you'd find in any church. A secretary. A teacher. A student. A hairdresser. A business owner. After they were trained, commissioned, and began their ministry, those Stephen Ministers saw the power of what they were doing—of the difference they were making in the lives of those they cared for—and insisted that Dr. Haugk share the ministry with other congregations.

So in 1975, Dr. Haugk and his wife, Joan, herself a psychiatric nurse and clinical social worker, founded Stephen Ministries St. Louis, the non-profit educational organization that would eventually bring the Stephen Ministry system of lay caring to thousands of congregations around the world, see over a half-million laypeople become Stephen Ministers, and enable care for millions of people inside and outside the church.

The Meaning of the Stephen Ministry Logo

The Stephen Ministry logo signifies that we are all broken people and it is only through the cross of Jesus that we can be made whole.

To this day, Stephen Ministry continues to spread to more congregations every year, led by people with a heart for caring ministry and a vision for expanding their congregations' pastoral care—for bringing Christ's healing love to those facing life's many challenges. And all the while, these congregations are constantly equipping new Stephen Ministers to listen, offer a caring presence, and provide emotional and spiritual support.

As you begin your Stephen Minister training, you are following in the footsteps of those Stephen Ministers who have come before you, entering into a rich tradition of high-quality, lay Christian care that will make a profound difference for you and those for whom you care. In so doing, you will make your own contribution to a ministry that truly changes lives.

The story of Stephen Ministry continues with you.

The *Stephen Minister Online Library*

Along with the *Stephen Minister Training Manual,* Stephen Ministers have access to an extensive set of additional resources: the ***Stephen Minister Online Library.***

This library, maintained and periodically updated with new content by Stephen Ministries St. Louis, includes:

- Information and educational material related to the topics covered in Stephen Minister training

- Ideas for ministry resources to use in your Stephen Ministry caring relationships or personal ministry

- Essential tools for Stephen Ministry Small Group Peer Supervision

- More items to enhance your caring ministry

We encourage you to access these resources for ongoing growth and support of your ministry.

How to Access the *Stephen Minister Online Library*

Use the following steps to log in to the *Stephen Minister Online Library* for the first time:

1. Go to stephenministries.org/library.

2. On this page, you'll have the option to log in with an existing account or create an account.

3. Follow the instructions on the page and, when prompted, enter this one-time access code:

> **J9X32Y**

You can return to the *Stephen Minister Online Library* anytime by visiting stephenministries. org/library and logging in.

For help accessing the *Stephen Minister Online Library,* contact the Customer Service Department of Stephen Ministries St. Louis at (314) 428-2600, Monday–Friday, 8 A.M.–5 P.M. Central Time.

Table of Contents

Volume 1

Your Stephen Minister Training Prayer Partner

PRAYER PARTNER SUGGESTIONS

Prayer partners can do together as much or as little as they desire. Here are some possibilities.

- Pray privately for each other.

- Share prayer concerns (in person or over the phone) once a week and pray for each other privately.

- Meet regularly to share prayer concerns and pray for each other.

- Talk regularly by phone to share prayer concerns and pray for each other over the phone.

- Practice a spiritual discipline, such as Bible study, together (see "Spiritual Practices That Strengthen Our Connection to Christ" on pages 11–18 of your *Stephen Minister Training Manual).*

The Person of the Caregiver

Module 1 | Presentation Outline

In all my prayers for all of you, I always pray with joy because of your partnership in the gospel from the first day until now, being confident of this, that he who began a good work in you will carry it on to completion until the day of Christ Jesus.
Philippians 1:4–6

 Devotion: Partnership in the Gospel

I. First Steps

A. Who You Are

B. Who You Will Become as a Stephen Minister

II. The Caregiver's Compass

A. The Meaning of the Caregiver's Compass

FOCUS NOTE 1

The Caregiver's Compass

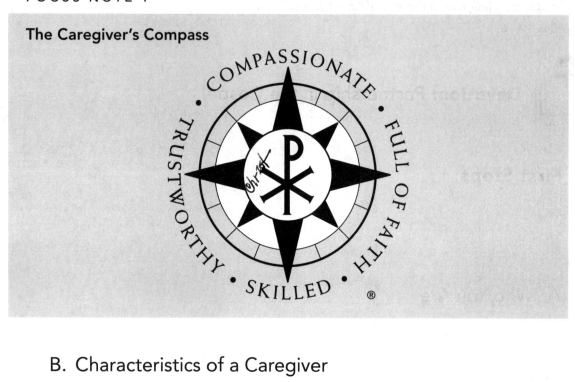

B. Characteristics of a Caregiver

FOCUS NOTE 2

Instructions for Characteristics of a Caregiver Activity

1. Choose a facilitator who will guide your group through this activity. This person needs to have a way to keep track of time.

2. In 2 minutes, brainstorm as many one-word or one-sentence answers as you can to question 1. Write your group's ideas in the spaces provided in this Focus Note.

3. At the end of 2 minutes, move immediately to question 2. Do the same for all five questions, spending 2 minutes on each one and writing the group's ideas in the spaces provided.

4. After each group has finished responding to these questions, you'll share your thoughts with the whole class and hear what others in the class have come up with.

1. What does it mean for a Stephen Minister to be *compassionate?*

No-Judgement Listening
To Share Love&Kindness
Acceptance   Share the Love of Christ
         S. to Experiencing

2. What does it mean for a Stephen Minister to be *full of faith?*

Total depaned on Christ   Full of faith
Not worried
Trusting IN Christ

3. What does it mean for a Stephen Minister to be *skilled?*

Listen
Know what you Are doing
No two people Are not Aw Al

4. What does it mean for a Stephen Minister to be *trustworthy?*

Private Info   Ensurane
Realible   To be healed
Not going to use them

5. How do Stephen Ministers keep *Jesus at the center* of their caring relationships?

Prayer   Non-believer
Word!
Talk About Jesus

FOCUS NOTE 3

Self-Evaluation

For each of the five characteristics of a caregiver, mark on the scale where you believe you are right now. Then write under each scale one way you may need to grow in that particular characteristic.

1. Compassionate

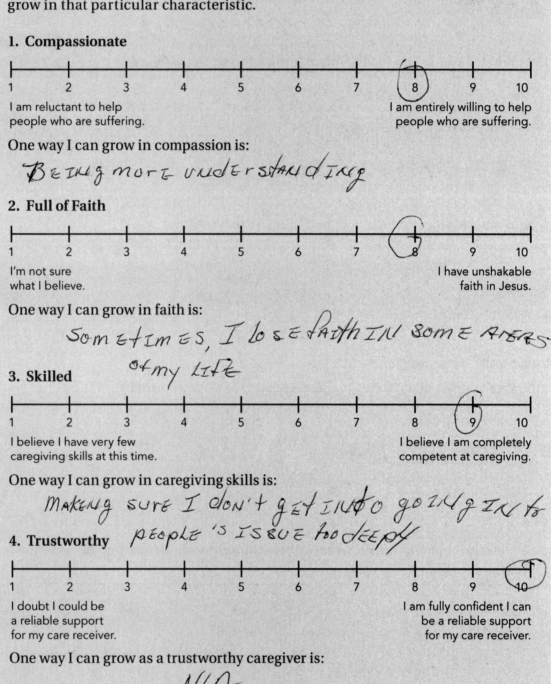

| 1 | 2 | 3 | 4 | 5 | 6 | 7 | 8 | 9 | 10 |

I am reluctant to help
people who are suffering.

I am entirely willing to help
people who are suffering.

One way I can grow in compassion is:

Being more understanding

2. Full of Faith

| 1 | 2 | 3 | 4 | 5 | 6 | 7 | 8 | 9 | 10 |

I'm not sure
what I believe.

I have unshakable
faith in Jesus.

One way I can grow in faith is:

Sometimes, I lose faith in some areas of my life

3. Skilled

| 1 | 2 | 3 | 4 | 5 | 6 | 7 | 8 | 9 | 10 |

I believe I have very few
caregiving skills at this time.

I believe I am completely
competent at caregiving.

One way I can grow in caregiving skills is:

Making sure I don't get into going into people's issue too deeply

4. Trustworthy

| 1 | 2 | 3 | 4 | 5 | 6 | 7 | 8 | 9 | 10 |

I doubt I could be
a reliable support
for my care receiver.

I am fully confident I can
be a reliable support
for my care receiver.

One way I can grow as a trustworthy caregiver is:

N/A

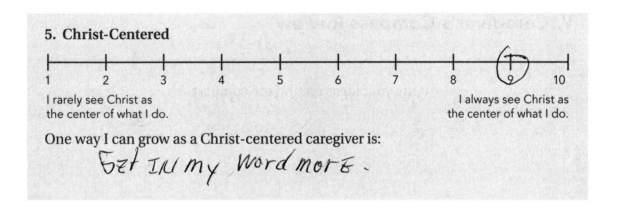

5. Christ-Centered

| 1 | 2 | 3 | 4 | 5 | 6 | 7 | 8 | 9 | 10 |

I rarely see Christ as
the center of what I do.

I always see Christ as
the center of what I do.

One way I can grow as a Christ-centered caregiver is:

Get IN my Word more.

III. Growing as Caregivers

A. Stephen Minister Training

B. Spiritual Practices for Spiritual Growth

IV. The Relationship-Building Activity

V. Caregiver's Compass Review

Write your ideas around the compass.

VI. Looking Ahead

Appendix A

Module 1

Well Done, Good and Faithful Servant

By Joel Bretscher

A good way to understand what it's like to serve as a Stephen Minister is to read an account of an actual caring relationship. Although each Stephen Ministry relationship is different, the Stephen Minister's caring process, personal growth, and connection with the care receiver in this story reflect the experiences of hundreds of thousands of Stephen Ministers over the years.

As I made my way up the sidewalk to his door, I whispered a prayer: "Please, God, let me find something I have in common with this man to talk about."

At the time, I was in my 20s and a newly trained Stephen Minister in my church in Arizona. I thought I might be paired with another young adult. However, when I met with the Referrals Coordinator[1] for our congregation's Stephen Ministry, she said, "The pastor and I have matched you with an 82-year-old man who was widowed 20 years ago and stopped attending church at that time. He visited our church recently and talked with our pastor afterward. He said he had been angry at the church and at God for a long time, but he figured it was time to make peace with both. The pastor told him about Stephen Ministry, and the man said he'd be open to having a Stephen Minister."

I called Henry (I have changed his name to preserve confidentiality[2]) to introduce myself and set up our first meeting. And that's how, a few days later, I found myself walking up to his front door, wondering what I could say and how I might help. As I stepped onto the porch, I noticed through the front window that he was watching a baseball game. "Baseball! We both like baseball," I thought, breathing a sigh of relief as I realized that God had given me the icebreaker I needed.

Building Trust

Baseball worked well as a conversation starter, and Henry and I began building a

---

1 The Referrals Coordinator is the Stephen Leader who oversees the process of identifying people in need of care and matching them with Stephen Ministers.

2 Confidentiality, a cornerstone of Stephen Ministry, is covered in depth in module 9.

friendship during that first visit.[3] Despite our age difference, we had a number of things in common. In addition to liking baseball, we were both from large families in small Midwestern towns, and we both went into that first meeting feeling a similar level of awkwardness. We spent that first caring visit getting to know each other, and then we decided to meet in his home for about an hour every Thursday evening.

We met regularly throughout the summer, and gradually Henry began to open up to me. I vividly remember one visit, as we were looking through his picture albums, when I asked him to tell me more about his wife. He began to share story after story about how they met, their life together, and how much they'd loved each other. He touched briefly on her death and his loneliness but seemed not to want to dwell on it. I just let him talk as I listened.

Difficulty Going Deeper

As summer turned to autumn, I began to feel a little frustrated. Henry and I were very good at small talk and occasionally broached deeper issues, but he never seemed to want to pursue them much. It didn't help that we were both brought up with the notion that we should not be emotional or talk about feelings.

I shared my frustrations with the Stephen Ministers in my Supervision Group.[4] They

---

3 Module 17, "How to Make a First Caring Visit," equips Stephen Ministers to be prepared and confident when they visit their care receivers for the first time.

4 Stephen Ministers meet twice monthly for Small Group Peer Supervision, where they offer support, guidance, and accountability to each other in their caring relationships. Stephen Ministers preserve confidentiality during supervision by not using names or any identifying details. Supervision discussions focus on the caring relationship, not on the care receiver. Supervision is covered in module 16.

encouraged me and reminded me to keep focused on the process of building the relationship, not the results of getting my care receiver to talk about deeper issues. "Be patient," they said. "It's okay to move slowly. God brought the two of you together, and God is right there with you in every caring visit." Their support helped me immensely.

Another thing that helped was that, from time to time, I'd tell Henry about the big event going on in my life at the time: preparation for my upcoming wedding in Indiana. As it turned out, this was the topic God used to prompt Henry to explore deeper issues. As my wedding day approached, we talked more and more about marriage, wives, and relationships, and our relationship progressed to a deeper level.

The Crisis

The week before I was to leave for my wedding, Henry surprised me by asking to come to church with me. But when I arrived to pick him up on Sunday morning, he met me at the door in his pajamas, saying he felt under the weather and couldn't go. I said I was sorry he didn't feel well and I'd call later to see how he was doing.

When I called that afternoon, I got no answer. I called again that evening—and again the next morning—still no response. I started to worry, so I drove to his house during my lunch break. His car was in the driveway, but no one was home. I left a note on the door with my phone number, asking him to call.

That evening Henry called me—from the hospital. He had suffered a heart attack. He had wanted to call me sooner but wasn't able to remember my phone number. His neighbor had found my note and relayed the information to Henry.

I immediately went to see Henry and visited him several times over the next few days.[5] The time we'd spent building trust and deepening our relationship—as well as everything I'd learned in my Stephen Minister training—began to bear fruit as Henry willingly dove into all the deep issues. We talked about life and death, about Jesus and salvation. He appreciated it when I held his hand, prayed aloud with him, and read psalms.

Henry steadily improved and was scheduled to go home the day after I left for my wedding. The evening before I left, he gave me some fatherly advice I will never forget: "Always, *always* love your wife, and never, *ever* take her for granted." We both had tears in our eyes as we embraced.

Surgery and Intensive Care

I called Henry from Indiana twice that week. He was eager to see me when I returned, and he promised he would go to church with my wife and me the first Sunday we were back. However, the day after we returned, he was readmitted to the hospital for bypass surgery.

This setback caught everyone by surprise. Henry did not like being in a hospital because it reminded him of his wife's death. The prospect of surgery and a stay in intensive care also troubled him. Henry wasn't the only one feeling anxious. I too was intimidated by the situation, the surroundings, and the postsurgical visits in intensive

---

5 A Stephen Minister typically meets with his or her care receiver once a week for about an hour. In crisis situations, a Stephen Minister may choose to visit more often to provide extra care and support.

care. It was my first time caring for someone in such circumstances.

Henry's son had flown into town for the surgery, and Henry introduced him to me. Our pastor came to visit Henry the night before surgery, and we all prayed together.

The surgery went fairly well. The doctors expected that Henry would be in intensive care for four or five days and then in the hospital another week. I resolved to visit him each of those days.

Henry was weak and couldn't talk much when I visited. I did a little bit of talking, but mostly I held his hand. I read psalms to him and prayed with him. His smile conveyed his appreciation as he nodded his head and squeezed my hand. I checked in with our pastor each day to let him know how Henry was doing. Given the size of our congregation, he wasn't able to visit Henry each day and was glad I could do so.

Henry Goes Home

I went to see Henry on his last scheduled day in intensive care to celebrate his progress and pending move to a regular hospital room, but I was startled to find someone else in that bed. I went to the nurses' station and asked, "Where's Henry?" She reviewed her paperwork and asked, "Are you a relative?" "No," I said, "I'm a very good friend from his church." She paused for a moment and then said, "I'm sorry, but Henry died this morning."

I left the hospital in a daze. My wife, Della, was waiting for me in the car since we had planned to go shopping after the visit. She saw in my face what had happened. She hugged me and asked, "Do you want to go home?" But I knew I couldn't just sit around at home; I had to do something active.

Walking around at the mall, I wandered into a Christian bookstore. Behind the register was a large painting of a man standing at the gates of heaven, receiving a welcoming embrace from Jesus. Below it were the words, "Well done, good and faithful servant." In that moment, I was able to smile because I knew that Henry was home.

Angels Ministering

Henry's funeral was two days later. Only a handful of people were there—Henry's son and daughter-in-law, a neighbor, a couple of friends, the pastor, and me. Riding home after the funeral, my pastor thanked me for what I had done. "You know, you made a big difference in Henry's life," he said. "I think this relationship has had an impact on your faith and who you are as well."

Coincidentally, my Stephen Ministry Supervision Group met the evening of Henry's funeral. I told them my care receiver had died. What happened next I can only describe with words from Matthew 4:11—". . . and the angels came and ministered to him." That night my tears became their tears, my sorrows their sorrows, my joys their joys.

Jesus' Promise Becomes Real

What does Stephen Ministry mean to me? It means growth. It means life. It means a faith that is practiced in giving care to others. Stephen Ministry made a difference in Henry's walk with Jesus—and in my own walk as I gave care in Jesus' name. Stephen Ministry offered me a way to be the personal presence

of Christ to Henry during his time of greatest need. It wasn't always clear at the time, but looking back, I now can see Christ was there with Henry and me every step of the way. Jesus' promise, "Where two or three are gathered, there I am also" (Matthew 18:20), became real to us in that relationship, and Christ's presence transformed us both.

ABOUT THE AUTHOR

Joel Bretscher serves as Program Director at Stephen Ministries. Prior to moving to St. Louis in 1995 to join the Stephen Ministries staff, he trained and served as a Stephen Minister at a church in Phoenix, Arizona.

Appendix B

Module 1

Spiritual Practices That Strengthen Our Connection to Christ

Stephen Ministry is a distinctively Christian ministry based on the biblical principle that Christ cares for people through people. Over the course of their training and service, many Stephen Ministers enjoy learning ways to strengthen their spiritual connection with Christ, who supports and sustains them. This appendix describes a number of spiritual practices that can help Stephen Ministers experience the transforming power of Christ in their own lives, which in turn will help them more effectively share the love and compassion of Jesus with their care receivers.

Christ Is the Source of Transformation and Ministry

Christ is the source of the hope and healing that Stephen Ministers offer their care receivers, so it's essential that Stephen Ministers stay connected to Jesus. Often, as they prepare for and participate in connecting care receivers to God's healing love, Stephen Ministers are surprised by the transformation and healing that occur in their own lives.

In your Stephen Minister training, you'll learn the practical skills necessary to provide effective care for people who are hurting.

In addition, you'll learn about being a Christ-centered caregiver and how to remain connected to Christ as he brings his care, compassion, and healing to care receivers through you.

Focus Note A shows how Jesus described the importance of remaining connected to him while doing ministry.

FOCUS NOTE A

Remaining Connected to Jesus

Jesus said, "Abide in me as I abide in you. Just as the branch cannot bear fruit by itself unless it abides in the vine, neither can you unless you abide in me. I am the vine, you are the branches. Those who abide in me and I in them bear much fruit, because apart from me you can do nothing" (John 15:4–5 NRSV).

God wants us to "abide in Christ" so that our ministry remains rooted and grounded in him. Apart from Christ, we can do nothing; with Christ, our caring ministry can bear much fruit. We are called to abide.

The question, then, is *how* do we abide in Christ? Focus Note B shows how theologian N.T. Wright describes abiding as involving two kinds of spiritual practices: community and private.

FOCUS NOTE B

How Do We Abide in Christ?

How do we "remain" in him? What does it look like in practice? . . . We must remain in the community that knows and loves him and celebrates him as its Lord. There is no such thing as a solitary Christian. We can't "go it alone." But we must also remain as people of prayer and worship in our own intimate, private lives. We must make sure to be in touch, in tune, with Jesus, knowing him and being known by him.[1]

Stephen Ministers looking to strengthen their connection with Jesus participate in those community and private spiritual practices that help them abide in Christ. When they faithfully engage in such practices, they experience God's blessings as he keeps them attentive and connected to Jesus.

Following are a number of spiritual practices, both community and private, that can help Stephen Ministers experience the transforming power of Christ and prepare for ministry.

Community Spiritual Practices

Some of the community spiritual practices that can help Stephen Ministers abide in Christ include regular participation in:

- worship;

- communion and other Christian sacraments or ordinances; and

- Christian fellowship.

Each of these community practices has a strong tradition in the Christian church and is often a fundamental part of congregational life.

Worship

For Stephen Ministers and anyone who wants to maintain and strengthen his or her connection with Christ, worship as a community is essential. Throughout Scripture, God's people are called to join together and lift their praises to God, as in Psalm 95:1–7a in Focus Note C.

FOCUS NOTE C

A Call to Worship: Psalm 95:1–7a

Come, let us sing for joy to the LORD;
let us shout aloud to the Rock of our salvation.

Let us come before him with thanksgiving and extol him with music and song.

For the LORD is the great God,
the great King above all gods.

In his hand are the depths of the earth,
and the mountain peaks belong to him.

The sea is his, for he made it,
and his hands formed the dry land.

Come, let us bow down in worship,
let us kneel before the LORD our Maker;

for he is our God
and we are the people of his pasture,
the flock under his care.

1 N.T. Wright, *John for Everyone, Part Two* (Louisville, KY: Westminster John Knox Press, 2004), 71.

We worship God together because God is worthy of our worship and because God instructs us to do so.

Community worship is an opportunity to join with others in expressing our thoughts and feelings about God the Father, Son, and Holy Spirit through liturgy, community prayer, and "psalms, hymns and spiritual songs" (Ephesians 5:19). By doing so, we give God honor and glory and strengthen one another in faith, hope, and love.

Worship is also an opportunity to hear God's word proclaimed through reading the Bible, preaching, and teaching. As we listen to Scripture, we are conscious of being in relationship with a God who speaks to his people. God's Word received into our lives brings about transformation and healing.

For many people, worship helps them to feel connected to something much larger than themselves. They experience a sense of awe, wonder, and joy as they gather for worship, especially as they consider the vast numbers of people around the world and throughout history who have engaged in similar practices, each worshiping God in his or her own language and out of his or her own experiences. Participating in worship helps people join countless others in experiencing the presence of Christ.

Since the early days of the church, worship with a community of believers has been part of the foundation of Christian life and ministry, and it's important that Stephen Ministers remain connected to God and his people in this way.

Communion and Other Sacraments or Ordinances

Another way that Stephen Ministers seek to remain in Christ is through observing the sacraments or ordinances of the church. The most universal of these spiritual practices is what the Apostle Paul called the Lord's Supper (1 Corinthians 11:17–26), also called Holy Communion or the Eucharist.

This observance is a direct response to Christ's command during the Last Supper he shared with his disciples before the crucifixion. Paul's account is in Focus Note D.

FOCUS NOTE D

The Last Supper: 1 Corinthians 11:23–26

For I received from the Lord what I also passed on to you: The Lord Jesus, on the night he was betrayed, took bread, and when he had given thanks, he broke it and said, "This is my body, which is for you; do this in remembrance of me." In the same way, after supper he took the cup, saying, "This cup is the new covenant in my blood; do this, whenever you drink it, in remembrance of me." For whenever you eat this bread and drink this cup, you proclaim the Lord's death until he comes.

While various Christian denominations understand communion in different ways, all agree that its observance was commanded by the Lord and that, as Christians participate in it, Christ strengthens our connection to him. Stephen Ministers regularly say they feel encouraged and empowered by observing communion, as it strengthens their faith in preparation to serve others.

Christian Fellowship

Another community spiritual practice that helps Stephen Ministers remain connected to Christ is the experience of Christian fellowship. An example of Christian fellowship is described in Focus Note E.

FOCUS NOTE E

Christian Fellowship: Acts 2:42–47

They devoted themselves to the apostles' teaching and to the fellowship, to the breaking of bread and to prayer. Everyone was filled with awe, and many wonders and miraculous signs were done by the apostles. All the believers were together and had everything in common. Selling their possessions and goods, they gave to anyone as he had need. Every day they continued to meet together in the temple courts. They broke bread in their homes and ate together with glad and sincere hearts, praising God and enjoying the favor of all the people. And the Lord added to their number daily those who were being saved.

The Greek word often translated as "fellowship," *koinonia,* also encompasses many other ideas: "to hold something in common," "to be in partnership with," "to be connected with," "to participate in something together," and "to share." Take another look at Focus Note E with all these meanings of koinonia in mind.

Focus Note F lists the ways in which Christians in the early church had koinonia.

FOCUS NOTE F

Examples of Koinonia in the Early Church

- Learning together
- Eating together
- Praying together
- Witnessing to Jesus' life, death, and resurrection together
- Sharing material goods with each other
- Providing for others' needs
- Meeting together regularly
- Sharing communion together
- Praising God together
- Reaching out to others with Christ's love

As you can see, Christians in the early church shared time, resources, care, and love for God and each other. They didn't try to be lone wolves; they knew they needed one another to be God's people and to truly love. They knew that Jesus was with them in the person of their sisters and brothers in Christ.

There are a variety of ways to find and experience Christian fellowship, but one way that works well for many people is participating in a small group. Small groups gather regularly for prayer, worship, Bible study, and sharing of each person's faith journey. Some groups may regularly share meals or participate in missional service together.

Christian fellowship is an important way that people in the church experience Christ's presence, as they learn to see Jesus at work in and through their brothers and sisters. Stephen Ministers find that participating in Christian community strengthens their relationship with Christ and supports them in their ongoing ministry.

Private Spiritual Practices

In addition to community spiritual practices, there are a number of private spiritual practices that can help Stephen Ministers abide in Christ. Some of the most common include regular participation in:

- reading for study and reflection;
- prayer; and
- meditation on Scripture.

Each of these practices can provide you with additional strength and encouragement in your ministry.

Reading for Study and Reflection

Reading Scripture, daily devotions, Christian literature, and material on the spiritual aspects of caring for others can be useful and helpful in your personal growth as well as your growth as a caregiver.

Many people find that reading and studying Scripture connects them to Christ in ways that help them to grow spiritually and empower them to minister more effectively to their care receivers. You might choose a daily Bible reading guide that takes you through part or all of the Bible in a certain amount of time, or you may find some other plan that works for you. There are also numerous Bible apps available to serve as a guide through Scripture.

There are many other books that can help people grow spiritually. Some daily devotional books concisely summarize a spiritual truth for each day. Other books explore in detail the life of Jesus, particular spiritual disciplines, the practices of Christians who've gone before us, discipleship, or the truths we believe. As you look for books to read and reflect on, it may help to get suggestions from others, including your pastor, Stephen Leaders, other Stephen Ministers, or Christian friends.

Prayer

Another private spiritual practice helpful for Stephen Ministers is prayer. Walter Wangerin, Jr., in his book *Whole Prayer,* suggests that prayer is communication that includes four acts, as explained in Focus Note G.

FOCUS NOTE G

Wangerin on Prayer

Simply, *prayer is communication.*

We talk *with* God, not just *to* him. God talks with us too, causing a circle to be whole and closed between us.

Complexly, the complete prayer is made up of four acts, four discrete parts, two of which are ours, two of which are God's. The parts may seem separated one from another by time or by the different nature of the acts; yet often all four acts occur in such swift succession that the complete prayer is revealed as a single, unbroken event. And so it is. It is communication:

—First, we speak,

—while, second, God listens.

—Third, God speaks,

—while, fourth, we listen.

If we initiate the first act, God will respond with the second. That is sure and certain. So is the third act absolutely certain to follow the first two, because God's love promises to speak to us by a Word.

But if we have never learned the fourth, if we are too impatient to perform the fourth act, too demanding and unsubmissive to watch and to wait upon the Lord, then we will never know that the second and the third acts have been accomplished. Without our truly listening, prayer will seem to have failed because communication, remaining incomplete, *did* in fact fail. The circle stayed broken, and love was left unknown.

Learn the circle. Trust in God to listen and to speak, and our own listening will follow as easily as the eyes of a child follow her father—in whom is all her good.[2]

Wangerin goes on to describe the many different ways God may speak to us, including scripture passages, sermons, corporate worship, devotions, friends, and everyday events. Prayer is like other forms of communication—it involves speaking and listening. Rather than just asking things of God, our communications with the Almighty should also involve hearing how God is responding to and speaking with us.

ACTS Prayers

People at times wonder what to focus on when praying. Although much about prayer depends on the individual and his or her unique circumstances, the acronym ACTS can offer helpful guidance for what to include:

Adoration—telling God the reasons why you love him and value his presence in your life.

Confession—acknowledging to God the ways you have fallen short in living a life that reflects Christ.

Thanksgiving—thanking God for all the good gifts he has given you, including mercy, grace, and love.

Supplication—asking God to address the issues and concerns that are on your heart, for yourself and for others.

As you pray, you might use this acronym as an outline for your conversation with God.

Guides to Prayer

Many people learn personal prayer through reading and using prayers from the Bible, particularly the book of Psalms, which has been called a school of prayer. Others have used guides such as *The Book of Common Prayer,* the *Daily Office,* or the *Liturgy of the Hours.* Still others have learned from the published prayers of other believers. A prayer from one classic work, *A Diary of Private Prayer* by John Baillie, is included in Focus Note H.

FOCUS NOTE H

A Prayer of John Baillie

Eternal Father of my soul, let my first thought today be of you, let my first impulse be to worship you, let my first word be your Name, let my first action be to kneel before you in prayer.

For your perfect wisdom and perfect goodness;

For the love you have for all people;

For the love you have for me;

For the great and mysterious opportunity of my life;

For your Spirit, who dwells in my heart;

---

2 Walter Wangerin, Jr., *Whole Prayer* (Grand Rapids, MI: Zondervan, 1998), 29.

For the seven gifts of your Spirit;

I praise and worship you, O Lord.

Yet when this morning prayer is finished, do not let me think that my worship is ended and spend the rest of the day forgetting you. Rather, from these quiet moments, let light and joy and power pour out and remain with me through every hour of this day.

May that light and joy and power:

Keep my thoughts pure;

Keep me gentle and truthful in all I say;

Keep me faithful and diligent in my work;

Keep me humble in my opinion of myself;

Keep me honorable and generous in my dealings with others;

Keep me loyal to every cherished memory of the past;

Keep me mindful of my eternal destiny as your child.

O God, you have been the refuge of your people through many generations; be my refuge in every moment and every need that I face today. Be my guide through all uncertainty and darkness. Be my guard against all that threatens my spiritual well-being. Be my strength in times of testing. Cheer my heart with your peace; through Jesus Christ my Lord. Amen.[3]

Meditation on Scripture

Christian meditation is the spiritual practice of listening for God's voice in Scripture. It involves focusing on a single truth or passage from the Bible, thinking deeply about how it relates to our lives, and allowing God to change us through our reflections and his grace.

Focus Note I shares Richard Foster's comments about various ways to meditate on Scripture.

FOCUS NOTE I

Foster on Meditating

The Bible uses two different Hebrew words . . . to convey the idea of meditation, and together they are used some fifty-eight times. These words have various meanings: listening to God's word, reflecting on God's works, rehearsing God's deeds, rumination on God's law, and more. In each case there is stress upon changed behavior as a result of our encounter with the living God.[4]

The purpose of meditating on Scripture is to let it affect not only our thinking but also our actions—to bring about life transformation. We meditate on Scripture because we know it's given for our benefit by someone who loves us and has our best interests at heart.

See in Focus Note J how Dietrich Bonhoeffer describes meditation as an act of receiving God's love.

FOCUS NOTE J

Bonhoeffer on Meditation

Just as you do not analyze the words of someone you love, but accept them as they

---

3 John Baillie, *A Diary of Private Prayer* (New York: Scribner, 2014), 3.

4 Richard J. Foster, *Celebration of Discipline*, rev. ed. (New York: Harper & Row, 1988), 15.

> are said to you, accept the Word of Scripture and ponder it in your heart, as Mary did. That is all. That is meditation.[5]

It's usually a good idea to set aside some time specifically for meditation; otherwise, distractions are likely to come up. When you meditate, seek out a place where you will be comfortable and undistracted. Read a little of the Bible passage or other material and think about it. Focus your attention on the content of your meditation, shutting out all other thoughts as best you can. It's all right if your mind wanders, especially at first; meditation takes practice. If you find that you've lost your focus, there's no need to feel bad about it. Simply direct your attention back to your meditation.

While you meditate, be open to God's presence. You will be joining a conversation already in progress, as God the Father, Jesus Christ, and the Holy Spirit are eternally engaged in a discourse of love into which you are admitted, embraced, and included. Participation in this communion is a unique Christian blessing.

Find the Practices That Work for You

You might choose to try out some of the spiritual practices listed in this appendix, as well as others that you learn about elsewhere. Find the spiritual practices that fit best for you, and then use them regularly to grow as a Christian and distinctively Christian caregiver.

---

5 Dietrich Bonhoeffer, *The Way to Freedom* (New York: Harper & Row, 1966), 59.

Feelings: Yours, Mine, and Ours

Module 2 | Pre-Class Reading

CONTENTS

Feelings Are God-Given

Our ability to experience feelings is a gift from God—it's a unique part of who we are as human beings. God doesn't want us to ignore or suppress our feelings, and we aren't expected as Christians to only feel happy and positive all the time. Rather, God wants us to recognize all our feelings and understand why they're present in our lives so we can handle them in the most beneficial ways possible.

Jesus Expressed Deep Feelings

Jesus demonstrated on many occasions the importance of having and expressing emotions.

For example, standing in front of the tomb of his friend Lazarus, Jesus broke into tears (John 11:35). The Greek word used to describe Jesus' crying, *dakruo*, focuses on the actual shedding of tears—in contrast to *klaio*, which describes the audible, public wailing common in expressions of grief at the time. This indicates that Jesus was not simply participating in a public display of sadness but was experiencing deep, genuine pain.

In addition, when Jesus had seen others expressing their grief moments earlier, it prompted intense feelings inside him (John 11:33). Two of the Greek words used in that verse, *embrimaomai* and *tarasso*, indicate that Jesus was feeling agitated and indignant. Some scholars think that Jesus may have been angry at death itself and perhaps anxious about his own impending death. Whatever his feelings, Jesus didn't keep them hidden.

The scene at Lazarus' tomb is just one example of Jesus as a man of deep feelings. Elsewhere, the Gospels describe times when Jesus showed compassion (including Matthew 9:36, 14:14, 15:32, and 20:34), anguish (Luke 22:44), anger (Mark 8:33), and joy (Luke 10:21). Jesus owned and expressed his feelings rather than holding them inside, and he invites us to do the same.

Feelings Can Help Us in Life

God has given us the capacity for feelings—pleasant, painful, and otherwise—to help us understand and live life in the best ways possible. For example, our emotions can help us recognize how our surroundings, interactions, and experiences are affecting us, in both positive and negative ways. They can show us how we're experiencing life and what we might need to address in order to experience life as God intended it. As we come to understand our feelings—and respond to them in productive ways—we can become more authentically the people God created us to be.

When we deal proactively and productively with our feelings, we can learn to choose words and actions that will bring hope and healing to others—and avoid words and actions that will cause ourselves and others pain. For example, when we realize we're feeling anger during a conversation with someone, it can remind us to be careful with our words so we don't say something we regret. Far from being something to ignore or avoid, God's gift of feelings can greatly enrich and help our lives.

Left Unattended, Feelings Can Cause Damage

Feelings that are adequately dealt with can help us respond to different situations in the best ways possible—but when feelings are left unattended, they can lead to problems in our attitudes and behaviors and cause real damage. For example, when we feed our anger toward someone rather than handling that anger in healthy ways, it can turn into an attitude of contempt or hatred, causing harm to the relationship and the people involved. That's why it's so important to recognize our difficult feelings, work through them, and seek to deal with them in the best ways possible.

Stephen Ministers Help Care Receivers Work through Feelings

Care receivers often encounter a wide range of difficult emotions, such as sadness, anger, fear, and despair—feelings they most likely wish they weren't experiencing. One of the ways Stephen Ministers support their care receivers is by helping them come to recognize and accept their feelings rather than ignoring, hiding, or suppressing them.

Stephen Ministers know that emotions are God-given and designed to help us. Based on that knowledge, they listen to care receivers and encourage them to share any and all feelings they may be experiencing, whether painful or pleasant. Giving care receivers the permission and opportunity to express and work through difficult feelings is a powerful way Stephen Ministers help them find hope and healing in the midst of their pain.

Seven Points about Feelings

Here are seven points Stephen Ministers need to keep in mind about feelings in order to help people experience, understand, and work through their feelings.

1. What Feelings Are Not

Sometimes people use the word *feel* when they aren't talking about feelings at all. They may say, "I feel . . ." but then describe something that isn't actually a feeling. A good place to start in understanding what feelings are is to look at what they are *not*—so Stephen Ministers can identify when their care receivers are expressing actual feelings and when they're not.

Feelings Are Not Opinions

People may describe their personal opinions by saying something like, "I feel he's the right person for the job" or "I feel we should choose another course of action." In both instances, the person is really expressing an opinion, so "I think" would fit better than "I feel."

Feelings Are Not Evaluations

Sometimes people may use the word *feel* when they're giving an evaluation. For example, when someone says, "I feel this restaurant is better than that one" or "I feel that this was not a wise choice," the person is expressing an evaluation, not a feeling. Whether or not someone's perspective is accurate, evaluations aren't the same as feelings.

Feelings Are Not Instructions or Commands

The word *feel* can be used to issue instructions or commands—for instance, "I feel like you'd better do the dishes," or "I feel you should get over here right now." Words like these may hint at feelings of frustration or impatience, but they aren't themselves feeling statements. It would be more accurate to say, "I'd like you to do the dishes."

Feelings Are Not Interpretations

People sometimes make statements like, "I feel that you're angry and that's why you're responding this way," or "I feel you're happy because of what happened earlier." Statements like these are *about* feelings, but they're actually interpretations of someone else's feelings, not expressions of the speaker's own emotions. In each case, "I think" would be more appropriate wording.

Feelings Are Not Something That Comes from the Head

Opinions, evaluations, instructions, and interpretations all have one point in common—they're thoughts that come from our *head*. Feelings, in contrast, come from the *heart*. Although feelings and thoughts can certainly influence each other, using the word *feel* to express thoughts confuses the issue. When you recognize the differences, you can help your care receiver get to his or her true feelings.

2. What Feelings Are

With a clear understanding of what feelings are not, we have a good foundation for looking at what feelings *are*.

Feelings Are Our Internal Responses to Life

Feelings are spontaneous internal responses that reflect our current experience of life. We may say, for instance:

- "I'm happy."
- "I'm uneasy."
- "I'm angry."

Responses like these indicate what we're *experiencing* in the moment—distinct from what we may be *thinking* or *believing* about the situation.

Feelings Are Personal

Feelings come from within us—from the heart. They're intrinsically personal, and they belong to us. No one can impose feelings on us or cause us to feel a certain way. Our feelings are ours, and we are responsible for them.

This means it's important for people to own their feelings. Even if we've been wronged by someone, for instance, it isn't accurate or helpful to say, "You make me angry." Although the person's actions may have affected us, they didn't make us feel the way we feel—our reaction to what they've done still belongs to us. It's better to say, "I feel angry because . . . ," or "I am angry because. . . ." When we own our feelings rather than blaming them on someone or something else, we can begin the process of working through those feelings.

Feelings Are Shaped by Our Unique Personality and Experiences

The feelings we may experience in any given situation are unique to us, shaped by our personality and past experiences. Two people encountering what appears to be the same situation may respond in two completely different ways; in fact, they may actually experience the situation differently.

For example, two people conversing at a party might have very different emotional responses—one person might feel happy and comfortable, enjoying the opportunity to relax and chat, while another might feel anxious and tense, hoping for the conversation to end quickly. Both people participated in the same conversation, but each had very different feelings about it, seeing it through the lens of a distinct personality.

3. Feelings Are Intended for Our Benefit

God gave us feelings for our benefit. Whether those feelings are pleasant, difficult, or a mix of the two, we can learn a lot about ourselves by paying attention to them.

- *Pleasant feelings* generally indicate a sense of well-being in one or more areas of life. Maybe we're feeling good about how much we're accomplishing at work, or maybe we're encouraged by having a new friend in our life. Pleasant feelings can add to our personal satisfaction and point toward what we value most. They can motivate us to strengthen relationships and reward us when we do well.

- *Difficult feelings* typically come up when something seems wrong in one or more areas of our life. Maybe we're feeling sad about a loss we've experienced, or we're angry about something that seems unfair. Maybe we feel guilty about something we've done—or something we haven't. Our difficult feelings can help us identify areas where we might need to make a change of some kind. They can be the catalyst for taking steps toward personal growth or reconciliation.

- *Mixed feelings* are when we have a combination of pleasant feelings and difficult feelings about a situation. Maybe we want to do something we know we shouldn't, or we don't want to do something we know we should. Mixed feelings serve as signals that we're conflicted about something, which can help us begin to sort out those feelings and determine the best way to proceed.

4. Feelings Are Meant to Be Expressed

Although feelings come from inside us and are an internal response to the circumstances of life, they are not meant to stay inside. Feelings are meant to be acknowledged and expressed to others, especially to those who are close to us and whom we trust.

People share feelings in many ways. They may tell others verbally or express their feelings nonverbally through laughter, sighs, moans, sobs, or wails. Often people convey emotions through facial expressions (like smiling or frowning), gestures (like shrugging or pointing), or other actions (like hugging or clenching a fist).

Sometimes people express their feelings through artistic or creative means like painting, crafting, singing, or writing. The Bible has many examples of people sharing a wide array of feelings with God and others through writing—especially in the Psalms, as Focus Note A shows.

FOCUS NOTE A

Expressing Feelings to God

Afraid:
"LORD, how many are my foes! How many rise up against me!" (Psalm 3:1)

Anxious:
"Search me, God, and know my heart; test me and know my anxious thoughts." (Psalm 139:23)

Brokenhearted:
"My sacrifice, O God, is a broken spirit; a broken and contrite heart you, God, will not despise." (Psalm 51:17)

Content:
"But I have calmed and quieted myself, I am like a weaned child with its mother; like a weaned child I am content." (Psalm 131:2)

Delighted:
"I delight in your decrees; I will not neglect your word. . . . Your statutes are my delight; they are my counselors." (Psalm 119:16, 24)

Despairing:
"Help, LORD, for the godly are no more; the faithful have vanished from among men." (Psalm 12:1)

Dismayed:
"So my spirit grows faint within me; my heart within me is dismayed." (Psalm 143:4)

Distressed:
"Answer me when I call to you, my righteous God. Give me relief from my distress; have mercy on me and hear my prayer." (Psalm 4:1)

Doubtful:
"Why, Lord, do you stand far off? Why do you hide yourself in times of trouble?" (Psalm 10:1)

Downcast:
"Why, my soul, are you downcast? Why so disturbed within me?" (Psalm 43:5a)

Frustrated:
"Why, Lord, do you reject me and hide your face from me?" (Psalm 88:14)

Grieved:
"When my heart was grieved and my spirit embittered, I was senseless and ignorant . . ." (Psalm 73:21–22a)

Guilty:
"My guilt has overwhelmed me like a burden too heavy to bear." (Psalm 38:4)

Helpless:
"Scorn has broken my heart and has left me helpless; I looked for sympathy, but there was none, for comforters, but I found none." (Psalm 69:20)

Joyful:
"When anxiety was great within me, your consolation brought me joy." (Psalm 94:19)

Lonely:
"Turn to me and be gracious to me, for I am lonely and afflicted." (Psalm 25:16)

Overwhelmed:
"Fear and trembling have beset me; horror has overwhelmed me." (Psalm 55:5)

Restless:
"My God, I cry out by day, but you do not answer, by night, but I find no rest." (Psalm 22:2)

Sorrowful:
"The cords of death entangled me, the anguish of the grave came over me; I was overcome by distress and sorrow." (Psalm 116:3)

Thankful:
"I will praise God's name in song and glorify him with thanksgiving." (Psalm 69:30)

Troubled:
"When I tried to understand all this, it troubled me deeply." (Psalm 73:16)

Trusting:
"In peace I will lie down and sleep, for you alone, O Lord, make me dwell in safety." (Psalm 4:8)

Weary:
"My soul is weary with sorrow; strengthen me according to your word." (Psalm 119:28)

When we understand and express our feelings, it benefits us and those around us in a number of ways:

- We are more authentic.

- We give others the opportunity to know and love us.

- We allow others the chance to serve and help us.

- We encourage others to understand and express their own feelings.

- We build deeper, stronger relationships.

- We help lay the foundation for community with those we've opened up to.

- We have the opportunity for spiritual growth.

5. Difficult Feelings Require Special Attention

Everyone experiences difficult, painful feelings at times. Their frequency and intensity can vary depending on an individual's personality and life experiences, but no matter the circumstances, difficult feelings require special attention.

What Can Happen When People Ignore or Avoid Difficult Feelings

When people have difficult feelings they don't know how to handle, they may begin to feel trapped by those feelings. For example, deep sadness and despair can leave people feeling hopeless and helpless. If they don't find ways to deal with those feelings, they may isolate themselves and become depressed.

People who ignore or suppress their difficult feelings can also end up acting in ways that hurt themselves and others. Many people have taken action based on feelings of rage, despair, infatuation, or fear—and later regretted their actions.

Painful feelings can affect people's understanding so that they lose sight of their responsibilities. Feelings of helplessness or hopelessness, for instance, can leave people with the sense that nothing they do really matters, and they might neglect caring for themselves and others.

Sometimes, when people can't bring themselves to acknowledge their difficult feelings, they project those feelings onto other people instead. They refuse to see the feelings in themselves and instead see them in others, even in people who don't actually have those feelings.

When feelings have been hidden for years, they often come out in unexpected ways. For example, a person may have felt anger or fear toward a parent or teacher in the past, but now he or she has transferred it onto a person in authority or even a caregiver.

To begin dealing with challenges like these, the person needs to learn how to express his or her difficult feelings.

The Importance of Expressing Difficult Feelings

Difficult feelings typically create problems when people don't express them fully. That's why it's so important that Stephen Ministers give people a safe place to express their feelings—and encourage them to do so in healthy ways.

When people express difficult feelings to someone they can trust, they experience a number of emotional and relational benefits. The act of sharing releases some of the pressure that's built up inside, reducing stress and helping them relax. Talking through their feelings may also help people gain perspective on why they feel a particular way and what they can do about it.

Of course, sometimes it's best to temporarily set difficult feelings aside until they can be expressed in a safe time and place. For example, if you're driving in heavy traffic in the middle of a severe storm, it's probably better to hold in tears of sadness until you can pull over to a safe place to release emotions. Or, during a crisis situation, such as when one's child has gotten lost in a department store, it's probably better to act first and address feelings later. At some point, though, it's necessary to pay attention to any strong feelings and let them out so they don't cause more pain.

6. We Can Decide What to Do with Our Feelings

It's important to keep in mind that our feelings are not under our direct, conscious control. They are involuntary responses that arise out of who we are, how we perceive the world around us, and what we are experiencing. There's no need to feel guilty about having particular feelings—no one can ever have complete control over whether he or she feels angry, happy, or sad.

What we can do, however, is decide what we do with our feelings. Feelings may motivate us to act, but they don't choose our course of action for us. That's a decision we make ourselves.

For instance, suppose someone feels irritated by a neighbor's gruff and unfriendly behavior. The person may feel an urge to do something unfriendly to the neighbor in return. But the person doesn't have to follow through on those feelings. In fact, he or she can choose to treat the neighbor with empathy, kindness, patience, and mercy instead. The person can make the decision not to let those negative feelings lead to negative actions.

Our feelings may influence us positively or negatively, but they don't make decisions for us. The responsibility for handling our feelings in the best ways possible remains with us.

7. Feelings Can Change

Feelings are not static. Often they change naturally as time passes, but we can change them ourselves as well. Even though our feelings are not under our direct, conscious control, we can think and act in ways that bring about changes in our feelings.

We can begin by identifying feelings we'd like to change. For example, we may decide that we want to move from being continually frustrated with someone to feeling compassion for that person. Then, we can talk through the difficult feelings with someone we can trust. Doing so helps us release those feelings so we can stop feeding them and/or allowing them to have control over us.

It's possible to change not only the feelings we have about others, but also those we have about ourselves. The process is a gradual one; if we are feeling discouraged, for instance, we can't flip a switch and make ourselves feel encouraged. However, we can talk with someone about the negative feelings we're having and, rather than judging ourselves and being self-critical, seek to have empathy for ourselves. Focusing on the process of caring for ourselves over time can result in a change in the way we feel.

Kinds of Feelings

Human beings have the capacity to experience a wide variety of feelings. The Feelings Word List on pages 31–32 gives just a sampling. Many of these words describe feelings that are either entirely pleasant or entirely difficult, although some could go either way.

Pleasant Feelings

A good number of feelings are pleasant—and some are so enjoyable that experiencing them can be a highlight of a person's life. Love for family and friends or joy at the birth of a child can provide pleasure for a lifetime. Feelings of accomplishment or achievement can provide satisfaction and motivate someone to set new goals. For many people, having a strong faith in God can bring feelings of hope and peace.

One of the most satisfying parts of your ministry may be sharing your care receivers' pleasant feelings. Be open to such feelings and encourage your care receivers to express them. The Apostle Paul encourages us to "Rejoice with those who rejoice; mourn with those who mourn" (Romans 12:15). While you will certainly spend a significant amount of time focusing on care receivers' difficult and painful feelings, it's important to also encourage care receivers to express what they feel good about—and rejoice with them in those moments.

Difficult Feelings

Because of the nature of Stephen Ministry, care receivers will generally have difficult feelings they need to talk about. Here are some of the more common ones.

Anger

Anger is not bad in itself, but it holds great potential to cause harm—both to those feeling the anger and to those receiving it. Care receivers who are dealing with anger need opportunities to talk through their anger so they can begin to understand where it comes from and how best to handle it.

Sometimes people react in anger beyond what a situation warrants. When this happens, it may be that the person's anger is being fueled by another feeling such as hurt, frustration, fear, or rejection.

People also become angry when they believe that they or their loved ones have been treated unfairly or unjustly. The more unfair a situation seems, the stronger a person's anger is likely to be.

In the process of dealing with anger, it's possible for a care receiver to inadvertently lash out at his or her Stephen Minister. This doesn't mean the Stephen Minister has done anything wrong—just that the care receiver isn't sure what to do with those feelings. When anger builds up, it can come out at an unexpected time and with much more intensity than circumstances seem to warrant.

Fear

People usually feel fear when they perceive a potential threat. They may also be afraid when they believe they have lost control over a situation or when they feel vulnerable and unable to protect themselves.

Fear may be in response to an actual or perceived threat. Even when the threat is not real, however, the fear is real and needs to be addressed. Fear can fuel feelings of anger, despair, and frustration.

Sadness

Sadness usually results from loss, either current or anticipated. For example, when a child leaves home, parents may grieve because the child is no longer a daily part of their lives—a current loss. Parents may feel sad when they think ahead about a child eventually leaving home—an anticipated loss. In both cases, the sadness is real.

The significance of a loss depends on the perspective of the person experiencing it. For example, when a pet dies, the owner may experience deep sadness and pain because he or she considered the pet a beloved family member. Someone who has never owned a pet may not have the same understanding of the significance of the loss, but that doesn't make it any less sad or painful for the owner.

Despair

People feel despair when they find their situation unbearable and believe they are powerless to change it. The despair may be because of current problems or expected problems.

For example, a person in a broken relationship may have tried to bring reconciliation a number of times, but the person's efforts were not matched or welcomed by the other person in the relationship. The person may eventually give up hope of reconciliation for the relationship, and his or her sadness may turn to despair.

Guilt

People may feel guilty for both rational and irrational reasons. *Rational guilt* is when the person feels remorse over something he or she did or neglected to do that resulted in hurt or harm to another person. To feel rational guilt is to be in touch with the negative impact of one's words and actions.

Irrational guilt, on the other hand, is a feeling of guilt that is not related to any actual wrongdoing. Rather, it comes from being overly self-critical. For example, a father may feel irrational guilt that his child has cancer, even though he did nothing to cause it and could not have done anything to prevent it. Or a woman who had an argument with her husband may feel guilty when he later ends up in a car accident, even though she was not involved in what happened on the road. Irrational guilt occurs when people disappoint themselves or fail to meet their own expectations, regardless of whether those expectations are realistic.

Focus Note B contains questions you can ask to determine whether a care receiver's feeling of guilt is rational or irrational.

FOCUS NOTE B

Questions to Differentiate between Rational and Irrational Guilt

1. What is it you've done that feels wrong or sinful?

2. If you had to, what particular thought or action would you ask forgiveness for?

3. If you had to ask forgiveness of a person, whom would you ask?

If a care receiver cannot clearly answer these questions, he or she may be dealing with irrational guilt. As the care receiver thinks about and talks through this issue over time, he or she may come to recognize that the guilt is irrational. If, however, you believe the care receiver may have a serious problem with irrational guilt—for example, if the sense of guilt doesn't go away and seems to impair his or her everyday life—then the care receiver might need to be referred to a mental health professional. Your Supervision Group can help with issues related to referrals, and the topic is covered thoroughly in module 11, "Using Mental Health Professionals and Other Community Resources."

Primary and Secondary Feelings

Feelings sometimes change over time, so a person may end up with a different feeling than the one he or she started with. In these situations, the initial feeling is the *primary feeling,* and the one it changes into is the *secondary feeling.* The secondary feeling is a reaction to—and often an attempt to protect oneself from—the initial feeling. Focus Note C shows a couple of examples.

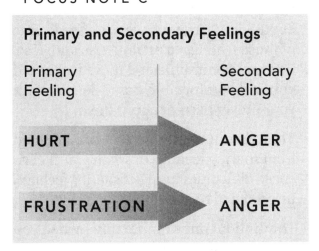

FOCUS NOTE C

Primary and Secondary Feelings

Primary Feeling	Secondary Feeling
HURT	ANGER
FRUSTRATION	ANGER

Often, when a person feels angry, that anger is actually a reaction to feeling something else, such as hurt or frustration. The person may have found the primary feeling so unacceptable that he or she refused to acknowledge and deal with it, and instead the feeling became anger. In this situation, the feeling of hurt, fear, or shame is still there and still needs to be dealt with—it's just been pushed to the side and overshadowed by the anger.

For example, two siblings get into a serious argument over the phone, and one abruptly hangs up on the other. Afterward, they both feel deeply hurt by what happened, but because they don't want to deal with that hurt, they each move toward anger, nursing a grudge and complaining about each other to the rest of the family. Although anger may give them an opportunity to vent, they need to address the underlying, primary feeling to fully deal with their emotions.

Although a secondary feeling is as real as any other, dealing with just that feeling isn't enough. The primary feeling fueling that secondary feeling needs to be addressed as well. If a person is experiencing anger as a secondary feeling, the underlying hurt, fear, shame, or frustration needs to be addressed first.

It's important for Stephen Ministers to acknowledge and validate a care receiver's secondary feeling—but also to help the care receiver get beyond the secondary feeling to deal with the primary feeling behind it, which is often at the core of the problem.

Cover-Opposites

Sometimes the emotions people show on the outside are a cover for feelings they have at the same time inside. These pairs of seemingly contradictory feelings are *cover-opposites.*

Cover-opposites differ from primary and secondary feelings in a key way. With primary and secondary feelings, one feeling comes out of another over time, pushing the original feeling into the background. With cover-opposites, however, the two opposite feelings exist at the same time at different levels. Generally, the cover or exterior feeling is meant to conceal the opposite or interior feeling, which is often the more painful of the two feelings.

Some examples of paired cover-opposite feelings are illustrated in Focus Note D.

FOCUS NOTE D

Cover-Opposite Examples

Example 1
A person who displays a great deal of bravado may have a lot of insecurity inside that he or she doesn't feel able to express.

COVER
Confidence
Insecurity
OPPOSITE

Example 2
A person who projects a sweet, cheery image to others may be covering up feelings of anger.

COVER
Cheerfulness
Anger
OPPOSITE

Example 3
A person who puts up a happy front may feel very sad inwardly.

COVER
Happiness
Sadness
OPPOSITE

Getting Ready for the In-Class Session

In order to get the most out of the In-Class Session, do the following:

- Read the Feelings Word List on pages 31–32, and choose three words that represent feelings you've experienced recently. Think about whether you have expressed some of those feelings to anyone else and, if so, how you communicated those feelings. If you feel comfortable doing so, talk with your prayer partner about them.

- Think about a time when you benefited from sharing feelings or when you experienced difficulties from not sharing feelings. Be prepared to share your recollections.

- Think about one or more times when you felt either safe or unsafe sharing your feelings. Be prepared to share your thoughts.

stephenministries.org/library

See the **Stephen Minister Online Library** for additional resources and downloads related to this Stephen Minister training topic.

As a Stephen Minister, as you acknowledge and validate your care receiver's feelings, keep in mind that exterior feelings may be covering other, opposite feelings. You can best care by listening, asking good questions, and letting care receivers know they can share *any* feelings they may have, without fear of being criticized or judged.

Appendix A

Module 2

Feelings Word List

PHYSICALLY ORIENTED

alert	exhilarated	on edge	tense
alive	famished	refreshed	tired
awake	fatigued	relaxed	uncomfortable
beat	full	restless	under the weather
breathless	hot	run down	unsteady
burned out	hungry	rushed	warm
charged	hurt	shaky	weak
cold	ill	sick	weary
comfortable	invigorated	sleepy	well
edgy	jittery	sore	wide awake
energetic	lethargic	spent	worn
enlivened	listless	steady	
excited	loose	stiff	
exhausted	nervous	strong	

SPIRITUALLY ORIENTED

alive	detached	helpless	pessimistic
apathetic	discouraged	hopeful	powerful
ashamed	disheartened	hopeless	powerless
awakened	dissatisfied	indifferent	proud
blessed	doubtful	insecure	redeemed
bored	downhearted	inspired	renewed
bound	empty	joyful	repentant
broken	enlightened	jubilant	satisfied
committed	enlivened	lonely	secure
complacent	faithful	lost	strong
complete	fearful	loving	sure
confident	free	moved	thankful
courageous	fulfilled	optimistic	touched
dead	full	overwhelmed	trustful
defeated	grateful	peaceful	unsure
despairing	guilty	penitent	whole

COGNITIVELY ORIENTED

absorbed	concerned	intrigued	skeptical
alert	confused	involved	suspicious
amazed	curious	optimistic	thoughtful
ambivalent	engrossed	out of touch	unconcerned
appreciative	fascinated	perplexed	uninterested
bewildered	hesitant	puzzled	unnerved
complacent	inquisitive	reluctant	vexed
composed	interested	scattered	

EMOTIONALLY ORIENTED

afraid	discouraged	grateful	rancorous
aggravated	disgruntled	grieved	relieved
agitated	disgusted	happy	resentful
alarmed	dismayed	horrified	sad
amused	displeased	hurt	scared
angry	distraught	infuriated	shocked
annoyed	distressed	irked	sorrowful
anxious	disturbed	irritated	spellbound
apprehensive	down	jealous	splendid
astonished	downcast	joyful	surprised
bitter	ecstatic	jubilant	taken aback
blue	elated	lonely	tense
brokenhearted	embarrassed	mad	terrified
calm	enthralled	melancholic	touched
comfortable	exasperated	merry	tranquil
concerned	excited	miffed	troubled
contented	exhilarated	miserable	undone
dejected	frightened	mortified	uneasy
delighted	frustrated	overjoyed	unhappy
depressed	furious	overwhelmed	upset
disappointed	glad	pleased	

Feelings: Yours, Mine, and Ours

Module 2 | Presentation Outline

Rejoice with those who rejoice; mourn with those who mourn.
Romans 12:15

 Devotion: Rejoicing and Mourning

I. Our Own Feelings

II. Why Feelings Need to Be Expressed

FOCUS NOTE 1

Instructions for Activity

Tell the other person about a time when you shared your feelings with someone and it was beneficial for you—or possibly about a time when you didn't share your feelings and it caused problems. Listen as the other person does the same.

III. A Model for Handling Feelings

A. Recognize

FOCUS NOTE 2

Reflecting Feelings

Care receiver:
I don't know what we're going to do about Matt. He doesn't listen to us, and lately he's been hanging out with the wrong crowd at school.

Stephen Minister:
It sounds as if you're worried about Matt and afraid of what choices he is making.

[or]

Care receiver:
It's been nearly a year since the funeral, but every time I think I've moved on, something comes up to remind me and then it all comes crashing in on me. I just can't stop thinking about it.

Stephen Minister:
It sounds as if you still have strong feelings about your loss.

Gently Pointing Out Inconsistencies

Stephen Minister:
That was a big sigh. I know you've said you feel happy in your relationship, but I'm wondering whether there might be more to it than that.

[or]

Stephen Minister:
Last week, you seemed very worried about your mother being in the nursing home. This week, you don't seem as concerned. Tell me more about that.

B. Accept

C. Express

FOCUS NOTE 4

Expressing Feelings

- Assure your care receiver that "It's okay to be real with me" or "It's okay to cry."

- Invite your care receiver to tell you more about his or her feelings, and then listen carefully.

- Let your care receiver know you can handle whatever feelings he or she needs to let out.

- When your care receiver expresses his or her feelings, encourage further sharing by saying something like, "Tell me more."

IV. Sharing and Listening to Feelings

FOCUS NOTE 5

Suggestions for Sharing Feelings

1. Talk about an event in your past you have strong feelings about.
2. Talk about a present concern you have strong feelings about.
3. Talk about a particular relationship you feel very happy or very sad about.
4. Talk about some big plans you're excited about, anxious about, or both.
5. Talk about a strong fear or hope you have for the future.

FOCUS NOTE 6

Discussion Questions

1. How comfortable did the speaker feel about sharing his or her feelings?
2. How comfortable did the listener feel in his or her role?
3. What feelings did the listener identify?
4. Does the speaker agree that these feelings were present?
5. What other feelings did the speaker have that the listener didn't identify?

V. The Mudhole

FOCUS NOTE 7

Carl Rogers's Definition of Empathy

Empathy is the ability "to sense the client's private world as if it were your own, but without ever losing the 'as if' quality."[1]

---

1 Carl R. Rogers, "The Necessary and Sufficient Conditions of Therapeutic Personality Change," *Journal of Consulting Psychology* 21:2 (1957), 99.

FOCUS NOTE 8

The Mudhole

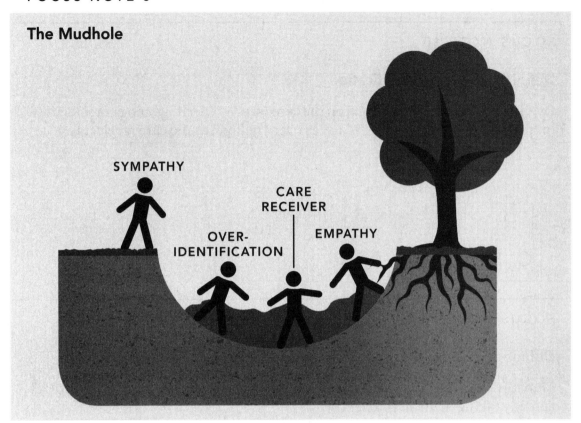

A. Sympathy

FOCUS NOTE 9

Definition of Sympathy

Sympathy is feeling concern for someone else without becoming involved in his or her life.

B. Overidentification

FOCUS NOTE 10

Definition of Overidentification

Overidentification means taking on the care receiver's feelings and characteristics to the point that the caregiver is just as overwhelmed as the care receiver is.

C. Empathy

FOCUS NOTE 11

Definition of Empathy

Empathy is feeling another person's problems as if they were your own without actually taking them on yourself.

FOCUS NOTE 12

The Meaning of the Tree

"He himself bore our sins" in his body on the tree, so that we might die to sins and live for righteousness; "by his wounds you have been healed."

1 Peter 2:24

VI. Creating a Safe Place for People to Recognize, Accept, and Express Feelings

A. Comfort or Discomfort Talking about Feelings

FOCUS NOTE 13

Instructions for Discussion of Comfort or Discomfort Talking about Feelings

1. Decide who will be Person A and Person B. Person A will share first.

2. Share a brief story about a time when you felt very *uncomfortable* talking about your feelings with someone. Identify anything the person in your story said or did that *decreased* your comfort with talking about feelings. In the space below, take notes on anything that decreased comfort for you.

What the person said or did that *decreased* comfort with talking about feelings:

3. Share a brief story about a time when you felt very *comfortable* talking about your feelings with someone. Identify anything the person in your story said or did that *increased* your comfort with talking about feelings. In the space below, take notes on anything that increased comfort.

What the person said or did that *increased* comfort with talking about feelings:

4. When the leader indicates that you're halfway done with the activity, switch roles and repeat steps 2 and 3, this time with Person B sharing. Continue to take notes in the space provided.

FOCUS NOTE 14

Comfort or Discomfort Talking about Feelings

Words or actions that *decrease* comfort with talking about feelings:

Words or actions that *increase* comfort with talking about feelings:

B. The Safe House

FOCUS NOTE 15

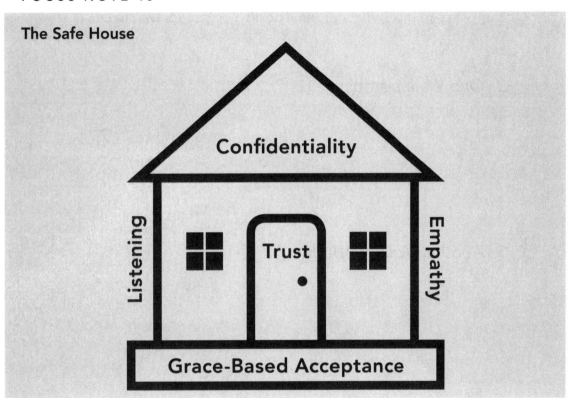

The Safe House

1. *The Foundation: Grace-Based Acceptance*

    a. Patience

    b. Being Nonjudgmental

    c. Unconditional Positive Regard

FOCUS NOTE 16

Rogers's Condition for Growth and Change

The therapist experiences unconditional positive regard for the client.[2]

2. One Wall: Listening

3. Another Wall: Empathy

4. The Roof: Confidentiality

5. The Door: Trust

---

2 Rogers, 96.

VII. Caregiver's Compass Review

Write your ideas around the compass.

VIII. Looking Ahead

The Art of Listening

Module 3 | Pre-Class Reading

CONTENTS

Listening Is Caring

Listening is perhaps the most important part of what a Stephen Minister does in a caring relationship. Effective caregiving begins with the ability to pay close attention to another person, to truly hear and understand what he or she is trying to say. Listening well communicates that you value the other person and that you're safe to talk with, which in turn encourages him or her to open up further and share more. The listening you'll do as a Stephen Minister is more than just one skill—it's a *set* of skills that work together. This kind of listening is the main way you'll provide care as a Stephen Minister.

Therapeutic Listening

The listening Stephen Ministers do can best be described as *therapeutic listening*. Here, the word *therapeutic* does not mean that Stephen Ministry is a substitute for professional therapy; rather, it means that Stephen Ministers listen as part of a process intended to bring emotional and spiritual healing.

The word *therapeutic* is based on the Greek word *therapeuo,* which means "to cause someone to recover health . . . to heal, to cure, to take care of, healing."[1] Stephen Ministers are not themselves healers; they rely on God to work through their listening to bring emotional and spiritual healing to care receivers.

Jesus Listened

While the Gospels focus more on Jesus' teaching and healing than his listening, they do show a number of examples of Jesus as a skilled listener.

- He was attentive to the needs of others and invited them to talk about those needs, such as when he called the blind man Bartimaeus to him and asked, "What do you want me to do for you?" (Mark 10:46–52).

- He helped people open up and tell him their story without judging them, such as when he asked the Samaritan woman at the well for a drink of water, which led to her sharing about her deepest need (John 4:7–26).

- He showed great empathy and compassion—important traits for effective, caring listening—such as when he shared in Mary's and Martha's grief over the death of Lazarus by weeping himself (John 11:33–35).

Although Jesus knew what people needed without them having to tell him, these examples show that he was aware of the benefits people experience when someone really listens to them. Jesus was an excellent listener who could help people find emotional and spiritual healing. Listening was an important part of Jesus' ministry, and it's central to what Stephen Ministers do as well.

STEPHEN MINISTER INSIGHT

"I used to think I was a good listener, but I now realize I was always listening to fix or to formulate a response. Now I listen to just hear what the person is saying—I listen with my heart."

Anyone Can Learn Listening Skills

Therapeutic listening isn't a talent or natural ability only a select few people are born with—it's not something you either have or don't have. In fact, it's a set of skills that *anyone* can learn.

---

1 J. P. Louw and E. A. Nida, eds., *Louw-Nida Greek English Lexicon of the New Testament Based on Semantic Domains,* 2nd ed. (New York: United Bible Societies, 1988), s.v. "therapeuo."

As you train to be a Stephen Minister, you'll first work on developing those skills through this Pre-Class Reading and the In-Class Session on "The Art of Listening." Then you'll have numerous opportunities to practice and build your listening skills throughout your training. By the time you complete Stephen Minister training and are assigned your first care receiver, you can be confident in your ability to do therapeutic listening.

Characteristics of Effective Listeners

Good listening requires three personal qualities in the listener:

1) presence;

2) empathy; and

3) composure.

1. Presence

Effective listeners are fully present with their care receivers—physically, mentally, emotionally, and spiritually.

- The best listening takes place when the Stephen Minister is *physically present* with the care receiver. This is why meeting with a care receiver in person is a foundational aspect of Stephen Ministry. When you are physically present with another person, you are able to listen with your eyes as well as your ears. You can learn a lot by observing the other person's facial expressions, body language, and interaction with the environment. At the same time, the care receiver is able to see that you are really listening, which will encourage him or her to continue talking.

- Presence also involves being *mentally present* for the care receiver. Your mind is fully engaged with and focused on what the care receiver is communicating—not drifting and thinking about what you might be doing later in the evening or what you want to say next. This mental attentiveness is critical because it affects so many of the other aspects of listening. When you're mentally present, you're able to process the information the care receiver is giving you and respond to that information, which helps you show that you're truly *with* the care receiver.

- Another important part of presence is being *emotionally present*. Rather than keeping your distance or remaining overly guarded, you become emotionally engaged as the care receiver shares his or her thoughts and feelings. Emotional presence is closely connected to mental presence, since in both you will voluntarily put aside your own thoughts and needs to focus on the world of the other person. Your emotional involvement communicates a depth of care that invites the care receiver to go deeper with you alongside him or her.

- Being *spiritually present* is the fourth aspect. With Christ at the center of your caring relationship, you pray for God to work through your presence and listening to provide care and hope to the other person. You pay attention to the care receiver's possible spiritual needs, listen to what's going on in his or her relationship with God, and pray over your care receiver's needs and concerns. Spiritual presence also involves bringing your own faith, hope, and loving care to the relationship.

There is no substitute for presence in a caregiving relationship. In order to listen well, it's essential that you be fully present—physically, mentally, emotionally, and spiritually—with your care receiver. Focus Note A contains an example of what can happen when a Stephen Minister is *not* fully present with a care receiver.

FOCUS NOTE A

What Can Happen When a Caregiver Isn't Fully Present

Drew was looking forward to meeting with his Stephen Minister, Ben, later that day. After getting to know Ben over the first couple of visits, Drew was starting to feel comfortable sharing his thoughts and feelings, and he had a number of things to talk about.

Around 4 P.M., though—an hour before they were scheduled to meet—Drew got a text message from Ben saying, "Hey, sorry. Busy day. How about we meet 7:30–8 tonight?"

Drew tried to be understanding, but he felt a little put off. He had intentionally kept his schedule open for this meeting, and now it was getting pushed back—and would last only a half hour! "Still," he thought, "things come up. This is better than nothing."

As promised, Ben showed up at 7:30, but based on how hurried and distracted he seemed, it was immediately clear to Drew that Ben's mind was elsewhere. Even so, Drew thought, "Okay, at least he's here. Let's just make the best of it."

Drew jumped right in, sharing about how things were going and some of what he'd been thinking about. After a while, he noticed that Ben's gaze seemed to be drifting to his phone on the side table. Ben kept nodding and saying "Mm-hm" as Drew talked, but Drew soon became convinced that Ben wasn't really paying attention. Drew paused and said, "Hey, man, are you with me?"

"What? Oh!" Ben said. "Yeah, I'm sorry. Today's just been crazy. What was it you were saying?"

Drew, frustrated, went back over what he'd already said. He'd really wanted to talk to Ben about some faith issues he was struggling with, but with how the conversation was going, he wasn't sure about bringing it up anymore.

Drew decided to go ahead anyway, but right as he began to broach the topic, Ben's phone rang. Ben grabbed it from the table, looked at the screen, and said, "Hey, I'm really sorry, Drew, but I'm going to have to take this call. It'll be just a minute."

Ben got up, turned away, and walked to the other side of the room to answer the call. Drew felt totally deflated. Was this how it was going to be? He had just started to believe that having a Stephen Minister might really help him. But now, it was just another item on his growing list of things he couldn't be sure about.

2. Empathy

Effective listeners possess and express great empathy for their care receivers. As described in module 2, *empathy* is "feeling another person's problems as if they were your own without actually taking them on yourself."

In the Mudhole diagram introduced in module 2, the empathetic caregiver reaches out to help the care receiver stuck in the mud, while keeping a firm grasp on the root of the tree. An empathetic person has a strong sense of self and thus is not overwhelmed or threatened when relating to someone who is in crisis or who has different perspectives and experiences. He or she enters into another person's experience, seeking to understand what the other person is thinking and feeling.

Focus Note B illustrates what can happen when a Stephen Minister shows empathy for a care receiver.

FOCUS NOTE B

Entering Another Person's Experience through Empathy

Ben knew he had really messed up during his last conversation with Drew. This time, when Ben arrived at Drew's house he was determined to be fully present and really try to understand what Drew was thinking and feeling about what he was going through.

Drew at first seemed reluctant to share in much depth—understandable, given how their last meeting had gone. As Drew started talking, though, Ben paid careful attention, following right along and asking good questions. He showed real interest and made a genuine effort to connect to Drew's experiences.

As the visit continued and Ben listened caringly and attentively, Drew appeared to grow less wary about sharing, and he eventually started to talk about the challenges he was encountering with his faith. That was an area where Ben hadn't had many struggles himself, so Ben knew he needed to really listen and try to understand what Drew was experiencing. He kept his focus on Drew, continuing to ask questions and invite further sharing so he could get a clear picture of what it was like to have those doubts.

When Drew finished sharing, Ben said gently, "Drew, I would think anyone who has been through what you've experienced would be thinking and feeling like that."

Drew could tell that Ben was truly interested in hearing and understanding what he was saying and feeling. Even after the frustration of their previous meeting, Drew felt comfortable sharing his private thoughts and feelings about God and faith thanks to Ben's listening.

3. Composure

Being an effective listener also involves the ability to maintain composure while caring for someone going through a crisis. As your relationship with your care receiver develops, you are likely to hear some raw, unfiltered thoughts and feelings. How you react to those thoughts and feelings will affect how the relationship progresses, so it's important to maintain your composure so you can respond in ways that encourage further sharing and foster a deeper caring relationship.

Composure in listening includes a number of important aspects.

• One key aspect is *calmness.* Even if you feel some shock or dismay over what the care receiver shares, it's crucial to maintain a peaceful exterior and to communicate in calming ways. Expressing frustration, anxiousness, displeasure, or other upset feelings communicates a lack of acceptance, even if that's not the intent, and will most likely bring the sharing to an end.

- Another part of composure is *accepting silence* when it occurs. Silence is a natural response when a person is hurting and doesn't know what to say. After Job suffered a series of devastating losses, he sat in silence with three friends for seven days and seven nights (Job 2:11–13). Sometimes people are nervous about silence, but when someone is suffering, it's a mistake to rush in and fill the silence with empty words. Instead, it's most caring to stay composed and wait until the care receiver is clearly ready to talk.

The book of Ecclesiastes reminds us that there is a time for speaking and a time for keeping silent (3:7b). Effective listening involves remaining patient as others struggle to express a feeling or pause to consider a thought. When you patiently listen during these silent moments, you encourage care receivers to take their time and share when they're ready.

- Composure also involves *not judging* the care receiver for what he or she expresses. Perhaps the quickest way to short-circuit the caregiving process is to jump in and suggest that certain thoughts or feelings are wrong or inappropriate, so it's important to be accepting and nonjudgmental. Your role as a Stephen Minister is not to teach or correct but to listen and care, letting God do the rest.

- In addition, a composed Stephen Minister is able to empathize while *not over-identifying* with the care receiver. If a Stephen Minister gets too caught up in the care receiver's story and lets it become his or her own story, it will interfere with providing effective care.

- A major part of maintaining composure is *being patient* with the care receiver and with the listening process. You'll want to take the time to listen and fully understand the person's needs as he or she works through the situation. People in crisis may already know exactly what they should or want to do, or they may need time to gain that understanding at their own pace. In either situation, what they need is not advice but a listening ear—someone who can be patient and completely present as they express their feelings.

Focus Note C shows what can happen when a Stephen Minister maintains composure as a care receiver shares difficult thoughts and feelings.

FOCUS NOTE C

Listening While Maintaining Composure

After their latest meeting, Drew was feeling more comfortable about meeting with Ben. He'd started to dig into his difficult feelings about God and faith, and he was encouraged that Ben had arrived right on time and stayed focused throughout. Drew was still uncertain, though, about how openly he should share. Some of what he'd been thinking about his faith got into uncomfortable territory, and he was worried that, if he let it all out, Ben might be shocked and condemn or dispute his thoughts and feelings.

At their next meeting, though, Drew decided to go ahead and open up—and Ben remained relaxed and understanding. He assured Drew that what he was thinking and feeling was a natural response to what he'd been through; it didn't mean he'd lost his faith. That gave Drew the confidence to go deeper still until he'd said everything on his mind and heart. Drew felt good being able to say all that while still feeling accepted.

As the meeting drew to a close, Drew told Ben, "I can hardly believe I could say those kinds of things out loud without being judged. Thanks so much for listening."

Establishing a Listening Environment

Besides the characteristics of the listener, another important factor for effective listening is *where* the conversation takes place. Effective listeners establish an environment where the care receiver can feel comfortable sharing deeply about what he or she is thinking and feeling. This includes choosing an appropriate physical setting and seating arrangements, as well as being ready to handle potential distractions or interruptions.

Physical Setting

The physical setting of the caring visit can greatly affect the quality of your listening. It needs to be a place where:

- you and your care receiver feel comfortable and at ease;

- the two of you are able to speak freely and confidentially;

- there are no major distractions; and

- your conversation is unlikely to be interrupted.

Plan ahead to ensure your caring visits take place in a setting that makes it easy to listen. Usually, a private setting such as the care receiver's home or a church office or meeting room works best. At times, Stephen Ministers and care receivers might meet in a more public setting, such as a park or a restaurant, but keep in mind that doing so increases distractions and creates privacy challenges, making it harder for a care receiver to share difficult emotions or shed tears.

If your care receiver suggests meeting somewhere that listening may be difficult, such as a restaurant with loud music and TVs, suggest that another setting may work better. You could say something like, "It might be difficult to have a good conversation there, since it tends to be crowded and noisy. I'm really interested in hearing what's going on with you, so a place where it's easier to talk may work better."

Seating Arrangements

Where you and your care receiver sit may affect your ability to listen. It's best to sit in close proximity to the other person so you can hear each other without having to speak loudly. At the same time, be aware of the care receiver's personal space and avoid sitting so close that the care receiver feels uncomfortable.

If you sit down first and the other person sits some distance away, feel free to ask, "Is it okay if I move closer so I can hear you better?" or something similar.

Some people find that facing each other creates the best environment for listening. Others prefer sitting side by side or at an angle to each other. There's no single right answer, so do what works best for you and your care receiver.

If necessary, ask permission to move a chair to improve the seating for your conversation. Also pay attention to other factors, such as whether the sun is shining in the care receiver's eyes or in your own. Your goal is to create the best possible situation for listening, so adapt the setting as needed.

When Distractions or Interruptions Occur

In spite of your best-laid plans, interruptions and distractions will sometimes happen. The phone will ring, children will come in from the yard, people will wander into the room where you are meeting, and so on. When interruptions happen, be patient. Make a mental note so you remember what was being said before the interruption occurred. After the interruption ends, you can help the care receiver to pick up where he or she left off.

When distractions are excessive, prolonged, and unavoidable, think through how best to continue the conversation, keeping in mind the urgency of the situation and the need for confidentiality. You may consider finding somewhere else to meet, if possible. You might ask the care receiver what he or she thinks is best, using words like these: "It's pretty difficult to talk here. What do you think about finding somewhere else where we could talk more easily?"

Use your own judgment about how to proceed, considering your care receiver's needs and desires as well as the overall listening environment.

What to Listen For

A good listener wants to receive all the information a care receiver communicates during a visit—to understand as completely as possible the care receiver's situation and what he or she is thinking and feeling. This includes listening for thoughts, feelings,

themes, patterns, and even what the person does not say.

Listening for Thoughts

Effective listening begins with paying close attention to the thoughts the care receiver shares. Focus Note D lists some possible types of thoughts.

FOCUS NOTE D

Some Types of Thoughts Care Receivers May Share

- Comments about recent events in their life

- Memories about a loved one

- Beliefs about life, relationships, faith, or other topics

- Perspectives on their current situation

- Ideas or plans for dealing with the situation

- Anything else that comes to mind

Listen carefully to your care receiver's words about his or her thoughts and to what those thoughts tell you about his or her current mindset, relationships, situation, and feelings. Your care receiver's thoughts are the foundation for much of what you'll be listening for, and paying careful attention to them is key in helping your care receiver share more deeply.

Listening for Feelings

In addition, listen carefully for the feelings that may be behind your care receiver's thoughts. Often, these feelings will come out not in the care receiver's words but through other cues. Focus Note E lists some cues that may point to your care receiver's feelings.

FOCUS NOTE E

Cues That May Reveal Feelings

- Facial expressions
- Eyes (tearful, closed, looking down at the ground or off into the distance)
- Tone of voice
- Rate of speech (rapid, slow, halting)
- Volume of speech
- Body language
- Voice tremors
- Gestures
- Rate and type of breathing (rapid and shallow, slow and deep, sighing)
- Muscle tension (clenched fists, shaking)
- Posture (rigid, relaxed, slouched)

Also ask yourself, "Is this person's nonverbal behavior consistent with the words he or she is saying?" For example, if the care receiver says, "I'm not angry about that!" in a harsh tone, it's likely he or she actually is angry. If the care receiver laughs or smiles while making a negative statement, he or she may have some anxiety about the situation.

Listening for Themes and Patterns over Time

As you regularly meet with your care receiver, recall your previous conversations with him or her. Listen for patterns of communication, recurring themes, or seeming contradictions. For example, if the care receiver has talked a number of times about being unwilling to make decisions, you might ask about this theme with a question like, "You've said sev-eral times lately that you're having a tough time making decisions. Could you tell me more about that?"

Good listening also involves noting when your care receiver thinks or behaves differently from his or her established patterns. You may notice that one week a care receiver is surprisingly talkative, but in the past he or she had been very quiet. In one visit, a person may speak highly of a job, but during the next visit he or she may talk about wanting to quit. Explore such changes by saying something like one of these statements:

- *[Smiling pleasantly]* "You seem more talkative than usual tonight. Do you think so? *[If yes]* What do you think may be the difference?"

- "Hmm. In the past, you've talked about liking your job. Tell me more about what you're thinking."

Listening to What Is Not Said

Part of effective listening is paying attention to what is *not* said. What is silently passed over may be what most troubles the person and what he or she needs to talk about. For example, suppose a care receiver has three children and regularly talks about two of them but hardly ever mentions the third child. You might say something like, "You've talked a lot about Travis and Lindsey. How has Ashley been doing?" An open-ended question like this can help lead people to express important feelings about issues they may at first be reluctant to address.

Or, when you ask your care receiver how his or her week went, the reply might be, "Great, for the most part," followed by a recounting of only the positive developments. If the care receiver holds back on indicating why it was only great "for the most part," it would be good to follow up with something like, "I'm glad to hear that *most* of the week went well. What didn't go as well?"

Using Active Listening Skills

Active listening is a way of understanding what others communicate and helping them understand themselves better. When you use active listening skills, you serve as a kind of mirror, helping your care receiver see him- or herself through what you hear and see.

Active listening involves four main skills:

1) paying attention;

2) validating;

3) asking questions; and

4) reflecting.

1. Paying Attention

Paying attention to others helps them feel valued. It lets them know that someone cares for them and is willing to focus entirely on them, setting aside everything else. The care you show by paying attention makes it easier for your care receiver to trust you and feel comfortable telling you about his or her personal thoughts, feelings, fears, joys, and hopes. Sharing at a deeper level then gives your care receiver the freedom to take a fresh look at his or her feelings, thoughts, and behaviors.

Paying attention is the only way to really hear what another person is saying. Here are some practical suggestions to help you pay attention and let others know you're doing so.

- Relax and make frequent eye contact. Keep in mind that it's normal to break eye contact occasionally, as long as you remain focused on the care receiver.

- Lean forward slightly, face the care receiver, nod your head, and use verbal cues like "Uh-huh" to show you're listening.

- Avoid fidgeting, doodling, looking at your phone, or engaging in other activities that indicate distraction.

- After an interruption, remind the care receiver what he or she was saying. For example, you might say, "You were telling me you had called your mother." This shows you were paying attention, helps the care receiver get back on track, and gets the conversation rolling again.

If you happen to get distracted during a caring visit, be quick to acknowledge the distraction, apologize briefly but sincerely, and quickly refocus on your care receiver.

2. Validating

As you listen, a powerful, effective active listening skill is to validate what the person says. A definition of validation is in Focus Note F.

FOCUS NOTE F

Definition of Validation

Validation is the process of learning, understanding, believing, and accepting another person's thoughts and feelings about his or her experience—and letting the other person know you've done so, which communicates that his or her thoughts really do matter.

By validating what your care receiver tells you, you let the person know you are not going to try to reinterpret that experience or talk him or her out of thinking and feeling that way. Validation builds trust, strengthens the relationship, and lets the care receiver know it's safe to continue sharing. Focus Note G contains some examples of validating statements.

FOCUS NOTE G

Examples of Validating Statements

Care Receiver:
"Sometimes it hurts so much I just don't know what to do with myself."

Stephen Minister:
"That sounds awful. I'm sorry you're going through that."

Care Receiver:
"I'm just so frustrated."

Stephen Minister:
"I'd be frustrated by that too."

Care Receiver:
"God feels so far away right now."

Stephen Minister:
"That must be a lonely feeling."

Validating people's thoughts and feelings doesn't necessarily mean you *agree* with those thoughts and feelings. What it means is you believe that their thoughts and feelings are true to their experience—so they don't have to pretend to think or feel any other way.

3. Asking Questions

Active listening encourages others to continue talking about their thoughts, feelings, or concerns. The more they share, the more you're likely to understand, and the better they can understand themselves. Open-ended and clarifying questions are excellent tools to encourage this kind of sharing.

Ask Open-Ended Questions Rather than Closed-Ended Questions

Open-ended questions require an extended answer. They encourage the care receiver to open up and share more fully about what he or she is thinking and feeling, making open-ended questions one of the most effective tools Stephen Ministers can use.

In contrast, *closed-ended questions* can be answered with a yes or no. Rather than inviting the other person to think and share more deeply, closed-ended questions tend to produce limited responses.

Focus Note H gives a number of examples of closed- and open-ended questions.

FOCUS NOTE H

Closed- and Open-Ended Questions

⊗ *Closed:*
"Were you angry about that?"

⊘ *Open:*
"How did you feel when that happened?"

⊗ *Closed:*
"Are you excited about your vacation?"

⊘ *Open:*
"What are you looking forward to doing on vacation?"

⊗ *Closed:*
"Are you feeling better?"

⊘ *Open:*
"How have you been doing this past week?"

⊗ *Closed:*
"Are you going to quit work?"

⊘ *Open:*
"What are you thinking about work?"

⊗ *Closed:*
"Did you feel honored?"

⊘ *Open:*
"How did you feel about that?"

This doesn't mean that you'll never use closed-ended questions with your care receivers. There are times when closed-ended questions are appropriate and helpful, such as when you want to confirm a particular fact. You might say something like, "You mentioned Tom—is that your cousin who lives overseas?" After the care receiver answers, you could follow up with an open-ended question to help him or her continue sharing. The key is not to overuse closed-ended questions, as open-ended questions are more effective in helping a care receiver to really share thoughts and feelings.

Ask Clarifying Questions

Clarifying questions help you better understand what the care receiver means. If someone says, "I can't stand my job another day," you could ask, "What's been happening at work?" You might find out the person wants to change careers, that he or she is having serious problems with a coworker, or any number of other possibilities.

Pay Close Attention to How You Ask

How you ask your questions has a significant effect on how a care receiver will hear and respond to them. Here are some guidelines for asking questions in the most caring and effective ways.

Ask in a Gentle, Non-Judgmental Way

Phrase questions in a way that shows your care and concern. When your questions are gentle and kindly express your interest, the care receiver is likely to tell you more. Abrupt or judgmental questions, on the other hand, tend to discourage sharing and raise the care receiver's guardedness. There's an example in Focus Note I.

FOCUS NOTE I

Asking in a Gentle, Non-Judgmental Way

⊗ *Don't say:*
"What made you do that?" [or] "Why would you do that?"

⊘ *Do say:*
"What happened?" [or] "What preceded the decision to do that?"

Allow the Other Person Enough Time to Respond

Once you have asked a question, be intentional about allowing time for the other person to respond. It's easy to ask a question and then keep talking, especially if the other person doesn't respond immediately. Focus Note J shows what this might look like.

FOCUS NOTE J

Allowing Enough Time to Respond

⊗ *Don't say:*
"You had some tests today. How did they go? [Short pause] I can see by the way you look that they were pretty rough on you. I bet you're feeling pretty bad right now. I had a

niece who had the same tests you had, and she said they were horrible. First they . . ."

⊘ **Do say:**
"You had some tests today. How did they go?" [Long pause]

Avoid Asking Rapid-Fire Questions

A closely related pitfall is overwhelming the care receiver with rapid-fire questions without giving him or her a chance to answer the first one. Avoid asking a long string of questions and instead ask one at a time. Focus Note K contains an example.

FOCUS NOTE K

Avoiding Rapid-Fire Questions

⊗ **Don't say:**
"How's it going for you today? Any better than yesterday? Did your physician see you yet today? What did the doctor say?"

⊘ **Do say:**
"How's it going for you today?" [Long pause]

Avoid Asking Multiple-Choice Questions

Sometimes people will ask a question and then list several possible responses. The other person might then feel constrained to choose one of those multiple-choice responses, even if his or her actual response is completely different—and possibly much longer. It's much better to leave the question open-ended, allowing the care receiver to respond how he or she wishes. You'll see an example in Focus Note L.

FOCUS NOTE L

Avoiding Multiple-Choice Questions

⊗ **Don't say:**
"How are you feeling right now—good, bad, or somewhere in the middle?"

⊘ **Do say:**
"How are you feeling right now?"

Ask What Questions Rather than Why Questions

Another potential pitfall is starting questions with the word *why*. Questions that begin with *why* can put a care receiver on the defensive so that he or she feels a need to explain, justify, defend, or give reasons for particular feelings or behaviors. People are unlikely to trust those who put them on the defensive. Instead of asking *why*, try asking *what* most of the time. *What* questions ask for specifics about the situation and help you and the care receiver get a clearer idea of what is going on. See Focus Note M for an example.

FOCUS NOTE M

Asking What Rather than Why

⊗ **Don't say:**
"Why did you make that decision?"

⊘ **Do say:**
"What led to that decision?"

---

4. Reflecting What the Care Receiver Says

Reflecting means listening to someone and then saying back in your own words what you heard the person saying. It's more than just repeating the person's words back to him or her—it's sharing how you've interpreted the person's words. Your reflecting can focus on the message itself, the feelings behind it, or both. Focus Note N shows one example.

FOCUS NOTE N

An Example of Reflecting

Care Receiver:

"I don't know what's wrong with my sister. If I call her, she doesn't want to talk to me. If I don't call her, she texts me and says I don't care about her."

Stephen Minister:

"It sounds like you're frustrated about how your sister is treating you."

Benefits of Reflecting

Reflecting what you heard helps you learn how well you understood what your care receiver was trying to say. For example, in response to the Stephen Minister's words in Focus Note N, the care receiver might say one of the statements in Focus Note O.

FOCUS NOTE O

An Example of Reflecting (continued)

Care Receiver:

"That's right. I just don't know what she wants from me."

[or]

"No, I'm not really frustrated with her—I'm just confused. I want to have a good relationship with her, but I don't know how."

Reflecting affirms the other person, confirms that you are listening and interested, and invites the person to tell you more and continue talking for as long as needed. It gives the care receiver a chance to hear how his or her thoughts and feelings are coming across to you. This can lead the care receiver to greater self-awareness and self-understanding. After stopping to think, "Yes, that's what I mean," or "No, it's not quite like that," the care receiver can clarify what he or she really meant—both to you and to him- or herself.

Reflecting takes some practice, but over time it can become second nature. As you focus on saying back what you understand someone to be thinking and feeling, the responses will come to you more naturally.

There are a number of phrases you can use to reflect what you hear your care receiver saying. Several possibilities are listed in Focus Note P.

FOCUS NOTE P

Reflecting Responses

- "It sounds to me as if you're wondering whether . . ."
- "It seems as if you're feeling . . ."
- "From what you're saying, I get the idea that . . ."
- "I get the impression that inside you're dealing with a lot of . . ."
- "As I understand it, you're planning to . . ."
- "If I understand what you're describing, the situation is . . ."

Two Kinds of Information You Might Reflect

There are two kinds of information you can reflect back to your care receiver: content and feelings. Content includes the who, what, why, when, where, and how of what the person said. Feelings may include emotions the person actually verbalizes—or unnamed emotions which you sense may be behind what the person is saying. The content and feelings people share may involve physical, emotional, relational, or spiritual concerns.

There's no set pattern for how a person will share content or feelings—most people will just share whatever comes to them or seems the most important. The key is to listen for both content and feelings and reflect back what you hear.

As you reflectively listen, keep in mind that your goal is not to fix your care receiver's situation. Instead, focus on listening to, caring for, and walking alongside your care receiver. As you do, trust that God is working through your caregiving to bring healing.

Getting Ready for the In-Class Session

Be very familiar with the content of this Pre-Class Reading for the In-Class Session, particularly the material on how to engage in reflective listening. During part of the next class, you will participate in a reflective listening skill practice.

stephenministries.org/library

See the *Stephen Minister Online Library* for additional resources and downloads related to this Stephen Minister training topic.

The Art of Listening

Module 3 | Presentation Outline

You must understand this, my beloved: Let everyone be quick to listen, slow to speak.
James 1:19a NRSV

 Devotion: Our Listening God

I. May I Have Your Attention, Please?

FOCUS NOTE 1

SOLAR Listening

Sit slightly forward

Maintain an **O**pen, relaxed posture

Look into the other person's eyes

Pay close **A**ttention to what the other
person is saying so that you are able to . . .

Reflect what the other person says

FOCUS NOTE 2

Discussion Questions

1. How did the speaker feel when the listener was not paying attention?

2. How did the speaker feel when the listener was really paying attention?

3. What did you learn from this activity?

II. Active Listening Discussion

FOCUS NOTE 3

Listening Discussion Questions

1. How much potential do you think people have to grow in their ability to be a good listener? Share your thinking.

2. Your Pre-Class Reading described three qualities of an effective listener. The first is the ability to be fully present with another person—physically, mentally, emotionally, and spiritually. What can make it personally challenging to offer that kind of presence?

3. The second quality of an effective listener, as described in your Pre-Class Reading, is empathy. What do you think helps a person have empathy?

4. The third quality of an effective listener is to maintain composure during a conversation. This includes remaining calm, accepting silence, not judging, not overidentifying, and being patient with the other person. What do you find the most difficult part of maintaining composure during a conversation?

5. Caring conversations need to take place in a physical setting that allows for confidentiality, personal comfort, and good listening. What settings do you think could be appropriate for a caring conversation?

6. Even when the setting seems suitable for listening, there sometimes may be some unexpected distractions or interruptions. What are some effective ways to deal with distractions or interruptions?

7. A key part of a Stephen Minister's role is to listen for the care receiver's feelings and help him or her recognize, accept, and express those feelings. What has helped you be effective in listening for others' feelings?

8. Part of active listening is paying attention to the other person. What does it mean to pay attention to your care receiver?

9. Another part of active listening is validation. What are some reasons people may be hesitant to validate others' sharing about their feelings?

10. Another part of good listening is asking questions, particularly open-ended questions. What makes an open-ended question more beneficial than a closed-ended question for listening?

III. Practicing Reflective Listening

FOCUS NOTE 4

Sharing Situations

1. Tell what you enjoyed doing on your last vacation.
2. Tell about a time in the last few months when you felt especially happy.
3. Tell about a time when you really needed God's presence and help.

FOCUS NOTE 5

Discussion Questions

1. How did the listener feel reflecting the speaker's experiences?
2. How did the speaker feel having his or her experiences reflected?
3. What were some instances when the listener reflected well?
4. What were instances when the listener could have reflected even better?

IV. Caregiver's Compass Review

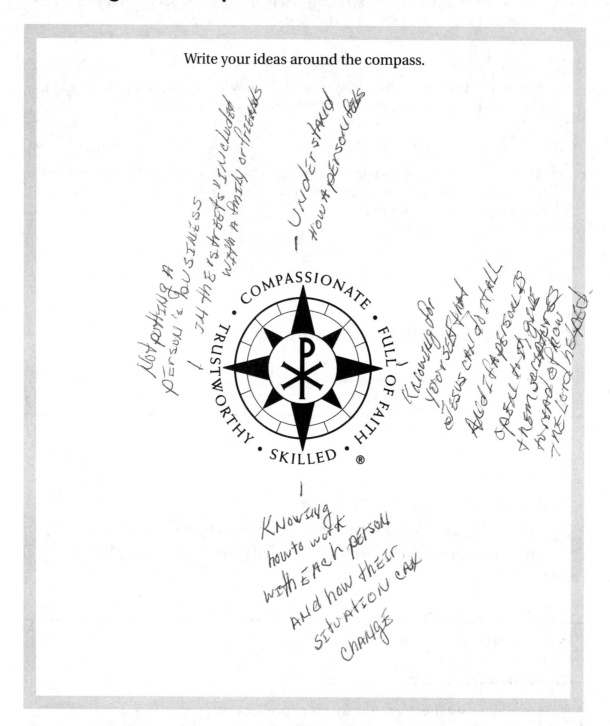

Write your ideas around the compass.

Handwritten notes around the compass:

Not putting a person's business in the streets/unless included with a family or friends

Understand how a person feels

Knowing for yourself that Jesus can do it all

About a persons beliefs to stay open to always remember to no head of prow the lord helped

Knowing how to work with each person and how their situation can change

V. Looking Ahead

VI. Listening to God

FOCUS NOTE 6

Listening to God

Exodus 4:10–12

Moses said to the LORD, "Pardon your servant, Lord. I have never been eloquent, neither in the past nor since you have spoken to your servant. I am slow of speech and tongue." The LORD said to him, "Who gave human beings their mouths? Who makes them deaf or mute? Who gives them sight or makes them blind? Is it not I, the LORD? Now go; I will help you speak and will teach you what to say."

Isaiah 55:10–12

As the rain and the snow
come down from heaven,

and do not return to it
without watering the earth

and making it bud and flourish,
so that it yields seed for the sower and bread for the eater,

so is my word that goes out from my mouth:
It will not return to me empty,

but will accomplish what I desire
and achieve the purpose for which I sent it.

You will go out in joy
and be led forth in peace;

the mountains and hills
will burst into song before you,

and all the trees of the field
will clap their hands.

Matthew 6:25–27

"Therefore I tell you, do not worry about your life, what you will eat or drink; or about your body, what you will wear. Is not life more than food, and the body more than clothes? Look at the birds of the air; they do not sow or reap or store away in barns, and yet your heavenly Father feeds them. Are you not much more valuable than they? Can any one of you by worrying add a single hour to your life?"

2 Corinthians 1:3–7

Praise be to the God and Father of our Lord Jesus Christ, the Father of compassion and the God of all comfort, who comforts us in all our troubles, so that we can comfort those in any trouble with the comfort we ourselves receive from God. For just as we share abundantly in the sufferings of Christ, so also our comfort abounds through Christ. If we are distressed, it is for your comfort and salvation; if we are comforted, it is for your comfort, which produces in you patient endurance of the same sufferings we suffer. And our hope for you is firm, because we know that just as you share in our sufferings, so also you share in our comfort.

Revelation 21:5–6

He who was seated on the throne said, "I am making everything new!" Then he said, "Write this down, for these words are trustworthy and true." He said to me: "It is done. I am the Alpha and the Omega, the Beginning and the End. To the thirsty I will give water without cost from the spring of the water of life."

Questions:

• What thoughts is God sharing?

• What feelings is God sharing?

• What thoughts and feelings do you have about what God is sharing?

Distinctively Christian Caring—Part 1

Module 4 | Presentation Outline

A new command I give you: Love one another. As I have loved you, so you must love one another.
John 13:34

 Devotion: Christlike Caregivers

I. God as the Curegiver

FOCUS NOTE 1

Pressure to Be the Curegiver

Describe a time in your life when you tried to be the curegiver rather than a caregiver for someone.

- How did you feel about it?

- What happened as a result?

- How might the situation have been different if you had let God be the Curegiver and you focused on being the caregiver?

II. God's Constant Presence

FOCUS NOTE 2

Three Ways of Recognizing God's Presence

- Through prayer
- Through a heightened consciousness or awareness of God's presence
- By verbalizing God's presence

FOCUS NOTE 3

Discussion Questions

1. What have you found most helpful for staying aware of God's presence in your own life?

2. What implications does God's presence have for our caregiving?

3. What are practical ways we can help our care receivers connect with God's presence in the caring relationship?

III. Tools of Your Trade: Their Use and Abuse

FOCUS NOTE 4

Questions on the Tools of Your Trade

Christian Caregiving—a Way of Life, chapter 5

1. In the opening story of the chapter (pages 53–54), one caregiver offers an awkward prayer and another spouts Bible verses at a person who is struggling spiritually. How might these "tools of the trade" have been used more appropriately?

2. A Stephen Minister needs to be careful not to treat the care receiver as an object (pages 58–60). What are some specific ways a caregiver might unintentionally do this?

3. What are some indications that your care receiver may welcome distinctively Christian tools in your caring and relating?

4. What are some indications that those tools may not be welcome in a particular situation?

5. What specific steps can you take so that you respectfully and appropriately match resources to people's needs?

IV. Prayer

V. Servanthood vs. Servitude

FOCUS NOTE 5

Descriptions of Servitude and Servanthood

Servitude implies bondage, slavery, and involuntary labor. *Servanthood,* on the other hand, indicates willingness, choice, and voluntary commitment.

There is a big difference between servanthood and servitude. Servanthood is acting out of commitment and love; it's healthy and uplifting. Servitude is acting out of duty and fear; it's unhealthy and even demeaning. While servanthood lifts up and benefits everyone involved, servitude actually creates more difficulties—for both the server and the one being served—than no service at all.

FOCUS NOTE 6

Servanthood vs. Servitude Discussion Questions

1. Overall, would you say your attitude doing this task was one of pure servanthood, pure servitude, or somewhere in between? What gives that impression?

2. Based on your experience, what makes it easier to maintain an attitude of servanthood? What makes it more challenging?

3. Based on your experience, what might be ways you can seek to consistently have an attitude of servanthood with your care receiver?

VI. Caregiver's Compass Review

Write your ideas around the compass.

VII. Looking Ahead

Distinctively Christian Caring—Part 2

Module 4 | Presentation Outline

Likewise the Spirit helps us in our weakness; for we do not know how to pray as we ought, but that very Spirit intercedes with sighs too deep for words. And God, who searches the heart, knows what is the mind of the Spirit, because the Spirit intercedes for the saints according to the will of God.

Romans 8:26–27 (NRSV)

 Devotion: The Spirit Intercedes for Us

I. Reaching Spiritual Depths

FOCUS NOTE 1

Questions about Meeting Spiritual Needs

1. What kinds of spiritual needs might Stephen Ministry care receivers have?

   1. Prayer
   2. Faith
   3. Understanding Scripture
   4. More specific Scripture

2. What signs might you observe that could point to spiritual needs in your care receiver?

   1. WhaWhat to obey & follow God.
   2. Ask for prayer or Bible.

   How to pray for a person?
   Several ways

3. Suppose you sense deep, underlying spiritual needs as your care receiver talks to you. How might you encourage your care receiver to talk about those needs?

II. Building a Prayer

FOCUS NOTE 2

Building a Prayer Discussion Questions

1. What went well?
2. What could have gone better?
3. What was different compared to when you prayed for each other in the last session?
4. What might be some key principles for building a prayer?

III. How the Bible Speaks to You

Literalic
Funfurtic
Traditionalic

FOCUS NOTE 3

My Favorite Bible Passages

A Bible passage is *any verse or series of verses that offer comfort, convey a truth, or otherwise speak to you in a personal way.*

Passage | What Makes It a Favorite

1. 1 John 4: 18 —

I HELPED ME IN A TIME OF A VERY TRUMAHA EXPERIENCENCE IN MY LIVE. I LEARNED THAT EVEN though THAT I HAD gone through such A thing, HE IS THE Prefrect LOVE that SAW ME through AND HEALED ME.

2. LUKE 18: 35 - 43

That JESUS WILL hear us EVEN IN the midst of everything ELSE that may BE going on Around US.

3. NEhEmiah 5

There are times IN our LIVES that we dEAL with vArious types of oppasion (Job, family, Church, Etc.) AND WE NEED God's guidance and wisdom to make A STAND AGAINST it.

4. Joshua 9: 3 - 27
Joshua 10: 1 - 15

ALthough PEOPLE CAN pLAY tricks ON A Person, GOD CAN revEALt but ALSO provide help EVEN WHEN It MAY NOT SEEM It IS desered

5. MATthEW 14: 13 - 14

The people who followed JESUS had SO much compassion for him After he found out that his cousin, John the Baptest was Executed, that they came by foot to a deserted place It WAS SO moved by such AN out pouring of compassion that HE HEAL their sick

Consider continuing to add to your list over time.

FOCUS NOTE 4

My Favorite Bible Stories

A Bible story is *an account of specific events involving people—a narrative with a beginning, middle, and end.*

Story	What Makes It a Favorite
1. MATTHEW 15: 21-28 A woman who (was NOT Jewish) asked Jesus to heal her daughter.	It would seem that either Jesus rejects her, but she proofs her faith in Him. Her daughter is healed
2. Joshua 5: 13-15 Joshua was near Jericho and looked up to see a man before him. He did not know friend or foe.	It was the commander of the Army of the Lord. Joshua worshipped as was to where he was holy.
3. Acts 26: 1-11 Paul comes before King Agrippa to make his case concerning his arrest. Paul was imprisoned for a few years by that time.	Paul confessed what he used to do before his conversion (shut saints in prison, receiving that permission from the chief priests, voted for saints to be killed, etc.
4. Daniel 1: 8-17 Daniel & his friends take a stand in the name of the Lord not to eat or drink food offered to idols.	This is a total stand for the Lord even in the face of danger, and against all odds.
5. Matthew 15: 32 Jesus provided for not only for 5,000 + recorded, but 4,000 + as well who was with him for 3 days with no physical food to eat (spiritual, yes!)	He had compassion on them as well as he has all and made so with very little, there was a lot. It should always be noted that he gave thanks.

Consider continuing to add to your list over time.

IV. Using the Bible in Caregiving

FOCUS NOTE 5

Three Questions to Ask Before Sharing Bible Stories or Passages with a Care Receiver

1. Is my care receiver open to hearing Scripture right now?

2. Is the Bible passage or story relevant to my care receiver's situation?

3. Is my care receiver likely to feel affirmed and validated by my sharing the Bible passage or story—rather than pressured, invalidated, or judged?

FOCUS NOTE 6

Key Guidelines for Sharing Scripture in a Caring Relationship

What guidelines from *Christian Caregiving—a Way of Life* seem especially important to you for sharing Scripture in a caring situation?

V. Caregiver's Compass Review

Write your ideas around the compass.

VI. Looking Ahead

78 |

A Process Approach to Caring

Module 5 | Pre-Class Reading

CONTENTS

Review Two Chapters in *Christian Caregiving— a Way of Life*

As background before you begin this Pre-Class Reading, review the following two chapters of *Christian Caregiving—a Way of Life:*

- Chapter 1, "God as the Curegiver"

- Chapter 12, "Celebrate Results—but Focus on the Process"

Both chapters, which explore a process approach to caring and what makes it distinctively Christian, will be discussed during class.

A Crossroads in Caring

The following situation paints a good picture of two very different approaches to caregiving.

Rebekah and Lindsey

Rebekah was assigned to be Lindsey's Stephen Minister after Lindsey's husband, Adam, was killed in a boating accident. Lindsey and Adam had celebrated their third wedding anniversary just days before the accident, and Lindsey was devastated by the loss.

Over the months that followed, Rebekah spent a lot of time listening to and caring for Lindsey, helping her recognize, accept, and express a lot of painful feelings. Numerous times Rebekah just held Lindsey's hand or sat with her when Lindsey could do nothing but cry. Rebekah felt good about the caring relationship and how it was helping Lindsey.

There was one area, however, where Rebekah wished they could make more progress. Lindsey had long been a person of strong faith—someone others would look to as an example. Since the accident, though, Lindsey had become bitter and angry with God, and she had come to church only a couple of times in the past several months.

Rebekah had asked Lindsey on occasion what she thought about her relationship with God. Each time, Lindsey clenched her jaw and quickly changed the subject.

Two Approaches

Rebekah was anxious to help Lindsey resolve these challenges with her faith. She believed it would contribute a lot to Lindsey's healing. Rebekah saw two ways she could approach the situation:

1. She could shift her focus to **results,** trying to resolve Lindsey's faith crisis by urging her to put aside her bitterness and anger, start regularly going to church again, and have more faith.

2. She could continue the **process** of caring for and supporting Lindsey, trusting that God would work through her presence and care to bring healing to Lindsey.

The Results Approach

Rebekah was tempted to push for a quick resolution to Lindsey's spiritual crisis. She wanted Lindsey to experience complete healing as soon as possible, and she wondered whether she should urge Lindsey to move past her anger and trust God more.

As Rebekah thought about it, however, she recognized the risks of relating to Lindsey this way. If Rebekah focused on getting results right away, Lindsey might feel:

- judged by Rebekah for not trusting God enough;

- guilty or embarrassed that she didn't have more faith;

- annoyed or angry that Rebekah was pressuring her into talking about faith before she was ready;

- compelled to put on a happy face and pretend her faith issues were resolved; or

- more determined not to open up about God.

Rebekah realized that pushing Lindsey for a resolution would do much more harm than good, most likely failing to produce the hoped-for results.

The Process Approach

Instead, Rebekah decided to continue with a process approach—focusing on effective caring and being present for Lindsey and leaving the results to God. By focusing on the process, Rebekah would show that she:

- didn't judge Lindsey for being angry at God;

- wanted to hear Lindsey's thoughts and feelings about God;

- was a safe person to talk with about God and faith;

- wouldn't pressure Lindsey to talk about faith before she was ready; and

- trusted God to work through the caring relationship at a comfortable pace.

Rebekah realized that a process approach would help Lindsey feel more comfortable talking about her faith—and ultimately would produce a better resolution than a results approach would.

As a Stephen Minister, you also may sometimes find yourself facing the choice to either push for a quick resolution to a particular challenge or continue to work the caregiving process. When this happens, it's good to keep in mind that a central part of what makes Stephen Ministry so effective is its *process approach to caring.*

The Best Way to Get Results: Focus on the Process

This isn't to say that results don't matter. Indeed, results are good in caregiving. All Stephen Ministers want to see their caring relationships come to a positive resolution, with their care receivers experiencing emotional, relational, and spiritual healing. All of us, caregivers and care receivers alike, want the best results possible from the relationship. The key to obtaining those results is to focus on the process.

As Rebekah and Lindsey's story demonstrates, your caregiving approach as a Stephen Minister plays a significant role in determining those results. It's an unexpected truth of caregiving: The best way to get results is to put results out of your mind as much as possible and instead focus on the process of caring.

Pressing for a resolution in a caring relationship—trying to fix the care receiver's problems and make him or her feel better as soon as possible—is most likely to end up with negative results. It can add to the care receiver's difficult feelings, foster a sense of dependence on the Stephen Minister, or increase the individual's resistance to change and growth.

Focusing on the process, on the other hand, is more likely to achieve the desired results. *Christian Caregiving—a Way of Life* puts it this way: *"Results start happening when you stop pushing for them!"* [1]

Elements of a Process Approach to Caring

Focus Note A gives an overview of five key elements that make up a process approach to caring and distinguish it from a results approach.

---

1 Kenneth C. Haugk, *Christian Caregiving—a Way of Life,* second edition (St. Louis: Stephen Ministries, 2020), 122.

Five Key Elements of a Process Approach to Caring

1. **Presence:** being with the care receiver

2. **Service:** helping the care receiver without expecting anything in return

3. **Skills:** using best caregiving practices

4. **Boundaries:** respecting the care receiver's personhood

5. **Trust:** leaving the results to God

1. Presence: Being with the Care Receiver

Module 3, "The Art of Listening," described how effective listeners are physically, mentally, emotionally, and spiritually present for their care receivers. This ministry of presence—the Stephen Minister being with and focusing fully on the care receiver—is a foundational part of a process approach to caring.

Another related aspect of presence is that the Stephen Minister consistently *shows up* for the care receiver. That consistency in being present is a key part of what makes a Stephen Ministry caring relationship work, letting the care receiver know he or she can count on the Stephen Minister to be there when needed.

A Stephen Minister's presence is beneficial in multiple ways:

- It lets the care receiver know he or she is not alone.

- It brings an element of reliability to the care receiver's life.

- It is a tangible reminder of God's presence in the care receiver's life.

If, instead, a Stephen Minister focuses on trying to fix the care receiver's situation, his or her attention shifts away from being with the care receiver in the moment to trying to figure out how to make something specific happen in the future. Also, by focusing on results instead of on the care receiver's needs, the Stephen Minister may subtly communicate that his or her presence is contingent on the care receiver's progress toward the Stephen Minister's goals—rather than demonstrating grace-based acceptance of the care receiver as a person.

God gives us the opportunity and privilege to minister to people in the present moment. It's up to us to make the most of it.

2. Service: Helping the Care Receiver without Expecting Anything in Return

Focusing on the process of caring involves service: helping the care receiver address his or her emotional, relational, and spiritual needs without expecting anything in return.

The service element of the process approach highlights a key difference between a friendship and a Stephen Ministry caring relationship. As Focus Note B illustrates, a friendship is mutual, with the focus on both people. A Stephen Ministry caring relationship, on the other hand, is focused solely on the benefit of the care receiver.

FOCUS NOTE B

The Difference between a Friendship and a Stephen Ministry Caring Relationship

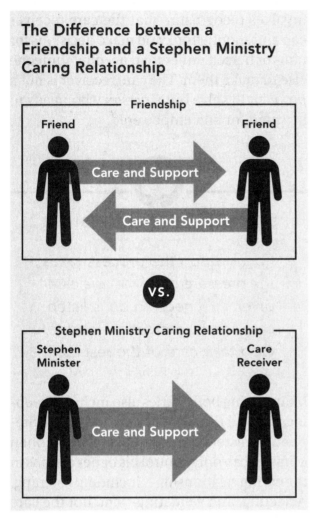

A process approach to caring focuses entirely on what's best for the care receiver. This might include:

- sharing a care receiver's pain and listening to a care receiver express the same thoughts or feelings over and over for as long as needed;

- spending time in silence with the care receiver until he or she is ready to share;

- continuing to listen and care even when the care receiver has made a choice or expressed opinions the Stephen Minister doesn't agree with;

- praying or sharing Bible passages with the care receiver only as he or she is open to it; or

- continuing to love, care for, and pray for a care receiver who may not be ready to follow Christ.

This kind of service helps the care receiver in such a way that he or she doesn't feel pressured to:

- hold the Stephen Minister's attention and make the Stephen Minister's time worthwhile;

- help with the Stephen Minister's anxiety about the care receiver's situation;

- think or act in ways that match the Stephen Minister's beliefs and values;

- make decisions based on what the Stephen Minister wants;

- find a resolution as soon as possible; or

- help the Stephen Minister feel successful as a caregiver.

Such pressure would interfere with the caring and healing process and could suggest incorrectly that the caring relationship is at least in part for the benefit of the Stephen Minister.

A process approach temporarily sets aside the needs of the Stephen Minister in order to focus fully on the care receiver. That doesn't mean that the Stephen Minister's needs are unimportant or have to go unmet—it's just that those needs are best addressed in Small Group Peer Supervision, which will be covered later in Stephen Minister training.

3. Skills: Using Best Caregiving Practices

A process approach to caring focuses on the *means* of care, not the ends or the ultimate resolution. Those means are the caregiving skills and practices the Stephen Minister brings to the caring relationship—skills and practices you'll learn and develop throughout your training.

Taking a process approach means focusing on what you can do using your caregiving skills in your time with your care receiver. At the same time, it includes recognizing that you *can't* and *don't have to* cure your care receiver or fix his or her problems. In fact, attempting to fix the situation would most likely set back the care receiver's movement toward healing and wholeness.

The effectiveness of a Stephen Minister's caregiving is not based on how quickly the care receiver starts feeling better or how soon the situation is resolved. Rather, it's based on the Stephen Minister's consistency in working the process and exercising caring skills—being focused and attentive during visits, reflecting and validating the care receiver's feelings, and so on. This emphasis helps keep Stephen Ministers from pressuring their care receivers to get better, as well as pressuring themselves to get results. Instead, they focus on making use of their caring skills during each visit, while trusting God to work through the process of caregiving to bring hope and healing to the care receiver. Following this approach helps you be maximally successful in your care.

4. Boundaries: Respecting the Care Receiver's Personhood

A process approach to caring is based on a clear understanding of the boundaries between the Stephen Minister and the care receiver. (Module 7 covers boundaries in greater detail.)

The Stephen Minister respects the personhood of the care receiver at all times. This involves recognizing that the care receiver can and should think and make decisions for him- or herself rather than needing someone else to make them. The care receiver is not a *problem* to solve but a *person* who needs to be cared for and empowered.

STEPHEN MINISTER INSIGHT

"Focusing on the process takes the pressure off of me as a caregiver. All I need to do is listen, care, and be present—and let God take care of the results."

Maintaining boundaries also includes keeping in mind there are limits to what the Stephen Minister has control over. The Stephen Minister can only control his or her actions in the caring relationship—including listening, reflecting, and validating—and not the care receiver's actions or the ways God works in and through the caring relationship. Rather than crossing boundaries and attempting to control those other factors, the Stephen Minister focuses on the process of caring and leaves the response to the care receiver and the healing to God.

If the Stephen Minister pushes for specific results and tries to get the care receiver to follow his or her lead, it may have one of two effects on boundaries.

1) The care receiver may see the Stephen Minister as intruding on his or her life and personhood. This could lead to defensive-

ness, unwillingness to address existing issues, a loss of trust, or even a premature end to the caring relationship.

2) The care receiver may feel powerless to go against the Stephen Minister's plans and may instead comply passively, trusting that the Stephen Minister knows best. The care receiver would probably make fewer and fewer independent decisions, leading to excessive dependence on the Stephen Minister and delaying healing.

However, when the Stephen Minister focuses on the process instead of results, the care receiver feels affirmed, respected, and empowered. That's a big part of what a person needs when moving through a difficult time in life.

Stephen Ministers encourage care receivers to become more self-reliant. Through the process approach of Stephen Ministry, care receivers begin to think through what they can do for themselves and how they can take responsibility for their own lives. More importantly, Stephen Ministers help their care receivers grow in their reliance on God by incarnating God's presence and modeling their own trust in God.

Sometimes Stephen Ministers may strongly believe they know what their care receiver needs better than the care receiver does. Even then, however, they remain focused on the process, allowing the care receiver to make his or her own choices.

5. Trust: Leaving the Results to God

The final component of a process approach to care is trust. Stephen Ministers trust that God will bring the results the care receiver needs. As *Christian Caregiving—a Way of Life* points out, we are the *caregivers* and

God is the *Curegiver*—so we trust God is working through our caring to meet the care receiver's needs.

Stephen Ministers can provide care in many ways, but only God can change lives, bringing about results such as these:

- *Healing.* Stephen Ministers and other caregivers play a crucial role in the process that paves the way for healing, but healing itself is in God's hands—including physical, emotional, and spiritual healing, as well as the healing of relationships.

- *Faith.* As much as Stephen Ministers may want their care receivers to trust God more fully, the only way people grow in faith is through the Holy Spirit's work. "I pray that out of his glorious riches he may strengthen you with power through his Spirit in your inner being, so that Christ may dwell in your hearts through faith" (Ephesians 3:16–17).

- *Forgiveness. Christian Caregiving—a Way of Life* talks about freedom from guilt and freedom to forgive as results that come only through faith in Jesus.[2]

- *Hope.* True hope comes from God. "May the God of hope fill you with all joy and peace as you trust in him, so that you may overflow with hope by the power of the Holy Spirit" (Romans 15:13).

- *Peace.* Only God can give the deep and lasting peace that comes from knowing that God is with us no matter what. "And the peace of God, which transcends all understanding, will guard your hearts and your minds in Christ Jesus" (Philippians 4:7).

---

2 Haugk, *Christian Caregiving—a Way of Life,* 127–128.

A Biblical View of a Process Approach to Caring

Focusing on the process is a thoroughly biblical approach. Here are 12 caring actions that take a process approach, as described in the Bible.

1. Caring

- "Bear one another's burdens, and so fulfill the law of Christ" (Galatians 6:2 ESV). The "law of Christ" is stated in John 13:34: "Love one another."

- "Each of you should look not only to your own interests, but also to the interests of others" (Philippians 2:4).

2. Listening

- "He who answers before listening—that is his folly and his shame" (Proverbs 18:13).

- "Let everyone be quick to listen, slow to speak, slow to anger" (James 1:19b NRSV).

3. Accepting

- "Accept one another, then, just as Christ accepted you, in order to bring praise to God" (Romans 15:7).

4. Understanding

- "One who spares words is knowledgeable; one who is cool in spirit has understanding" (Proverbs 17:27 NRSV).

- "The purposes in the human mind are like deep water, but the intelligent will draw them out" (Proverbs 20:5 NRSV).

5. Respecting

- "Honor one another above yourselves" (Romans 12:10b).

- "Show proper respect to everyone" (1 Peter 2:17a).

6. Acting with Kindness

- "Let love and faithfulness never leave you; bind them around your neck, write them on the tablet of your heart" (Proverbs 3:3).

- "And be kind to one another, tenderhearted, forgiving one another, as God in Christ has forgiven you" (Ephesians 4:32 NRSV).

7. Acting with Gentleness

- "Pleasant words are a honeycomb, sweet to the soul and healing to the bones" (Proverbs 16:24).

- "I . . . beg you to lead a life worthy of the calling to which you have been called, with all humility and gentleness" (Ephesians 4:1–2a NRSV).

8. Acting with Patience

- "Love is patient" (1 Corinthians 13:4a).

- ". . . be patient, bearing with one another in love" (Ephesians 4:2).

9. Acting with Sympathy

- "Finally, all of you, have unity of spirit, sympathy, love for one another" (1 Peter 3:8 NRSV).

10. Acting with Empathy

- "Rejoice with those who rejoice, weep with those who weep" (Romans 12:15 NRSV).

11. Acting with Compassion

- "If one member suffers, all suffer together with it" (1 Corinthians 12:26a NRSV).

- "Therefore, as God's chosen people, holy and dearly loved, clothe yourselves with compassion . . ." (Colossians 3:12).

12. Praying for and with Others

- "Therefore confess your sins to one another, and pray for one another, so that you may be healed" (James 5:16a NRSV).

- "Pray without ceasing" (1 Thessalonians 5:17 NRSV).

You can pray *for* your care receiver at all times and pray with your care receiver when it is appropriate, natural, and timely.

STEPHEN MINISTER INSIGHT

"When your job is focused on fixing things, it can be hard to flip the switch for your caring visits. So, before I get out of my car and walk up to my care receiver's house, I pause, take a deep breath, and say, 'God, help me trust you to be the Curegiver.' A little prayer like that goes a long way toward helping me stay focused on the process."

Getting Ready for the In-Class Session

Be very familiar with the ideas in this Pre-Class Reading and chapters 1 and 12 from *Christian Caregiving—a Way of Life*. You will use these concepts in class.

stephenministries.org/library

See the **Stephen Minister Online Library** for additional resources and downloads related to this Stephen Minister training topic.

A Process Approach to Caring

Module 5 | Presentation Outline

I planted the seed, Apollos watered it, but God made it grow.
1 Corinthians 3:6

 Devotion: Paul, Apollos, and God

I. A Vivid Example

FOCUS NOTE 1

Care Receiver Profile

Create a description of a care receiver who is the same gender as the person playing the role. Make sure that the caregiving need is *entirely fictional*—not based on your own life or on the life of a friend or loved one.

1. What is the care receiver's age and primary need for care?

2. How long has this need been going on?

3. What feelings is the care receiver experiencing?

4. What does the care receiver most want from his or her caregiver?

Discussion Questions

1. How did the care receiver feel?

2. How did the caregiver feel?

3. What body language and feelings did the observer notice?

4. What did this exercise tell you about caregiving?

II. Process Goals

A. Definition of Process Goals

A Definition of Process Goals

Process goals are *actions* ...

Verb

They focus on
the means, not the end.

FOCUS NOTE 4

A Definition of Process Goals

Process goals are actions *I can do* . . .

They focus on
what I can control.

I can be too who I am AND I can control that, but it may not ~~it not~~ help others.

FOCUS NOTE 5

A Definition of Process Goals

Process goals are actions I can do ***now*** . . .

They focus on
the present.

To be there to be know that Jesus is there, focus . . .

FOCUS NOTE 6

A Definition of Process Goals

Process goals are actions I can do now
that concentrate on the other person's needs . . .

They focus on
servanthood.

Focus on other's person's needs

FOCUS NOTE 7

Jesus' Attitude of Servanthood

Do nothing out of selfish ambition or vain conceit, but in humility consider others better than yourselves. Each of you should look not only to your own interests, but also to the interests of others.

Your attitude should be the same as that of Christ Jesus: Who, being in very nature God, did not consider equality with God something to be grasped, but made himself nothing, taking the very nature of a servant, being made in human likeness. And being found in appearance as a man, he humbled himself and became obedient to death—even death on a cross!

Philippians 2:3–8

FOCUS NOTE 8

A Definition of Process Goals

Process goals are actions I can do now that concentrate on the other person's needs *and leave the results to God*.

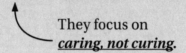

They focus on *caring, not curing*.

B. Examples of Process Goals

FOCUS NOTE 9

Examples of Process Goals

1. As a caregiver, I will be physically and mentally present with the care receiver.

2. I will actively listen.

3. I will focus on the care receiver's feelings.

4. I will strive to understand the care receiver's frame of reference—to see the care receiver's situation as he or she sees it.

5. I will be nonjudgmental and accepting of the care receiver as a person deeply loved by God.

6. I will share a prayer, Bible passage, or other Christian resource when appropriate, natural, and timely.

C. A Possible Challenge: When a Care Receiver Asks for Advice

---

FOCUS NOTE 10

Process Responses to Requests for Advice

- "What seems best to you right now?"
- "What are you thinking about that?"
- "Given everything you know, what are you leaning toward doing?"
- "What might be some of the pluses and minuses of doing that?"
- "What options do you see? Are there any other options you might consider?"

III. The Importance of Results

FOCUS NOTE 11

Sincere Results Goals

- My care receiver will share his or her feelings.
- My care receiver will feel better about him- or herself.
- My care receiver's painful feelings will go away.
- My care receiver will resolve his or her situation.
- My care receiver will relate better to other people.
- My care receiver will feel more hopeful about the future.
- My care receiver will grow spiritually and be closer to God.

FOCUS NOTE 12

Negative Results That Can Come from Focusing on Results

- The care receiver might become resentful of the Stephen Minister for trying to force a particular solution or result on him or her.

- The care receiver might simply go along with the Stephen Minister's efforts and become dependent on him or her, which would get in the way of personal growth.

- The care receiver might feel pressured or manipulated into making changes or acting differently so as not to disappoint the caregiver.

- The care receiver might not be emotionally ready to make those changes and may end up feeling worse when they don't happen.

- The care receiver might feel the Stephen Minister's love and acceptance was conditional on thinking, acting, or feeling a certain way.

IV. How to Focus on the Process of Caring

FOCUS NOTE 13

Caregiving Situation 1

Evan was recently fired from his job and is dealing with a lot of difficult feelings. He's married and has two young children, and he feels as if he's let them all down because he and his wife are now struggling to make ends meet on just her salary. He's embarrassed and ashamed to have been fired, and he is also very angry with himself because he knows his own lack of focus and effort are the main reasons he lost his job. At this point, he's not sure anyone else will ever want to hire him, so he hasn't been able to start thinking about taking any next steps.

Process goals:

1. Present Attentive
2. Allow him to talk about him he is feeling if he would like to
3. Options?
4. In Crisis
5. Listening
6. Non-Judgemental

FOCUS NOTE 14

Instructions for Discussing Focus Notes 15 and 16

1. Have someone in your group read aloud the caregiving situation in Focus Note 15.

2. Brainstorm at least five process goals a Stephen Minister could have in that situation.

3. Recorders: Write your group's ideas in the space provided in the Focus Note.

4. Evaluate your ideas to make sure they are focused on the process of caring.

5. After your group has worked through the caregiving situation, the whole class will discuss the situation.

6. Repeat steps 1–5 with Focus Note 16.

FOCUS NOTE 15

Caregiving Situation 2

Everything had been going great for Emma and Josh. Their youngest child had just left for college, and they were planning a cross-country vacation together. But then, Josh was diagnosed with late-stage cancer and died just a few months later. Emma is feeling overwhelmed by her grief, covering her child's tuition, and trying to figure out how to manage everything alone.

Process goals:

1.

2.

3.

4.

5.

FOCUS NOTE 16

Caregiving Situation 3

Anna's mother-in-law, Clara, has seen her health decline in recent years. About a year ago, when it became clear that Clara could no longer get by on her own, Anna had suggested that Clara move in with her and her husband, Jonathan. They'd all agreed that it seemed like the best arrangement.

Since that time, the burden of caregiving has fallen largely on Anna. She has had to cut back her work hours significantly and rarely has time for her own interests. Anna and Jonathan have always enjoyed traveling together, but since Clara moved in, they haven't wanted to leave her with anyone else for any length of time. Increasingly, Anna is overwhelmed by difficult feelings—regret over lost time and missed opportunities, anger and resentment at her mother-in-law for making her feel trapped, and guilt over that anger and resentment.

Process goals:

1.

2.

3.

4.

5.

V. Practicing a Process Approach to Caring

FOCUS NOTE 17

Discussion Questions

1. How did the caregiver focus on the process of caring?

2. How else could the caregiver have focused on the process of caring?

3. How did the caregiver feel about focusing on the process of caring?

4. How did the care receiver feel about receiving care that focused on the process?

VI. Caregiver's Compass Review

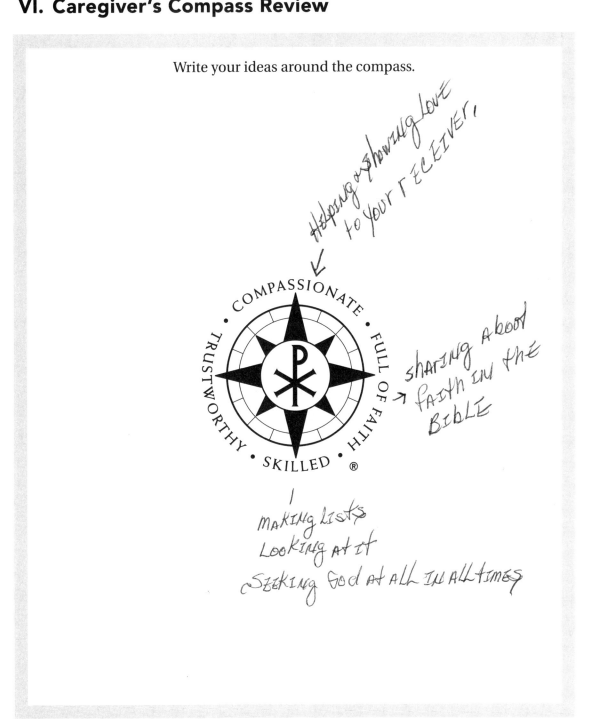

Write your ideas around the compass.

Helping & showing love to your RECEIVER!

sharing about faith in the BiBLE

MAKINg lists
Looking at it
SEEKING God at ALL IN ALL timES

VII. Looking Ahead

Assertiveness: Relating Gently and Firmly—Part 1

Module 6 | Presentation Outline

Instead, speaking the truth in love, we will in all things grow up into him who is the Head, that is, Christ.

Ephesians 4:15

Devotion: The Power of Speaking the Truth in Love

I. Defining Assertiveness

A. What Assertiveness Is

FOCUS NOTE 1

Definition of Assertiveness

Assertiveness is a positive, constructive way of relating in which a person clearly, directly, and confidently expresses his or her own needs, wants, feelings, and opinions—while also respecting the needs, wants, feelings, and opinions of others.

1. Assertiveness Is a Positive, Constructive Way of Relating

2. Assertiveness Is about Expressing Yourself Clearly, Directly, and Confidently

3. Assertiveness Is about Expressing Your Own Needs, Wants, Feelings, and Opinions

4. Assertiveness Respects the Needs, Wants, Feelings, and Opinions of Others

B. What Assertiveness Is Not

1. Assertiveness Is Not Passive

FOCUS NOTE 2

Definition of Passive Behavior

Passive behavior is when a person holds back from expressing his or her needs, wants, feelings, and opinions. The person is reluctant to make decisions, hold any particular position, or take appropriate action—and instead often goes along with the wishes of others regardless of what he or she personally wants or what is in his or her best interests.

2. Assertiveness Is Not Aggressive

FOCUS NOTE 3

Definition of Aggressive Behavior

Aggressive behavior is when a person relates in a forceful, harsh, or controlling manner. The person puts his or her own needs, wants, feelings, and opinions above others' and may use demands, insults, sarcasm, manipulation, and other tactics to get his or her own way.

FOCUS NOTE 4

Definition of Passive-Aggressive Behavior

Passive-aggressive behavior is when a person uses covert, hidden, or indirect means of opposition to get his or her way. While on the surface appearing compliant, the person uses stubbornness, pouting, excessive rigidity, veiled criticism, or other stealthy means to undermine the decisions or actions of others.

II. Assertive, Passive, and Aggressive Bible Stories

A. Concepts with a Long History

B. A Modern-Day Prodigal Son

FOCUS NOTE 5

A Modern-Day Prodigal Son (Inspired by Luke 15:11–32)

The Roles:

- Narrator
- Father
- Younger Son
- Older Son

Narrator: One day after dinner, the owner of a small business was talking with his younger son.

Younger Son: Dad, I'm 18 now. Give me my share of the inheritance so I can get on with my life.

Father: Your inheritance? Well, I guess I can pull it together—it'll take me a few days to make the arrangements, though.

Younger Son: The sooner, the better.

Father: What are you thinking you'll do with it?

Younger Son: I don't know yet, but it's my business, not yours.

Father: You know, I was going to offer you a job at the family business.

Younger Son: Ugh, not this again. I don't want to be stuck in that job forever. Let me do what I want.

Narrator: So the father got the money together to give the younger son his share of the inheritance. A few days later, the younger son came to him again, his bags packed.

Younger Son: Well, Dad, I'm out of here. I'm going to see what the real world is like.

Narrator: So the son headed off to the city, where he squandered all the money he had on expensive meals and constant partying. Before long, he had nothing, and the people he'd met and befriended in the city left him. The son was relegated to scrounging for food in the garbage and sleeping on park benches. Eventually, he came to his senses.

Younger Son: How could I be such an idiot? Here I am, practically starving to death, while the employees at my dad's business all get a decent paycheck! I'm going back home and apologizing. I don't even deserve to be called his son, but maybe he'll at least have some job for me—I'd take anything.

Narrator: So he set off to return to his father.

The Assertive Ending

Narrator: When the father saw his son step off the bus, he was filled with compassion. The father ran out of the house toward him and embraced him.

Father: My son! Thank God, you're back!

Narrator: The young man fell exhausted into his father's arms.

Younger Son: Dad, I really messed up. I'm so sorry. You probably don't think of me as your son anymore, and I know I don't deserve it, but—

Father: You'll always be my son, no matter what. We've got to celebrate! Come inside and get changed. Those clothes are rags—I've got new clothes for you! We're throwing some steaks on the grill tonight!

Narrator: A while later, the older son, after a long day at the family's business, pulled into the driveway and heard the sounds of laughter coming from the backyard and saw the smoke from the grill. He looked over the fence to see what all the noise was about.

Older Son: What's he doing here? And Dad is celebrating with him after he walked out on us? You've got to be kidding me!

Narrator: Furious, the brother stormed into the house. When the father saw him through the kitchen window, glaring at them and refusing to join the celebration, he went in to talk with his son.

Father: Son, what are you doing just sitting in here? Come out and celebrate with us. Your brother's home!

Older Son: Celebrate? For him? All these years I've always worked hard for you. I've never complained. And when was the last time you threw me a party? But when your good-for-nothing son leaves, wastes everything we worked so hard to earn, and comes back broke, here you are grilling steaks for him!

Father: Son, you're always with me, and everything I have is yours. But we lost your brother, and now he's come back to us. That's something worth celebrating.

FOCUS NOTE 6

The Passive Ending

Narrator: The young man's father saw him get off the bus, but although he was overjoyed to see his son, he was hesitant to show his emotions.

Father: Oh, my son is back! What should I do? I mean, I should probably welcome him back, but I don't know what to say.

Narrator: So the father waited in the house until at last the young man staggered up and rang the doorbell.

Younger Son: Dad, I really messed up. I'm so sorry. You probably don't think of me as your son anymore, and I know I don't deserve it, but . . . *(His voice trails off. When his father doesn't say anything, he continues tentatively.)* So, um, I was hoping you might have a job for me at the shop—I'll take anything. Would that be okay?

Father: Well . . . I guess so.

Younger Son: Dad, I feel terrible about all that happened.

Father: Forget about it.

Younger Son: Can you ever forgive me?

Father: I suppose. For now, you can get out of those clothes and get cleaned up.

Younger Son: Thank you. I want to earn your trust.

Father: We can figure that out later.

FOCUS NOTE 7

The Aggressive Ending

Narrator: The older brother was pulling into the driveway after a long day of work when he saw his younger brother at the other end of the street, walking toward the house. He was filled with anger that his younger brother would return after wasting their father's money and disgracing their family.

Older Son: That worthless brother of mine sure has some nerve showing his face around here again! I've got to stop him before he tries to worm his way back into the family.

Narrator: The older brother, his fists clenched, ran down the road to intercept the younger brother.

Younger Son: Brother!

Older Son: Don't "brother" me! How dare you come back here!

Younger Son: I just came to apologize to Dad. I know I don't deserve to be called his son; all I want is to ask for a job, any job.

Older Son: Well, at least you got one thing right—you don't deserve to be his son. And there's no way we'd hire you either, as lazy as you are! You should just go back the way you came!

Younger Son: Whoa, whoa! I'm just here to talk to Dad! I only need to earn enough for a place to stay and a little food.

Older Son: Oh, you need food? That's rich. I've heard all about how you've been partying day and night, and now that the money's all gone, you come slinking back here looking for sympathy? Pathetic. Don't waste Father's time—you're dead to the family already.

Younger Son: I'm sorry, I just hoped—

Older Son: You hoped! I couldn't care less about that. I've been working myself to the bone since you left, doing your share of the work on top of mine. Thanks a lot for that, by the way! Now get out of here!

III. Simple Assertions

Eight Simple Assertion Situations

Situation 1

Person A: You're at a reunion with a group of friends, about to have your picture taken. You notice your friend, Person B, has a tuft of hair sticking up that would be noticeable in the picture. Make an assertive statement.

Person B: Respond assertively.

Person C: Observe. After the situation concludes, lead a discussion for 30 to 60 seconds based on the questions in Focus Note 9.

Situation 2

Person C: While at the store, you run into one of your favorite teachers, Person A, whom you haven't seen in many years. Let Person A know how much you appreciate the difference he or she made in your life.

Person A: Respond assertively.

Person B: Observe. After the situation concludes, lead a discussion for 30 to 60 seconds based on the questions in Focus Note 9.

Situation 3

Person B: You want to borrow Person C's truck for a couple of hours to pick up some secondhand furniture you bought. Make an assertive request.

Person C: Person B is a good friend, and you normally wouldn't mind lending your truck, but there is somewhere you have to be in an hour, so you need your truck right now. Respond assertively.

Person A: Observe. After the situation concludes, lead a discussion for 30 to 60 seconds based on the questions in Focus Note 9.

Situation 4

Person A: You planned to visit Person B's house on Saturday to help move some furniture. You just found out that your child has a concert at school on Saturday, and you want to reschedule to Friday. Make an assertive request.

Person B: You are willing to reschedule, but you are busy Friday. Respond assertively.

Person C: Observe. After the situation concludes, lead a discussion for 30 to 60 seconds based on the questions in Focus Note 9.

Situation 5

Person C: You and your spouse want to sit together at the movie and the theater is very crowded. You notice an empty seat next to Person A and another empty seat on the other side of the person sitting right next to Person A. You cannot see any other seats together in the theater. Make an assertive request.

Person A: You and your spouse are seated together with empty seats on either side of you. Respond assertively.

Person B: Observe. After the situation concludes, lead a discussion for 30 to 60 seconds based on the questions in Focus Note 9.

Situation 6

Person B: You are meeting your friend, Person C, for lunch, but you had a busy morning and lost track of time. You are 20 minutes late when you arrive at the restaurant and sit down at the table with your friend. Make an assertive statement.

Person C: You and Person B meet for lunch every few weeks, and this is the third time in a row he or she has been late. His or her lateness has been an inconvenience for you, since you meet during your lunch break at work and have limited time. Respond assertively.

Person A: Observe. After the situation concludes, lead a discussion for 30 to 60 seconds based on the questions in Focus Note 9.

Situation 7

Person A: Person B is a cashier at a convenience store. You paid for your purchase with a $20 bill, but he or she only gave you change for a $10 bill. Make an assertive statement.

Person B: When you check the register, you see that Person A is right—there's a $20 bill on top of the stack of $10 bills. Respond assertively.

Person C: Observe. After the situation concludes, lead a discussion for 30 to 60 seconds based on the questions in Focus Note 9.

Situation 8

Person C: You're standing in line at a coffee shop waiting to order, and a stranger, Person A, steps in line in front of you. You're not sure whether the person did this intentionally or not. Make an assertive statement.

Person A: You were distracted by a message on your phone and inadvertently got in line in front of Person C. Respond assertively.

Person B: Observe. After the situation concludes, lead a discussion for 30 to 60 seconds based on the questions in Focus Note 9.

106 |

FOCUS NOTE 9

Simple Assertion Discussion Questions

- Was the interaction assertive? If not, what made it not assertive?
- How could the interaction have been more assertive?

IV. When, Where, and How to Be Assertive

A. Situations When a Stephen Minister Needs to Be Assertive

FOCUS NOTE 10

Examples of Situations When Stephen Ministers Need to Be Assertive with Their Care Receivers

- Setting up regular, weekly, in-person caring visits
- Encouraging a care receiver to share his or her feelings
- Asking whether you can pray for the care receiver during a caring visit
-
-
-
-
-
-
-

B. Three Steps to Relating More Assertively

1. Decide Whether to Be Assertive

FOCUS NOTE 11

Five Questions to Ask When Deciding Whether to Be Assertive

1. Is this a real problem—and how do I know it is?

2. Is this the time and place to respond assertively?

3. What are my chances of at least a small measure of success initially?

4. Am I willing to invest time and energy and face some possible risk in order to make the change?

5. Will I stay relatively calm while I try new, assertive behaviors, not letting fears or anxieties overwhelm me?

FOCUS NOTE 12

A Hypothetical Caring Relationship

Steve became Jake's Stephen Minister about a month after Ruth, Jake's wife of 48 years, had a heart attack and passed away. Steve has been meeting weekly with Jake for about three months, and they've built a good relationship. Steve has noticed that, although Jake occasionally talks about Ruth, he seems reluctant to explore his difficult emotions in any depth. Whenever Jake begins to get emotional, he quickly changes the subject.

Steve sees that Jake is really struggling with a lot of deep feelings, but they never seem to get beyond the surface. Steve begins wondering whether it's time to be more assertive in helping Jake open up about his feelings.

FOCUS NOTE 13

Steve's Assertiveness Challenge

1. Decide Whether to Be Assertive

Steve's Response to the Five Questions:

- Is this a real problem—and how do I know it is?

- Is this the time and place to respond assertively?

- What are my chances of at least a small measure of success initially?

- Am I willing to invest time and energy and face some possible risk in order to make the change?

- Will I stay relatively calm while I try new, assertive behaviors, not letting fears or anxieties overwhelm me?

2. Decide What to Say

Steve's Main Concerns:

What Steve Decided to Say:

See Focus Note 15

3. Decide What to Do

Nonverbal Aspects Steve Wanted to Work On:

2. Decide What to Say

Principles for Deciding What to Say
(Look Back at Focus Note 13, Number 2)

- Say something rather than nothing
- Be honest
- Use "I" messages
- Make "I want" statements
- Combine "I want" statements and "I" messages
- Avoid labeling
- Be concise
- Don't apologize for asserting yourself
- Avoid sarcasm
- Be as persistent as necessary

Ways to Invite Jake to Talk about His Feelings

- "I noticed you paused for just a moment there and then changed the subject. I'm interested in knowing what you were thinking or feeling just then."
- "You said you were feeling [sad, lonely, etc.]. Tell me more about that."
- "You mentioned Ruth just now. I'd be interested in hearing more about her."
- "I've gotten to know you pretty well these past few months, but you haven't said much about Ruth. I'd be interested in learning more about her."
- "It sounds like this may be a pretty difficult subject. Could you say more about what you're thinking?"
- "We've talked about a lot of things in our time together, but I am wondering whether we could talk more about Ruth."

3. Decide What to Do

FOCUS NOTE 16

Keeping Your Nonverbal Communication Assertive
(Look Back at Focus Note 13, Number 3)

- Look the way you feel
- Use assertive gestures
- Speak clearly
- Face the person
- Maintain eye contact
- Be aware of your physical position
- Pay attention to your tone of voice
- Actively listen

C. Assertiveness in Our Own Lives

FOCUS NOTE 17

Assertiveness in Our Own Lives

Briefly describe a situation where you find it difficult to be assertive.

When I am dealing w/ someone on the phone (customer service) sometimes.

1. Decide Whether to Be Assertive

Write your answers to the following questions about whether to be assertive. This will help you determine whether this is a situation that warrants an assertive change in your behavior.

- Is this a real problem—and how do I know it is?

This is a very real problem because the person on the line is trying to help.

- Is this the time and place to respond assertively?

Yes, most certainly!

- What are my chances of at least a small measure of success initially?

~~Bes~~ Before I make a call, to relax, write out what I want to say and try to listen

- Am I willing to invest time and energy and face some possible risk in order to make the change?

I may be willing to invest time but energy is another thing. There will be risk until I let Jesus take control.

- Will I stay relatively calm while I try new, assertive behaviors, not letting fears or anxieties overwhelm me?

I

And Another one too for 24th

2. Decide What to Say

Based on the principles in the box to the right, think about what you might say in order to respond assertively to the situation. It may help to write a brief dialogue, including what the other person might say in response to you.

My Main Concerns: (For instance, to speak truthfully and lovingly and to communicate your message in the least threatening way possible.)

What Will I Say? (You might write a full statement or some notes to help you remember what you want to say.)

Principles for Deciding What to Say

- Say something rather than nothing
- Be honest
- Use "I" messages
- Use "I want" statements
- Combine "I want" statements and "I" messages
- Avoid labeling
- Be concise
- Don't apologize for asserting yourself
- Avoid sarcasm
- Be as persistent as necessary

3. Decide What to Do

Think about the aspects of nonverbal communication in the adjacent box. Decide which ones you need to practice or pay special attention to and write them below.

Keeping Your Nonverbal Communication Assertive

- Look the way you feel
- Use assertive gestures
- Speak clearly
- Face the person
- Maintain eye contact
- Be aware of your physical position
- Pay attention to the quality of your voice
- Actively listen

V. Caregiver's Compass Review

Write your ideas around the compass.

VI. Looking Ahead

FOCUS NOTE 18

Assertiveness Assignment

Before the next class, make a point of responding assertively in a situation where you normally would have responded passively or aggressively. This situation might be the one you wrote about in Focus Note 17 or another situation that requires assertiveness. You'll have a chance in the next class session to tell others about your assertive action, if you feel comfortable doing so.

Assertiveness: Relating Gently and Firmly—Part 2

Module 6 | Presentation Outline

When he saw Peter and John about to enter, he asked them for money. Peter looked straight at him, as did John. Then Peter said, "Look at us!" So the man gave them his attention, expecting to get something from them.

Then Peter said, "Silver or gold I do not have, but what I do have I give you. In the name of Jesus Christ of Nazareth, walk."

Acts 3:3–6

 Devotion: What Does It Mean to Be an Assertive Christian

I. Assertiveness Experiences

II. Assertively Making, Granting, Refusing, and Negotiating Requests

A. Responding to Requests from Your Care Receiver

FOCUS NOTE 1

Examples of Requests Care Receivers Might Make of Stephen Ministers

1. "Can we get together on Tuesday instead of Wednesday next week?"

2. "Could we meet for an hour and a half this time instead of our usual hour? This week has been especially difficult."

3. "Could we find another place to get together? I'm feeling uncomfortable meeting with you in my home because my family might overhear."

4. "I appreciate all you've given me, and I'd like to do something for you. Could I give you a small token of my gratitude and appreciation?"

5. "One visit a week just doesn't seem enough. Couldn't we start getting together two or three times a week?"

6. "Could you watch my children Thursday evening while I go to a movie?"

7. "My husband is really struggling too right now. Could you meet with both of us together so you could care for him too?"

1. Saying Yes to Care Receiver Requests

2. Saying No to Care Receiver Requests

3. Negotiating Requests with Your Care Receiver

B. Making an Assertive Request

The DESC Model: Four Steps in Making a Request

1. *Describe* the Situation

   Describe your experiences and observations accurately without judging or accusing.

2. *Express* Your Feelings about the Situation

   Speak personally about what feelings you have connected with the situation. Own your feelings, and avoid blaming the other person for the way you feel.

3. *Specify* What You Want

   Ask specifically for what you want. Make your requests manageable and reasonable, and make only one or two requests at a time.

4. Describe the *Consequences* Associated with Your Request

   Whenever possible, describe the positive consequences associated with your request. Show how cooperating with your request will be in the other person's best interest as well as yours. If you must specify negative consequences, make sure they're appropriate, as well as consequences you're willing to carry out.

Example of the DESC Model

Describe the Situation: "A couple of weeks ago, you asked me to give you a ride so that you could do some errands. While I didn't mind you asking, I did point out that providing transportation goes beyond what a Stephen Minister does. As an alternative, I gave you information about some local transportation services."

Express Your Feelings about the Situation: "I'm glad to hear that you tried out one of the services I suggested, even if it didn't seem like it would quite work out for you to use it regularly."

Specify What You Want: "Since I'm not able to provide transportation for you, I'd encourage you to contact another of the services I suggested to see whether it can better meet your transportation needs."

Describe the Consequences Associated with Your Request: "A transportation service will give you a more reliable way of getting around."

C. Skill Practice: Making and Responding to Requests

FOCUS NOTE 4

Situation 1

The Stephen Minister and care receiver have met just about every Tuesday for the past six months since the care receiver's divorce. The care receiver prefers meeting on Tuesdays because childcare is not an issue on that night.

On the upcoming Tuesday, the Stephen Minister's child will be singing in a choir concert at school. The Stephen Minister would like to change the day of the visit, so he or she can attend the concert.

FOCUS NOTE 5

Discussion Questions for Situation 1

1. How does the care receiver feel about the conversation?

2. How does the Stephen Minister feel about the conversation?

3. How did the Stephen Minister use the DESC steps in making his or her request? What consequence did he or she describe?

4. How did the Stephen Minister demonstrate assertiveness throughout the conversation? How could the Stephen Minister have been even more assertive in the conversation?

FOCUS NOTE 6

Situation 2

The Stephen Minister and care receiver have been meeting for about two months, ever since the care receiver found out that he or she was being laid off.

Tonight, the Stephen Minister plans to meet his or her care receiver for their weekly visit and then quickly head over to meet up with a longtime friend who happens to be in town for the day. The Stephen Minister hasn't seen this friend in years, and tonight is the only opportunity to get together, since the friend flies out of town very early tomorrow morning.

Meanwhile, the care receiver has had a difficult day. The job search has been slow to produce promising leads, and today he or she received several bills in the mail that he or she isn't sure how to pay. With about five minutes left in the caring visit, the care receiver was still feeling overwhelmed and asked whether the Stephen Minister could extend their visit.

FOCUS NOTE 7

Discussion Questions for Situation 2

1. How does the care receiver feel about the conversation?

2. How does the Stephen Minister feel about the conversation?

3. What were the Stephen Minister's reasons for responding to the care receiver's request the way he or she did?

4. How did the Stephen Minister demonstrate assertiveness throughout the conversation? How could the Stephen Minister have been more assertive in the conversation?

FOCUS NOTE 8

Situation 3

The Stephen Minister and the care receiver have been meeting regularly since the care receiver's cancer diagnosis a little over a month ago.

The care receiver has shared many fears, frustrations, and uncertainties, while receiving needed support from the Stephen Minister. At this meeting, the care receiver mentions that his or her spouse is experiencing some difficult emotions and might benefit from being with them during their times together. The care receiver asks whether the spouse could start sitting in on their meetings so the Stephen Minister could minister to him or her too.

Discussion Questions for Situation 3

1. How does the care receiver feel about the conversation?

2. How does the Stephen Minister feel about the conversation?

3. What were the Stephen Minister's reasons for responding to the care receiver's request in the way that he or she did?

4. How did the Stephen Minister demonstrate assertiveness throughout the conversation? How could the Stephen Minister have been even more assertive in the conversation?

III. Assertively Dealing with Anger

A. Exploring Anger

1. Expressing Anger

FOCUS NOTE 10

Passive and Aggressive Expressions of Anger

Passive expressions of anger include:

• Internalizing anger

• Stewing

• Refusing to participate in discussions or activities

• Withdrawing from relationships

• Not responding to phone calls or messages

Aggressive expressions of anger include:

- Verbal attacks
- Sarcasm
- Harsh comments
- Disrespectful gestures
- Threats or intimidation
- Physical violence

FOCUS NOTE 11

Guidelines for Assertively Expressing Anger

- Take responsibility for your anger
- Take a moment to think before responding to a situation
- Pray about the situation and your feelings
- Substitute "it would be nice if" for "should"
- Channel your angry energy by using it in productive activities
- Be concise and stick to the issue
- Use "I" and "I want" statements
- Avoid labeling, name calling, and sarcasm
- Stay focused on the here and now
- Give others a chance to respond, and listen carefully
- Work toward resolution, not your own victory
- Deal with issues as they arise, without stewing

2. Receiving Anger

FOCUS NOTE 12

Guidelines for Assertively Receiving Someone Else's Anger

- Refuse abuse and violence
- Realize that you may not be the real target
- If you are wrong, apologize
- When appropriate, validate the person's feelings
- Continue to actively listen and reflect feelings

B. Your Own Experiences of Anger

FOCUS NOTE 13

Thinking about Your Own Experience of Anger

1. Identify a current situation in your life that involves anger. This might be a situation where you're angry with another person or where someone is angry with you.

2. Try to figure out what caused the feelings of anger. Write down your thoughts if you like.

3. What change do you think needs to take place to remove the cause of the anger? Write down your thoughts if you like.

4. Pray for God's help and wisdom in dealing with this situation.

IV. Assertively Expressing and Receiving Compliments

V. Assertiveness Is Christian

VI. Caregiver's Compass Review

Write your ideas around the compass.

VII. Looking Ahead

Maintaining Boundaries in Caregiving

Module 7 | Pre-Class Reading

CONTENTS

Amy, a Stephen Minister, had begun meeting her care receiver, Michelle, not long ago. Michelle's mother had moved into her family's house due to deteriorating health, and the stress of being her mother's primary caregiver, on top of taking care of her school-age kids and managing the house, had become overwhelming for Michelle.

Knowing that Michelle's husband wasn't able to help much because of his job, Amy was determined to support Michelle in any way she could. It didn't take long for her to become deeply involved in Michelle's life—visiting multiple times a week, helping with chores, taking care of errands, and picking up the kids from activities. In addition, Amy was a nurse and sometimes even drew on her professional training and experience to help Michelle care for her mother.

Because their meetings often ended up involving practical tasks instead of talking and listening, Amy also called Michelle frequently to offer advice and encouragement. Some of their phone conversations lasted well past midnight.

Then, Amy's shift times changed at the hospital. When she called to let Michelle know about the change and that she wouldn't be able to come over as planned that week, Michelle said, "But I need you to be here on Wednesday and Friday! I was counting on you watching Mom while I took the boys to baseball practice. How could you just spring this on me?"

Startled by Michelle's distraught response, Amy said, "I'm really sorry, but I have to be at work those days."

"Well, I don't know what I'm going to do then." Michelle took a deep breath, and when she started speaking again she was sobbing. "I'm stressed enough without having to figure this out too. I thought you said you'd be there for me whenever I needed you."

"I am here for you," Amy tried to reassure her. "I'm sure there's some way we can help you figure things out this week."

But Michelle went on, "If this is going to be your schedule going forward, the problem isn't just this week. I knew it was a mistake not to just take care of everything myself. Bye."

"Wait, Michelle!" Amy said, but Michelle had already hung up.

The story of Amy and Michelle illustrates a deeply troubled caring relationship—one in which the caregiver did not maintain boundaries, instead providing care beyond what is appropriate for a Stephen Minister. As a result, Michelle developed unrealistic expectations for the caring relationship and became upset when those expectations weren't met.

The Significance of Self

A crucial foundation for boundaries in caregiving is understanding the concept of *self*. That understanding can help Stephen Ministers avoid becoming entangled in their care receivers' situations. Supervision Groups offer valuable support in this area, helping Stephen Ministers recognize when boundaries are becoming blurred.

Focus Note A contains a simple definition of *self*.

FOCUS NOTE A

A Simple Definition of *Self*

Our *self* is that which makes us uniquely who we are and distinguishes us from others, including our physical, mental, emotional, social, and spiritual attributes.

God has created each of us as a unique individual—a distinct self, separate from every other person. Each person has ownership of and responsibility for his or her own thoughts, feelings, beliefs, and actions. Maintaining good, strong boundaries and healthy relationships involves recognizing everyone's unique personhood and demonstrating respect for ourselves and others.

- Respect for *ourselves* means we don't allow others to impose their thoughts, feelings, or beliefs on us or to take control of our actions. We are responsible to choose for ourselves who we are and how we live.

- Respect for *others* means we don't impose our thoughts, feelings, or beliefs on other people or attempt to control their actions. We recognize they are distinct individuals with their own responsibility to choose who they are and how they live. We may not always agree with their choices, but we understand they can choose for themselves as long as those choices do not risk serious harm to themselves or others.

STEPHEN MINISTER INSIGHT

"I frequently want to jump in and get emotionally wrapped up in other people's problems. The Mudhole from the Feelings session reminds me to empathize without overidentifying. Instead of taking on my care receiver's problems, I come alongside to listen and care, hanging on to the root of the tree and maintaining my boundaries. That's the best way I can help."

What Are Boundaries?

Every relationship, including a Stephen Ministry caring relationship, involves interactions between distinct persons, each with a unique self. Some people are more aware of their self, with a clear sense of who they are and are not, while others are less so. Some are naturally inclined to define and protect their self in any relationship, and others are more vulnerable to allowing people to affect their self. These differences are part of why it's so important for Stephen Ministers to understand what boundaries are and how they function in a relationship.

Boundaries are how we differentiate our own self from others. In their book *Boundaries,* psychologists Henry Cloud and John Townsend define boundaries as the distinctions between *"what is me and what is not me."* [1] Each of us assumes ownership for what lies within our personal boundaries.

Well-Defined Boundaries and Blurred Boundaries

Sometimes people have well-defined boundaries. They take responsibility for themselves, and they expect and allow others to take personal responsibility as well. At other times people are susceptible to blurring boundaries. They can become confused about "what is *me* and what is not *me*" and begin to assume responsibility for how another person thinks, feels, believes, or acts.

The images in Focus Note B illustrate the difference between well-defined and blurred boundaries in a relationship.

---

1 Henry Cloud and John Townsend, *Boundaries: When to Say Yes, How to Say No to Take Control of Your Life* (Grand Rapids, MI: Zondervan Publishing House, 1992, 2017), 31.

FOCUS NOTE B

Well-Defined Boundaries and Blurred Boundaries

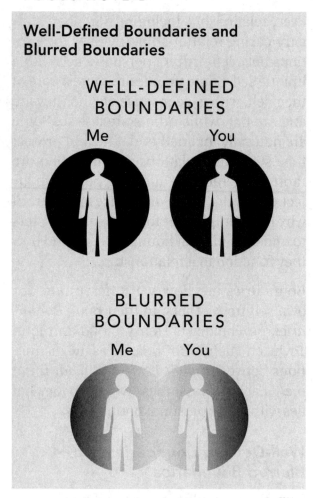

The image on top illustrates a relationship between two people whose boundaries are well defined. Each person takes responsibility for his or her own thoughts, feelings, beliefs, and actions. The space between them shows where one person begins and the other ends. The two may have similar thoughts, feelings, beliefs, and actions, but each person takes responsibility only for him- or herself, not for the other person.

The image on the bottom shows what it may look like when boundaries are blurred. It's much less clear where one person's self, ownership, and responsibility end and the other person's begin. For instance, one per-son might pressure the other to think and act the same way as him or her, and the other person might give in to that pressure.

The Value of Well-Defined Boundaries

Boundaries are important for defining, protecting, and preserving our sense of self. They allow us to take responsibility for our own thoughts, feelings, beliefs, and actions, and they help us avoid internalizing those of others.

Well-defined boundaries can alert us when people are intruding on our self or trying to unduly influence or even take control of some part of us. They also help us know when we're with a person we can trust—someone who respects our boundaries and doesn't seek to impose on us or take control of something that belongs to us.

In addition, well-defined boundaries help us avoid intruding on someone else's sense of self, especially when the other person's boundaries may not be well defined. They can keep us from pushing our thoughts, feelings, and beliefs onto someone else. With clear boundaries, we can see where our responsibilities end, helping us refrain from imposing our will on others.

Moreover, boundaries help us recognize God's work in each person's life. They remind us that while we may be a *caregiver* to another person, God is the *Curegiver*.

Two Areas Where People May Struggle with Boundaries

Maintaining appropriate boundaries can become an issue in any relationship, so it's important to be aware of potential problems in order to recognize and avoid them. Following are descriptions of two boundary challenges people may face. After reading each description, take a moment to reflect on your own experience with that particular challenge, and then indicate where you'd place yourself on the personal assessment scale at the end of the description—keeping in mind that we all have room to grow in these areas.

1. Not Maintaining One's Own Boundaries

The first challenge is when people have trouble maintaining their own personal boundaries. They may not be sure who they are, what makes them unique, why they're worthy of respect, or how they stand in relation to others—or they may have an idea about those issues, but they're not sure how to assertively communicate their thoughts and feelings.

People who lack well-defined boundaries tend to be passive and may not have the confidence to assert themselves. When people have trouble maintaining well-defined personal boundaries, they are especially vulnerable to letting others take advantage of, control, and possibly mistreat them. They may feel paralyzed and unable to stand up for themselves, their hopes, or their plans.

Focus Note C lists some indications that people may not be maintaining their personal boundaries.

FOCUS NOTE C

Indications of Not Maintaining Personal Boundaries

People who are not attending to their boundaries might at times:

- have difficulty making decisions
- have difficulty asking others for help
- have difficulty saying no to people
- rely on other people for personal happiness
- frequently get hurt, manipulated, or taken advantage of by others
- readily accept others' ideas and opinions rather than expressing their own
- spend so much time meeting others' needs that they often neglect their own needs
- feel responsible for other people's feelings
- tend to get caught up in other people's problems
- find it difficult to articulate their own faith apart from what others think

Take a moment to reflect on your own experience with maintaining personal boundaries. Then, circle a number on the personal assessment scale in Focus Note D to indicate how well you do.

Personal Assessment Scale 1: Maintaining Your Own Personal Boundaries

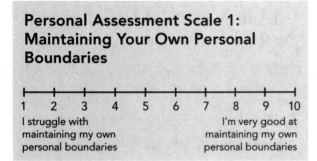

1	2	3	4	5	6	7	8	9	10

I struggle with maintaining my own personal boundaries

I'm very good at maintaining my own personal boundaries

2. Not Respecting Others' Boundaries

The second type of boundary challenge is when people don't respect others' boundaries. They may take responsibility for the other person rather than respecting his or her right to make personal decisions. They may make unrealistic demands or seek to impose their own thoughts, feelings, or beliefs on the other person.

People who do not respect others' boundaries tend to be aggressive and may push past the boundaries set by others. They might try to take advantage of, control, or mistreat others, especially those who have trouble maintaining their own boundaries.

STEPHEN MINISTER INSIGHT

"Giving in to inappropriate requests can cause you to begin feeling resentful toward your care receiver, which can hinder your caring relationship. Saying no to those requests is really what's best for your care receiver and for you."

Focus Note E lists some indications that someone is having trouble respecting others' boundaries.

Indications of Not Respecting Other People's Boundaries

People who do not respect others' boundaries may at times:

- make decisions for others

- jump in to do something for the other person without asking first

- interrupt others before they can finish sentences or thoughts

- have difficulty allowing others to say no to them

- hurt, manipulate, or take advantage of other people, perhaps without being fully aware of it

- discount or minimize others' ideas and opinions, expecting others to adopt theirs instead

- feel their insight is superior to others and should be followed without question

- expect others to feel the same way they do

- project their faults onto others

- pressure others to believe the same way they do

Take a moment to reflect on your own experience with respecting others' boundaries. Then, circle a number on the personal assessment scale in Focus Note F to indicate how well you do.

FOCUS NOTE F

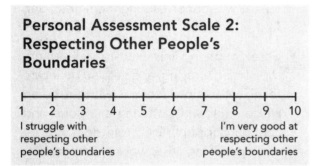

Personal Assessment Scale 2: Respecting Other People's Boundaries

1	2	3	4	5	6	7	8	9	10

I struggle with respecting other people's boundaries

I'm very good at respecting other people's boundaries

Avoiding Boundary Issues in a Caring Relationship

It's important for Stephen Ministers to proactively address these two potential boundary challenges for themselves within a caring relationship:

- the Stephen Minister does not maintain his or her own personal boundaries; or

- the Stephen Minister does not respect the care receiver's boundaries.

Often, these boundary challenges are due to blurred lines between a Stephen Ministry caring relationship and a friendship. Appendix A on page 135 takes a closer look at the difference between the two.

While care receivers may encounter their own boundary challenges, the best way for a Stephen Minister to help with those challenges is to focus on his or her own role in the caring relationship.

1. The Stephen Minister Does Not Maintain His or Her Own Personal Boundaries

Sometimes, Stephen Ministers give in to pressure to go beyond the normal expectations of a Stephen Ministry caring relationship.

As a result, even though they know what a Stephen Ministry caring relationship is supposed to look like, they begin to do more than is needed or appropriate, such as committing more time to their care receiver than is expected or doing tasks that are not part of Stephen Ministry.

This kind of pressure may come externally from the care receiver or internally from the Stephen Minister's own thoughts and feelings. Wherever the pressure comes from, regularly doing more than what's appropriate for Stephen Ministry is a strong indication that the boundaries between Stephen Minister and care receiver have become blurred.

2. The Stephen Minister Does Not Respect the Care Receiver's Boundaries

Other times, a Stephen Minister might encroach on the boundaries of the care receiver, pressuring the care receiver to take specific actions, pushing him or her to think or feel a certain way, attempting to make decisions for him or her, or taking ownership over aspects of the care receiver's life. The Stephen Minister may believe it's his or her responsibility to fix the care receiver or to solve the care receiver's problems. Taking control in this way may bring the Stephen Minister a sense of satisfaction or fulfillment. These instances of crossing boundaries typically arise when a Stephen Minister focuses too heavily on getting results rather than focusing on the process of caregiving and leaving the results to God.

Respecting the care receiver's boundaries means allowing your care receiver to maintain ownership of his or her own feelings, needs, and actions—not taking charge of them yourself.

Defining Boundaries for You and Your Care Receiver

The best time to establish appropriate boundaries between a Stephen Minister and care receiver is at the very start of the caring relationship. The groundwork is laid even before a Stephen Minister is assigned, when a pastor or Stephen Leader meets with a potential care receiver to explain Stephen Ministry and what a Stephen Minister does and doesn't do. Focus Note G contains an excerpt from the Agreement to Receive Care, which is typically shared with the potential care receiver in that initial conversation to provide that key understanding.

FOCUS NOTE G

What Does a Stephen Minister Do?

A Stephen Minister provides one-to-one, lay Christian care.

- **One-to-one:** Each Stephen Minister is matched with one care receiver of the same gender. The two meet in person, typically once a week for about an hour, in a setting they have both agreed on. The caring relationship will be brought to closure when the need for care has been addressed.

- **Lay:** Stephen Ministers are well-trained, supervised volunteers who provide a high level of care. They are not professional care-givers—their role is different from that of a counselor, therapist, pastor, or physician.

- **Christian:** A Stephen Minister's care is an expression of Christ's love and an extension of the pastoral care we offer. When it comes to spiritual matters, Stephen Ministers meet their care receivers where

they are, helping them work through challenges without pressuring them or forcing faith on them.

- **Care:** Stephen Ministers care by listening, supporting, praying, and helping their care receivers explore feelings without being judgmental, while offering emotional and spiritual support. Their role does not include providing other types of assistance—such as shopping, transportation, childcare, and other such types of help—although at times they may help care receivers identify ways to fill those needs.

In addition, the Stephen Minister needs to communicate these boundaries up front and then reinforce them, as necessary, throughout the caring relationship, through both words and behavior. Establishing, communicating, and maintaining appropriate boundaries in the caring relationship is the Stephen Minister's responsibility, not the care receiver's.

The Stephen Minister's Covenant to Care

As a Stephen Minister, one of the most important ways you can help your caring relationships get off to a good start is by reflecting on and committing to the Stephen Minister's Covenant to Care in appendix B on page 137. This covenant provides guidance for establishing effective personal boundaries so you and your care receiver avoid imposing on each other, helping to keep your unique personhoods intact and respected.

If a Stephen Minister struggles in the area of boundaries, his or her Supervision Group will be there to provide care, guidance, and support. No Stephen Minister is alone in working to maintain well-defined boundaries.

Helping Care Receivers Establish and Maintain Boundaries

People are often more vulnerable to boundary issues when experiencing life difficulties than they would be at other times. They may be using a significant amount of energy to deal with their struggles, leaving them without the resources to effectively maintain personal boundaries. Or, they may feel so helpless over their current situation that they turn to others to fix their problems. Because of that, part of your caregiving might be to help your care receiver build or restore boundaries.

The best way you can help your care receiver establish or maintain appropriate boundaries is by modeling healthy personal boundaries yourself. If your care receiver asks you to do something that goes beyond what a Stephen Minister typically does, respond assertively—most often by declining to do so and briefly explaining the reasons. By honoring your own boundaries, you show your care receiver that it's okay for him or her to do the same.

Another way to help with boundaries is simply through your commitment to your care receiver. People need to feel cared for and confident in order to maintain their boundaries. Your listening, prayers, and unconditional positive regard will help your care receiver build up his or her ability to establish and maintain boundaries.

Throughout, respect your care receiver's boundaries and be careful not to overstep them. Your respect gives your care receiver permission to set boundaries in order to feel safe in the caring relationship. By practicing that skill with you, your care receiver can become better able to establish and maintain boundaries in daily life.

STEPHEN MINISTER INSIGHT

"I see a close relationship between staying focused on the process and boundaries. When I get caught up in results and try to fix my care receiver's situation, I have all sorts of boundary issues. But when I focus on the process of caring—being present, listening attentively, reflecting feelings, showing compassion, and relying on God to provide the cure—it becomes a whole lot easier to maintain boundaries."

Good News for People Struggling with Boundary Challenges

Boundary issues often emerge due to feelings of fear or inadequacy. Christians have good news that speaks directly to these underlying causes:

- "There is no fear in love, but perfect love casts out fear . . . " (1 John 4:18a NRSV).

- "Therefore, since we have been justified through faith, we have peace with God through our Lord Jesus Christ, through whom we have gained access by faith into this grace in which we now stand. And we rejoice in the hope of the glory of God" (Romans 5:1–2).

- "We were therefore buried with him through baptism into death in order that, just as Christ was raised from the dead through the glory of the Father, we too may live a new life" (Romans 6:4).

These assurances of God's faithfulness and love are certainly good news—for us and for others. However, as *Christian Caregiving—a Way of Life* makes clear, distinctively Christian caring resources like these verses need to be shared in other-centered, sensitive ways, based on the care receiver's needs instead of your own. It won't help to pressure care receivers to think, feel, or believe this way.

Rather, caregivers need to communicate the love, hope, and new life of the gospel through their actions, their listening, and their care. Caregivers who treasure God's message and have experienced God at work in their own lives are in the best position to help others find that same powerful foundation for a life with appropriate boundaries.

Stephen Ministers need to respect and maintain their own boundaries. They neither allow care receivers to become dependent on them nor give in to unrealistic demands of their time and service. They are assertive about letting care receivers and others know what they can and cannot do. Overall, they recognize that maintaining well-defined boundaries is a vital component in building a caring relationship that helps the care receiver move toward greater wholeness.

Stephen Ministers also respect other people's boundaries by remaining process-oriented and allowing care receivers to make their own decisions. Stephen Ministers strive to be sensitive to what others are comfortable or uncomfortable with and then act accordingly. They use the tools of Christian faith as appropriate, in ways their care receivers will welcome. They provide a sense of safety and security for their care receivers as well as for themselves. In doing so, Stephen Ministers embody the good news of God's caring love for their care receivers.

Getting Ready for the In-Class Session

Between now and your In-Class Session, read and study the Stephen Minister's Covenant to Care in appendix B. This covenant is a way to define appropriate boundaries for you as a Stephen Minister. You will have a chance to talk about the covenant in class, and your Stephen Leader will ask you to sign your copy of the covenant to show your commitment to these guidelines in your caring ministry. Be familiar with the covenant so you can discuss it and commit yourself to it.

Also, make sure that you have completed the self-assessment scales in Focus Notes D and F. You won't be asked to share your scores, but thinking through and completing the self-assessment will help prepare you to participate in a discussion with another trainee in class.

stephenministries.org/library

See the *Stephen Minister Online Library* for additional resources and downloads related to this Stephen Minister training topic.

Appendix A

Module 7

The Differences between a Friendship and a Stephen Ministry Caring Relationship

A Stephen Minister is a trained Christian caregiver who is assigned to walk alongside a hurting person during a difficult time. Although there are similarities between a Stephen Ministry caring relationship and a friendship, the differences between the two are significant—and Stephen Ministers need to know and communicate those differences in order to maintain boundaries effectively.

Friendship	Stephen Ministry Caring Relationship
An informal, mutual relationship	A formal, helping relationship
Started by the friends themselves	Arranged by the Referrals Coordinator
Intended for the benefit of both people involved	Intended for the benefit of the care receiver
Independent of any formal supervision	Supervised by the congregation's Stephen Ministry
Not based on any specific schedule	Involves meeting once a week for about an hour
Might meet purely for enjoyment or leisure	Meet specifically for caring visits
Might involve meeting practical needs	Involves meeting emotional and spiritual needs, not other types of needs
May involve more than two people in the relationship	Strictly a one-to-one relationship
Not focused solely on one person—each feels free to talk about his or her thoughts, feelings, and needs	Focused entirely on the care receiver and his or her thoughts, feelings, and needs, not on the Stephen Minister
A relationship without a specific, concrete purpose or predetermined endpoint	A relationship with the purpose of addressing a specific need for care, coming to a close when that need is met

Appendix B

Module 7

Stephen Minister's Covenant to Care

As a Stephen Minister . . .

1. I will seek to glorify God with a grateful heart.

Stephen Ministers are people of faith who seek to glorify God in all they say and do.

- "Love the Lord your God with all your heart and with all your soul and with all your mind and with all your strength" (Mark 12:30).

2. I will depend on God for results in my caregiving.

Stephen Ministers demonstrate their dependence on God by praying for and with their care receivers, focusing on the process of care, and keeping in mind their role as caregiver and God's role as Curegiver.

- "My help comes from the LORD, the Maker of heaven and earth" (Psalm 121:2).

- "Pray continually" (1 Thessalonians 5:17).

- "I planted the seed, Apollos watered it, but God made it grow" (1 Corinthians 3:6).

3. I will worship God regularly.

Stephen Ministers faithfully participate with God's people in worship and trust the Holy Spirit to renew and transform their lives and the lives of their care receivers.

- "You also, like living stones, are being built into a spiritual house . . . offering spiritual sacrifices acceptable to God through Jesus Christ" (1 Peter 2:5).

- "And let us consider how to provoke one another to love and good deeds, not neglecting to meet together, as is the habit of some, but encouraging one another, and all the more as you see the Day approaching" (Hebrews 10:24–25 NRSV).

4. I will promote respect among fellow ministers and church leaders.

Stephen Ministers promote a spirit of gentleness and peace among other Stephen Ministers, Stephen Leaders, pastors, church staff, and congregation members by behaving appropriately and respectfully toward them, speaking well of all, and thinking the best of others.

- "But we appeal to you, brothers and sisters, to respect those who labor among you, and have charge of you in the Lord and admonish you; esteem them very highly in love because of their work. Be at peace among yourselves" (1 Thessalonians 5:12–13 NRSV).

- "The fruit of the Spirit is love, joy, peace, patience, kindness, generosity, faithfulness, gentleness, and self-control" (Galatians 5:22b–23a NRSV).

5. I will help my care receiver find necessary care if he or she needs more than I can give.

If Stephen Ministers recognize signs of a need for care beyond what they can give, they seek help and supervision from Stephen Leaders and pastors in determining how best to proceed. They recognize their limitations as lay caregivers and, following the guidance of their Stephen Leaders, encourage a care receiver to accept help from a professional caregiver when the care receiver needs care beyond what a Stephen Minister can provide. In all these matters, Stephen Ministers do what is right in the sight of God and in accordance with applicable laws.

- "Do not think of yourself more highly than you ought" (Romans 12:3).

- "Do not withhold good from those to whom it is due, when it is in your power to do it" (Proverbs 3:27 NRSV).

6. I will guard against any form of physical or sexual misconduct.

Stephen Ministers—in their relationships with care receivers, fellow Stephen Ministers, and Stephen Leaders—guard against inappropriate comments, physical contact, or other sexual behavior that could harm individuals and families and threaten the reputation and effectiveness of Stephen Ministry in the congregation.

- "Let us behave decently, as in the daytime. . . . Clothe yourselves with the Lord Jesus Christ" (Romans 13:13a, 14a).

- "For this is the will of God, your sanctification: that you abstain from sexual immorality; that each one of you know how to control his own body in holiness and honor. . . . For God has not called us for impurity, but in holiness" (1 Thessalonians 4:3–4, 7 ESV).

7. I will serve without expecting or accepting reward.

Stephen Ministers give care freely without expecting anything in return—never abusing the caring relationship by asking for favors, gifts, money, or other material benefits, or by receiving anything more than a small token of appreciation from their care receivers.

- "Keep your lives free from the love of money and be content with what you have" (Hebrews 13:5a).

- "And whatever you do, in word or deed, do everything in the name of the Lord Jesus, giving thanks to God the Father through him" (Colossians 3:17 NRSV).

- "Since you know that from the Lord you will receive the inheritance as your reward; you serve the Lord Christ" (Colossians 3:24 NRSV).

8. I will maintain confidentiality.

Stephen Ministers understand the importance of confidentiality and trust in the caring relationship, faithfully maintain confidentiality, and encourage other Stephen Ministers to do the same.

- "Set an example for the believers in speech" (1 Timothy 4:12).

- "Reckless words pierce like a sword, but the tongue of the wise brings healing" (Proverbs 12:18).

9. I will discipline myself to meet my care receiver's needs.

Stephen Ministers commit themselves to serving the needs of their care receivers and not their own needs within the context of the caring relationship. They strive to understand themselves and their own motives, maintain clear boundaries in caring relationships, and graciously accept the guidance, decisions, and constructive comments of their Stephen Leaders and fellow Stephen Ministers.

- "If it is serving, let him serve; . . . if it is showing mercy, let him do it cheerfully" (Romans 12:7–8).

- "Pay close attention to yourself and to your teaching; continue in these things, for in doing this you will save both yourself and your hearers" (1 Timothy 4:16 NRSV).

10. I will willingly receive direction and supervision.

Stephen Ministers receive their caregiving assignments from Stephen Leaders, visit their care receivers faithfully, and participate in regularly scheduled supervision in order to ensure quality Christian care for their care receivers.

- "But everything should be done in a fitting and orderly way" (1 Corinthians 14:40).

Signature _____

Date _____

Maintaining Boundaries in Caregiving

Module 7 | Presentation Outline

Bear one another's burdens, and in this way you will fulfill the law of Christ. . . . For all must carry their own loads.
Galatians 6:2, 5 (NRSV)

 Devotion: Burdens and Loads

I. Your Own Susceptibility to Boundary Issues

FOCUS NOTE 1

Questions for Discussion

- What would you say about how well you currently do in the area of maintaining your own boundaries?

- What would you say about how well you currently do in the area of respecting other people's boundaries?

- Which of these two areas is likely to be more challenging for you in a caring relationship? What do you think makes it more of a challenge?

II. Ways Boundaries Can Be Blurred in Caring Relationships

A. What a Stephen Minister Does

FOCUS NOTE 2

What Does a Stephen Minister Do?

A Stephen Minister provides one-to-one, lay Christian care.

- **One-to-one:** Each Stephen Minister is matched with one care receiver of the same gender. The two meet in person, typically once a week for about an hour, in a setting they have both agreed on. The caring relationship will be brought to closure when the need for care has been addressed.

- **Lay:** Stephen Ministers are well-trained, supervised volunteers who provide a high level of care. They are not professional caregivers—their role is different from that of a counselor, therapist, pastor, or physician.

- **Christian:** A Stephen Minister's care is an expression of Christ's love and an extension of the pastoral care we offer. When it comes to spiritual matters, Stephen Ministers meet their care receivers where they are, helping them work through challenges without pressuring them or forcing faith on them.

- **Care:** Stephen Ministers care by listening, supporting, praying, and helping their care receivers explore feelings without being judgmental, while offering emotional and spiritual support. Their role does not include providing other types of assistance—such as shopping, transportation, childcare, and other such types of help—although at times they may help care receivers identify ways to fill those needs.

B. Ways Care Receivers May Overstep Boundaries

FOCUS NOTE 3

Examples of Ways a Care Receiver Might Overstep or Attempt to Overstep Boundaries

- The care receiver wants his or her spouse or friend to sit in on a caring visit.

- The care receiver pushes the Stephen Minister to regularly meet for over an hour or more frequently than once a week.

- The care receiver expects the Stephen Minister to carry on extended conversations by phone or text between caring visits. (Module 10 will cover the appropriate and inappropriate uses of various communication technologies.)

- The care receiver asks the Stephen Minister to run errands, help with housework, provide transportation, babysit, or perform other tasks outside of Stephen Ministry.

- The care receiver wants the Stephen Minister's help in an area where the Stephen Minister has professional expertise—for instance, as an accountant, nurse, or mechanic.

- The care receiver wants the Stephen Minister to continue being the sole care provider when he or she really needs the help of a mental health professional. (Module 11 will cover what to do when a care receiver requires professional care.)

- The care receiver asks the Stephen Minister for financial assistance.

- The care receiver wants to give money or large gifts to the Stephen Minister.

- The care receiver tries to make the Stephen Minister feel guilty for not doing something outside the boundaries of the caring relationship.

C. Ways Stephen Ministers May Overstep Boundaries

FOCUS NOTE 4

Examples of Ways a Stephen Minister Might Overstep or Be Tempted to Overstep Boundaries

- The Stephen Minister overcommits his or her time to the caring relationship—for instance, meeting more than once a week, consistently meeting for much longer than an hour, or carrying on extended conversations by phone or text between caring visits.

- The Stephen Minister helps in ways that are outside the bounds of Stephen Ministry, such as running errands, providing transportation, or offering physical or financial assistance.

- The Stephen Minister is tempted to provide care or services that require professional help.

- The Stephen Minister overidentifies with the care receiver and becomes emotionally wrapped up in the care receiver's situation.

- The Stephen Minister tries to minister to the care receiver's spouse or another family member as well.

- The Stephen Minister tries to fix the care receiver's situation, give advice, or impose solutions on the care receiver.

- The Stephen Minister invites the care receiver to a movie, a family meal, or another enjoyable activity.

- The Stephen Minister feels guilty for not doing something for the care receiver, even though doing it would overstep the boundaries of the caring relationship.

- The Stephen Minister spends excessive time and energy making phone calls, conducting research, and consulting professionals or agencies to remedy the care receiver's situation.

- The caring relationship continues long after the need for care no longer exists.

D. Diagnostic Questions for Stephen Ministers and Boundaries

Diagnostic Questions to Assess Stephen Minister Boundaries

- Am I doing tasks that are outside of what a Stephen Minister should be doing?

- Am I committing more time during or between my weekly caring visits than what is appropriate for Stephen Ministry?

- Am I trying to provide a type or level of care above what a Stephen Minister should be providing?

- Is my caring relationship moving toward a friendship rather than a relationship between a caregiver and a care receiver?

III. How Maintaining Boundaries Relates to Earlier Modules

A. The Mudhole

FOCUS NOTE 6

The Mudhole

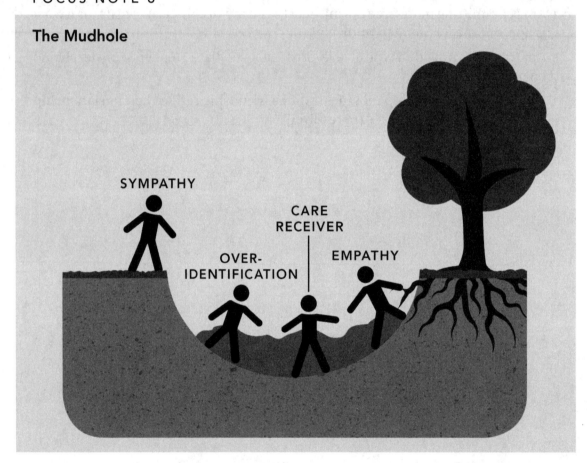

B. Servanthood versus Servitude

C. We Are the Caregivers, God Is the Curegiver

D. Focusing on the Process of Caring

E. Assertiveness

IV. What Boundaries Are Needed Here?

A. Assessing Caring Relationship 1

FOCUS NOTE 7

Caring Relationship 1: Aaron and Mark

Aaron was in his mid-40s when his father unexpectedly passed away. The two had been very close, and the loss was a big shock for Aaron. Mark, who was in his 50s, became Aaron's Stephen Minister during his grief.

The third time they met, Aaron said he needed to do some repair work on the garage and asked Mark whether he'd mind having their visit in the backyard. Mark agreed and even pitched in with the repairs as they talked.

The next two times, Aaron continued working on the garage, and Mark offered a hand. Mark realized their visits were starting to get off track, so he suggested to Aaron that the next time they meet at a coffee shop so they could focus just on talking. Aaron agreed, and the visit went very well.

The next time they met, however, Aaron said he needed to put up some shelves in the basement and asked Mark to help him. Although Mark felt a little frustrated, he figured it would be a short project and agreed to help.

That weekend, Mark got a call from Aaron, who said he was having some trouble with his van. He said it would be a big help to have Mark take a look at it.

Mark had had a busy week and wanted to enjoy his time off, but he didn't want to disappoint Aaron, so he suggested a good shop that could work on the van. Aaron dismissed the idea, saying that it would only take a couple of hours and that he and his father always used to handle those issues together.

Although Mark had some misgivings, he felt bad about saying no, so he gave in and drove over to Aaron's house to help.

FOCUS NOTE 8

Discussion Questions

1. Who in Caring Relationship 1 is struggling with boundaries?

2. How would you describe the boundary issues?

3. What could Mark, the Stephen Minister, do to address the boundary issues?

B. Assessing Caring Relationship 2

FOCUS NOTE 9

Caring Relationship 2: Katie and Melissa

Since graduating from college, Katie had been employed at a large company for several years, and she greatly enjoyed her work there. Then, during a round of downsizing, Katie was laid off. She quickly became stressed about her family's finances and wasn't sure how to go about looking for a new job.

Melissa became Katie's Stephen Minister shortly afterward. Melissa came into the caring relationship ready to do whatever she needed to help Katie navigate the challenges of unemployment and find a new job. They spent the first couple of meetings talking about Katie's feelings about the situation, but after a while Melissa began to ask fewer questions about feelings and more about job prospects.

During one caring visit about two months into the caring relationship, Katie was sharing how she felt down because she hadn't been able to get an interview for a promising position. Right in the middle of Katie's sharing, Melissa jumped in and asked, "What's your résumé look like?" Katie was surprised and a bit hurt about being interrupted, but she went and got a copy of her résumé. After looking at it for a minute, Melissa started making notes all over it and pointing out where Katie could improve it.

They spent the rest of the visit talking about the résumé. Then, when Melissa was getting ready to leave, she offered to take Katie's résumé home with her and find ways to improve it. Katie wasn't sure that she should let Melissa do that, but she felt like she'd hit a wall, so she reluctantly agreed.

FOCUS NOTE 10

Discussion Questions

1. Who in Caring Relationship 2 is struggling with boundaries?

2. How would you describe the boundary issues?

3. What could Melissa, the Stephen Minister, do to address the boundary issues?

C. The Role of Your Supervision Group

V. The Stephen Minister's Covenant to Care

VI. Caregiver's Compass Review

Write your ideas around the compass.

VII. Looking Ahead

Crisis Theory and Practice

Module 8 | Pre-Class Reading

CONTENTS

Crises are inevitable. Whenever a person faces a change or challenge that creates inner turmoil and requires new attitudes, behaviors, or ways of living, that person is experiencing crisis.

Crisis can be brought on by many different kinds of circumstances—predictable life events, such as a graduation or retirement, as well as unpredictable events, such as a car accident or the sudden death of a loved one. In your initial Stephen Minister training and continuing education, you will learn more about many types of situations that can lead to a state of crisis, including:

- Ministering to Those Experiencing Grief

- Understanding Suicide: How to Help People Get the Care They Need

- Ministering to the Dying and Their Family and Friends

- Caring for People Experiencing a Major Medical Crisis

- Ministering to Those Experiencing Losses Related to Aging

- Ministering to Persons Needing Long-Term Care

- Ministering to Those Experiencing Divorce

- Crises of Pregnancy and Childbirth

Regardless of the situation, every crisis has many characteristics in common. This module explores those common points, describing what crisis is, what causes it, what people in crisis experience, and effective ways to care for them.

Defining *Crisis*

Crisis occurs when a person is faced with an event, expected or unexpected, that requires new ways of thinking, acting, or relating to others. Focus Note A contains a definition of *crisis.*

FOCUS NOTE A

Definition of *Crisis*

Crisis is a state in which a person faces such overwhelming stress and anxiety that his or her established ways of thinking, acting, and relating in response are inadequate for the current challenge. Rather than being an *external event* that happens to a person, crisis is a person's *internal response* to an event and the mental, emotional, physical, relational, and spiritual pressures the person experiences as a result. The state of crisis ceases when the person settles on a strategy to deal with the new circumstances brought on by the precipitating event.

Many mental health professionals over the years have researched crisis and the best ways to respond to it. Focus Note B shows how a pioneer in crisis theory and intervention, psychiatrist Gerald Caplan, M.D., defined *crisis.*

FOCUS NOTE B

Caplan's Definition of *Crisis*

"People are in a state of crisis when they face an obstacle to important life goals—an obstacle that is, for a time, insurmountable by the use of customary methods of problem solving. A period of disorganization ensues, a period of upset during which many abortive attempts at a solution are made."[1]

"Crisis results from impediments to life goals that people believe they cannot overcome through customary choices and behaviors."[2]

According to Caplan's definition, crisis arises when something sets up a roadblock between a person and an important goal. The goal may be broad, such as having a comfortable retirement, or more specific, such as graduating

---

1 Gerald Caplan, *Principles of Preventive Psychiatry* (New York: Basic Book, 1964), 18.

2 Ibid., 40.

from college. The obstacles that might block these goals can vary widely, such as a cancer diagnosis that upsets retirement plans or a lost scholarship that forces someone to leave college. Whatever the specifics of the event, the obstacle upsets a person's life greatly and isn't possible to deal with effectively using his or her current approaches.

People in crisis feel like their lives have been turned upside down. They may see the changes they face as a threat to their values, lifestyle, relationships, or dreams. They are in a state of disequilibrium, of ongoing instability and uncertainty, as illustrated in Focus Note C. This disequilibrium may last several weeks, and people may respond to it in many different ways, such as withdrawing into themselves, experiencing strong emotions, or engaging in behaviors that alienate others.

FOCUS NOTE C

The Instability of Crisis

1. Life before Crisis

2. Life during Crisis

STEPHEN MINISTER INSIGHT

"You aren't responsible for fixing the crisis—that's not a burden you need to take up. All you need to do is to offer care and support and trust God while your care receiver finds ways to handle the situation."

Your Experience with Crisis

A good starting point for this topic is to look back on a time of crisis you have personally experienced. Pages 165–166 contain a Crisis Self-Inventory. Take a few minutes right now to reflect on a situation when you were in crisis—when you experienced a life challenge that required you to adopt new attitudes or behaviors or that resulted in a new way of living. Then, in the space provided on those pages, write answers to the questions about that crisis. During the In-Class Session, you'll have an opportunity to share some of your experiences with one other person, as you feel comfortable doing so.

Events That Can Lead to Crisis

Crisis is often the result of changes occurring in a person's life. Some changes are rather predictable; other changes happen unexpectedly. Either way, change can bring on a crisis.

Developmental Crises

Most people go through a number of fairly predictable changes in their lives, such as graduation, leaving home, starting a new job, having a family, aging, retiring, and facing death. Each of these events, including the more positive ones, can leave a person feeling disoriented and uncertain of what to do next, forcing him or her to find new ways to deal with stress.

These predictable circumstances can lead to what's called a *developmental crisis*. Even though people can typically anticipate when such events will happen, adapting to the stress and discomfort they cause can still be a challenge.

Situational Crises

In the face of an unanticipated event, a person may feel threatened, overwhelmed, disorganized, and unable to deal with what's happening. This event could be something like a serious illness, natural disaster, the loss of a job, an unexpected pregnancy, or the death of a loved one. When a surprising situation leaves a person in need of new ways of thinking or acting to address the situation, he or she enters what's called a *situational crisis*.

In some instances, a person may experience something that drastically and irreversibly changes his or her life, such as the loss of a loved one. When this kind of situation occurs, the crisis involves adjusting to a *new normal*, usually an unwanted change.

Crises Stemming from Multiple Events

Sometimes crisis comes not from any single event but out of the cumulative effect of multiple events. When a person has experienced a number of stressful events in succession, the next stressful event could be the one to throw him or her into disequilibrium. Even positive events such as marriage or an increase in income can create stress. While many of these events may be manageable on their own, when combined with other events, they can push a person into a state of crisis.

People Respond Differently to Stressful Events

Two people facing a similar event may experience different amounts of stress from it due to personality, life experiences, self-worth, abilities, support system, and other circumstances. For instance, one person may adapt quickly to a broken leg, while another person may experience a profound crisis after such an injury. Someone may also experience a similar event multiple times and perceive it differently each time.

More important than the event itself is how disruptive or threatening the person perceives the event to be, his or her unique emotional response, and the personal resources he or she has available. The way someone perceives an event affects the amount of stress it generates, which in turn affects how likely that event is to bring about crisis.

The Course of a Crisis

Crises can vary widely, but they usually follow a fairly predictable course, as illustrated by the diagram in Focus Note D.

FOCUS NOTE D

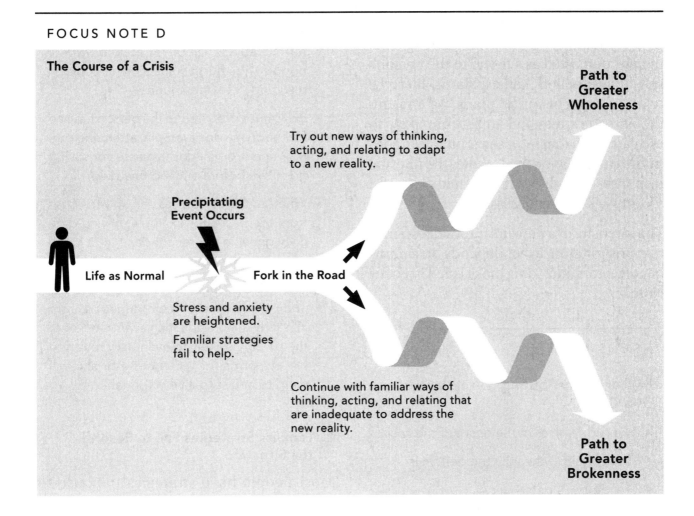

The Course of a Crisis

Path to Greater Wholeness

Try out new ways of thinking, acting, and relating to adapt to a new reality.

Precipitating Event Occurs

Life as Normal

Fork in the Road

Stress and anxiety are heightened.

Familiar strategies fail to help.

Continue with familiar ways of thinking, acting, and relating that are inadequate to address the new reality.

Path to Greater Brokenness

Precipitating Event Occurs

The stage is set for crisis when a situation or event brings unexpected change to someone, perhaps altering the person's self-perception or otherwise affecting his or her life and world. This precipitating event may be a sudden, unexpected occurrence, such as an automobile accident with serious injuries, or it may have been building for a while, such as a job loss after months of rumors about possible layoffs.

Note that this precipitating event is not a crisis itself; it merely sets the stage for a possible crisis. What ultimately determines whether the event leads to a crisis is the individual's internal response to it.

Person Enters Crisis

A person enters a state of crisis when he or she becomes overwhelmed by the event and is unable to respond in a way that restores a sense of calm and stability. This state is sometimes described as a crucible because it can feel as if the heat has been turned up.

Two main characteristics of this state are:

1) heightened feelings of stress and anxiety; and

2) an inability to resolve the situation using familiar strategies.

1. Heightened Stress and Anxiety

A precipitating event introduces change that may be perceived as a threat to the person's self-image, beliefs, values, status, lifestyle, relationships, or future plans. As a result, the person's stress and anxiety are likely to escalate, such that he or she is unable to continue with life as normal. Again, the internal response—the state of heightened stress and anxiety—is the actual crisis.

The intensity of a person's internal response to a precipitating event depends on a number of factors, including those listed in Focus Note E.

FOCUS NOTE E

Factors Contributing to the Intensity of a Crisis

- The suddenness of the onset of the crisis

- How physically healthy the person is

- The person's personality

- The person's self-esteem

- How strong the person's sense of identity is

- Whether the person feels a sense of purpose and meaning in his or her life

- Whether the person has others to provide support, such as family, friends, a Stephen Minister, a pastor, or another caregiver

- How effectively those others provide support

- Whether the person has ever experienced less severe crises in the past and learned new ways of thinking and acting to respond to them

- The person's relationship with God

- The perceived severity of the situation—for example, a minor car accident where nobody was hurt versus a major collision resulting in severe injuries

- How much preparation the person has had for the crisis—for example, attending pre-retirement or childbirth classes or saying goodbye before a loved one died

- Whether the person has unresolved issues from the past—for example, having difficulty grieving the recent death of a loved one because of not grieving another death in the past

- The permanence of the changes brought about by the precipitating event—whether the person is likely to eventually return to life as normal or whether he or she will need to adjust to a new normal

2. Familiar Strategies Fail to Resolve the Situation

Most people have strategies they use to cope with the everyday difficulties and disappointments of life. These activities vary widely from person to person, and while they don't always solve everything, they can help restore a much-needed sense of calm, stability, and perspective. By alleviating stress, they can also help a person gradually adjust to an unexpected change, averting a crisis or reducing its intensity.

One of the defining characteristics of crisis, however, is that the person's familiar ways of dealing with change are incapable of reducing the stress and anxiety caused by the new circumstances and fail to help restore a sense of stability and calm. When changes overwhelm a person while also undercutting that person's typical strategies, his or her overall stress and anxiety are likely to remain and possibly even escalate. The person is in the crucible of crisis, and new ways of thinking and behaving are needed to move forward.

STEPHEN MINISTER INSIGHT

"During a crisis, your care receiver might not be able to feel God's presence. That makes your presence so important. God can work through you to bring hope and healing to your care receiver."

The Fork in the Road

No one stays in crisis forever; eventually, a person has to adapt for better or for worse to the new situation. Someone in crisis faces a fork in the road and must choose to go in one of two directions. In fact, the English word *crisis* comes from the Greek *krisis,* which can refer to a person's decision-making ability or to the actual decisions he or she makes.[3]

As illustrated in Focus Note F, crisis is a crossroads. When a person's normal ways of responding to change fail, he or she faces a crucial decision:

- either try new ways of thinking, acting, or relating to others in an effort to adapt to the new reality; or

- continue using ineffective strategies, even though they're inadequate to address the new reality.

___

3 *The Abridged Liddell-Scott Greek-English Lexicon*, s.v. "krisis."

FOCUS NOTE F

Crisis Is a Crossroads

Fork in the Road

Although both paths lead out of immediate crisis, they are not equally desirable. The first path leads to greater wholeness, and the second leads to greater brokenness. When people are at that crossroads, choosing which path to take, your ministry can make a significant difference.

Path to Greater Brokenness

A person chooses the path to greater brokenness, shown in Focus Note G, when he or she continues to rely on ineffective ways of addressing the problem. Since those current strategies for dealing with the change in his or her life have proven inadequate, simply doing more of the same will inevitably lead to greater brokenness. Even worse, in some instances a person might turn to destructive ways of responding to the new reality, such as abuse of alcohol or other substances. Someone on this path cannot expect a satisfactory resolution to the crisis; in fact, the approach is likely to trigger additional crises.

FOCUS NOTE G

Path to Greater Brokenness

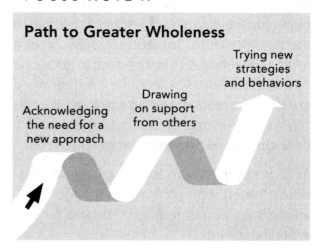

Reliance on ineffective ways of dealing with change

Possibly turning to destructive ways of responding

Potential to trigger additional crises

The path to greater brokenness is the one most people will naturally take if they don't receive the help they need. One reason is that it doesn't require anything of people other than continuing to do what they've been doing. Another reason, even more significant, is that people in crisis may not have anyone they trust to listen to their painful feelings without minimizing, criticizing, or judging. They need care and support as they tell their story, perhaps multiple times, and try to discover new ways of thinking, feeling, and relating that will help them better deal with the changed realities in their life.

This need is why the care and support that Stephen Ministers offer is so crucial. By listening, validating, and helping a person in crisis explore his or her feelings, a Stephen Minister helps the care receiver stay in the crucible long enough to gain hope that he or she can adapt as necessary to the new reality.

It's important to note that even when a person is currently on the path to greater brokenness, he or she is not without hope. There

will continue to be opportunities to choose new ways of thinking, acting, and relating, which can place a person on the path to greater wholeness.

Path to Greater Wholeness

A person chooses the path to greater wholeness, shown in Focus Note H, by adapting and trying new strategies to seek a place of calm and stability—a new normal. Taking this path requires intentional effort. It involves finding the desire, courage, and determination to try out new approaches for dealing with the stress and anxiety brought on by the precipitating event. Having the right type of care and support is crucial for that to happen—and that's what you offer as a Stephen Minister.

FOCUS NOTE H

Path to Greater Wholeness

Trying new strategies and behaviors

Drawing on support from others

Acknowledging the need for a new approach

The first step on this path is sometimes a painful one. The person must acknowledge his or her need to find a new approach. At first, this recognition may bring up feelings of fear, frustration, discouragement, or anger at oneself. It takes courage to make this step toward greater wholeness.

Most often, people draw on the support of others to find the courage they need to take this path. It can be difficult to admit a need for help. Doing so, however, is one of the most constructive steps that a person in crisis can take. While the path toward greater brokenness is a solitary one, the path to greater wholeness is one that people travel together, side by side.

Once the person acknowledges a need for change and help, he or she has greater freedom to begin trying new, more effective strategies and to adopt new behaviors to deal with the crisis. This often means changing the way one sees the world and what one thinks is most important. For instance, if a person's sense of purpose came largely through his or her career—and that person then faces a prolonged period of unemployment—he or she may need to develop a new sense of purpose. Or, someone whose self-identity was tied in to being a husband or wife may need to develop a new self-identity after losing a spouse.

When people find a new way of thinking and living, they embrace the opportunity for growth. Throughout the process of coming to greater wholeness, people grow and gain additional skills to help them deal with life's challenges. This does not mean that the difficult feelings or struggles connected to the precipitating event will go away—for instance, a person who has lost a loved one is likely to continue grieving even while on the path to greater wholeness. It *does* mean, however, that the person has gained new strategies and behaviors to weather both the current storm and those that may come in the future.

As a Stephen Minister, the best way for you to help a care receiver move toward greater wholeness is to be present in his or her life, empathize with and validate the thoughts and feelings he or she shares, support him or her in finding new coping strategies, and continue to focus on the process of care throughout the period of crisis.

Common Responses to Crisis

While each person's response to crisis is unique, there are some thoughts, feelings, questions, and behaviors people tend to have when in the crucible of crisis. Some of the most common are described here.

Anxiety

The most basic human response to crisis is heightened anxiety. Anxiety is a potentially overwhelming sense of worry, concern, uncertainty, or unease about a problem or issue, whether actual or potential. During a crisis, people may experience a potentially debilitating state of anxiety in response to the disequilibrium of their situation. This anxiety can lead to a variety of other responses described below.

Uncertainty and Lowered Self-Concept

Crisis often brings a sense of personal failure, inadequacy, incompetence, or uncertainty. For example, a person in crisis might think, "I thought I was a strong person, but I can't handle all the stress from my dad's illness. Am I not that strong after all?" In a crisis, as people find that their customary ways of dealing with stress and discomfort no longer work, they can be left uncertain about themselves and their ability to deal with difficult situations. This confusion and self-doubt may lead to a downward spiral of passive behavior and reduced self-esteem.

STEPHEN MINISTER INSIGHT

"The best way for you to help a care receiver during a crisis is to show up, listen, and listen some more."

Disorganized Functioning

When people are in crisis, they generally experience much more stress than usual, which can lead to increasingly disorganized thinking and behavior. People in crisis may have difficulty thinking clearly, concentrating, or remembering, causing them to take more time than usual to do common tasks. This experience has been described in a number of ways, such as "being on a 10-second delay," "going through the motions," or "functioning at 50 percent." Those in crisis may be more susceptible to their own or others' questionable judgment, since they aren't thinking as clearly and cannot evaluate their options as well as they usually would. They may allow others to make decisions for them, even when those decisions may not be in their best interests.

Disorganized behaviors can take many forms. People in crisis may:

- become less productive;

- engage in behavior that others would consider eccentric or strange;

- make rash or unwise decisions;

- keep a less well-maintained home or personal appearance than normal;

- have difficulty fulfilling commitments; or

- be less dependable than usual.

Withdrawal

When the human body is badly injured, blood tends to concentrate in and around vital organs in an attempt to maintain functions essential to life. Similarly, when people are seriously in crisis, they focus their mind and energies on managing the crisis, which may lead them to withdraw from other activities.

People in crisis often spend a lot of emotional energy adjusting to their circumstances, leaving them with little energy to invest in relationships. Although they can benefit greatly from receiving care and support, they may not have the energy to reach out and ask for it—so they're likely to struggle on their own if others don't proactively offer to help.

As a result, people in crisis often end up temporarily withdrawing from relationships, social groups, and religious communities. This withdrawal can actually contribute to the intensity or length of the crisis by preventing them from receiving care and support through those relationships, activities, and communities.

Difficult Feelings

People in a state of crisis typically experience a whirlwind of emotions. They may also be irritable and highly sensitive to what others say, and they may act aggressively if they feel threatened. Strong feelings may build up inside, increasing in pressure until those feelings are let out—sometimes in ways that hurt or drive away the very people who could provide much-needed support.

Life Perspectives Shaken

Crises tend to shake a person's view of life, often causing the person to readjust his or her attitudes, opinions, and perspectives. People in crisis may find that life seems surreal or think that the life they once knew is no more. For example, a person who found meaning in financially supporting his or her family may be terribly shaken by an injury that leaves him or her unable to work. Resolving such a crisis would require finding a new mindset about his or her place in life.

People in crisis may find themselves doubting or questioning long-held beliefs. Sometimes, they seek answers from religion or philosophy. Other times, they may spend more time lost in thought, trying to make sense out of their lives. Still other times, they may seek meaning in new experiences or relationships. Because their former perspective no longer seems to fit, they are compelled to find a new understanding of life.

STEPHEN MINISTER INSIGHT

"Your steadfastness, care, and encouragement can bring a sense of calm to your care receiver in the midst of chaos. You offer God's peace in the storm."

Changes in Relationship with God

Crises often have an effect on people's faith. While some people in crisis may find themselves drawing closer to God, for many others, crisis leads to a period of doubt. They may question God's love and forgiveness, or they may wonder whether God has abandoned them or even whether God is really there.

People in crisis sometimes experience guilt. They may feel guilty for questioning God or for struggling in their faith. They may wonder whether the events they've experienced are divine retribution for something they've done or not done. They may think they should have done more to prevent the event, or they might believe it's their fault that the people they love are affected. The guilt may be rational and connected to something the person did wrong, or it may be irrational and not based on any wrongdoing.

People may also feel anger at God for allowing the events that led to the crisis. Such anger doesn't mean that a person has lost faith—just that he or she has strong feelings to deal with. The best way to offer care in such circumstances is to listen and provide support—without lecturing or trying to change the person's perspective—while the person talks through his or her thoughts and feelings about God.

How Stephen Ministers Help People in Crisis

For a person in crisis, a Stephen Minister can be a source of certainty and stability when the rest of life feels completely out of control. By listening, reflecting, offering the ministry of presence, and giving a safe, non-judgmental place to express difficult feelings, a Stephen Minister offers peace and comfort in the midst of life's storms—and serves as a tangible expression of God's compassion and love. The Stephen Minister is present with the care receiver in the crucible of crisis, helping him or her work through any thoughts and feelings and choose the path to greater wholeness.

Getting Ready for the In-Class Session

In your In-Class Session, you will talk about how to care for someone in crisis. You will have a chance to analyze crisis situations and discuss in depth how you can care for people in crisis.

Have your Crisis Self-Inventory ready to share in class.

stephenministries.org/library

See the *Stephen Minister Online Library* for additional resources and downloads related to this Stephen Minister training topic.

Crisis Self-Inventory

1. How would you name or label the crisis?

2. What happened to bring on the crisis?

3. What made the crisis challenging for you?

4. What was your immediate reaction to the crisis?

5. How did you initially try to deal with the crisis? What were the results of those initial efforts?

6. Did others try to help when you were in crisis? If so:
   - How were their words and actions helpful in dealing with the crisis?

- How were their words and actions unhelpful?

If not, how did you feel about the lack of help?

7. What familiar ways of thinking and acting were unhelpful during the crisis?

8. What new ways of thinking and acting helped you move beyond the crisis?

9. How did your life change, for better or worse, as a result of your crisis?

10. In what ways did you grow as a result of your crisis?

Crisis Theory and Practice

Module 8 | Presentation Outline

Therefore I will boast all the more gladly about my weaknesses, so that Christ's power may rest on me. That is why, for Christ's sake, I delight in weaknesses, in insults, in hardships, in persecutions, in difficulties. For when I am weak, then I am strong.
2 Corinthians 12:9b–10

 Devotion: Finding Comfort in Christ

I. Crisis Self-Inventory

II. Caring for Someone in Crisis

A. The Course of a Crisis:
   Mini-Review of Key Information

FOCUS NOTE 1

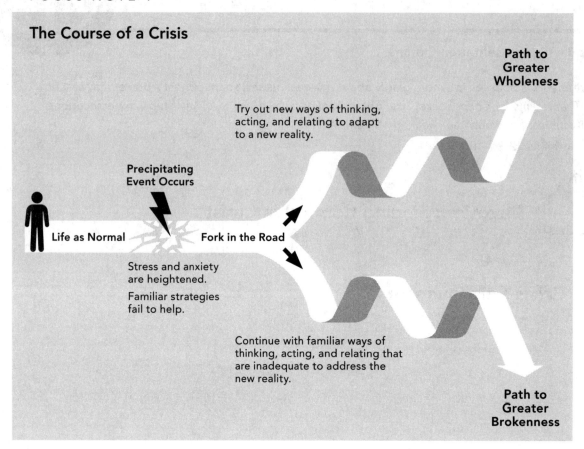

The Course of a Crisis

Path to Greater Wholeness

Try out new ways of thinking, acting, and relating to adapt to a new reality.

Precipitating Event Occurs

Life as Normal

Fork in the Road

Stress and anxiety are heightened.

Familiar strategies fail to help.

Continue with familiar ways of thinking, acting, and relating that are inadequate to address the new reality.

Path to Greater Brokenness

1. Precipitating Event Occurs

2. Person Enters Crisis

3. The Fork in the Road

4. Hope for Those on the Path to Greater Brokenness

B. Seven Ways to Care for People in Crisis

1. Begin Providing Care as Soon as Possible

2. Take the Crisis Seriously

3. Be Calm, Consistent, and Dependable

4. Help the Care Receiver Stay in the Crucible

5. Provide Essential Support

6. Remain Focused on the Process

7. Pray with the Care Receiver, as Appropriate

III. An Example of Caring during a Crisis

Evan's Crisis

The Situation

The Stephen Minister is caring for Evan, who was recently fired from his job. Evan has taken the dismissal hard. It has significantly affected his feelings of self-worth, and he's worried about his family's financial situation. Evan is married and has two young children, and he knows that his family won't be able to get by only on his wife's salary for long.

Dialogue

Stephen Minister: Hey, Evan. Good to see you.

Evan: Yeah, you too. It's nice to talk with the one person I haven't let down yet. Well, at least as far as I know.

Stephen Minister: You haven't let me down at all. But tell me more about this feeling that you've let people down.

Evan: [laughs bitterly] I mean, what's there to say? I've failed Jenna and the kids, for starters. We really need both Jenna's and my paychecks to make ends meet, so money's already getting tight. On top of that, Jenna was hoping to go part-time to spend more time with the kids, and we were really counting on my career to keep us going long-term. But now the pressure's all on her. It wasn't supposed to be like this. I totally screwed up.

Stephen Minister: It can really hurt to feel that way.

Evan: Yeah. I don't think I've ever felt this worthless. Do you know what it's like to have to tell your family and friends you got fired? It was a good job too. I liked what I did, and I could have done well and moved up. But I just didn't stay on top of things and lost one of our biggest accounts. After that, I'd probably fire me, too. It's my own fault, and the more I think about it all the worse I feel.

Stephen Minister: I hear how tough this is for you. You lost a good opportunity and feel responsible. How do you see yourself moving ahead from here?

Evan: I haven't been able to even think about that. Why would any other company want me now? I wouldn't want me. And if someone did hire me, I'm sure I'd mess that up too.

Stephen Minister: That's a lot of negative feelings you're holding onto.

Evan: Well, sure, why wouldn't I? I had a good job—but couldn't keep it. And now I can't even support my own family.

Stephen Minister: It sounds like this whole thing has completely knocked you off your game.

Evan: I mean . . . yeah. And it's also that I know I made mistakes, but deep down, I don't really think I'm totally useless. I was doing a good job before I started slacking—so I know what I'm capable of. It's just . . . I just keep kicking myself over what I threw away and what I should've done differently. If only I hadn't messed this up. . . .

Stephen Minister: You really seem down on yourself, but you also mentioned that you know what you're capable of. What are some things you might do to turn things around?

Evan: I don't know. I feel pretty lame just moping around like this. Other guys I know who lost their jobs were out applying at new places the next day. And here I am, just throwing a pity party for myself. Why can't I just bounce back like they did?

Stephen Minister: Well, you might just need that first step to get you going. It sounds like you want to change things. What do you think might be a good first step?

Evan: I wish I knew . . . *[pause]* I guess I should probably update my résumé, huh?

Stephen Minister: Sounds like a good start. In fact, that might even help you start feeling better about things. And if you're still stuck after that, another possibility might be to consider seeing a career counselor.

Evan: Yeah, I don't know about that. I'm not real big on counselors. They're not like you; you're easy to talk to.

Stephen Minister: Well, I'm going to keep on meeting with you, but a career counselor could get you connected with different resources that I can't. They're focused on helping think through who you are, what skills you have to offer, and what kinds of jobs might be a good fit for you. I just wanted to mention that option.

Evan: Sure, I see where you're coming from. I'll keep it in mind.

Stephen Minister: You don't have to decide anything tonight. Take your time and figure out what you want to do. *[pause]* What else are you thinking about?

Evan: Well, I'm still worried about how we're gonna pull through with the money stuff, but I guess I don't feel as hopeless as I did before. It's just one job, and even if I screwed it up, that doesn't mean I can't get it right next time. I don't want to just give up on everything here.

Stephen Minister: Losing a job's rough on anyone. But you're a capable person, and I believe you'll find another soon. I like your idea of updating your résumé. What do you think about making that your first step?

Evan: Yeah, it's been a while since I last looked at it, but I can do it. I helped a bunch of the guys with their résumés back in college, so I know what I'm doing. I'm still not totally sure about going to a career counselor, but I'll keep it in mind. Maybe I'll see how I do job-hunting on my own and then decide.

Stephen Minister: Fair enough. If you want, I can check our Stephen Ministry community resource guide at church to see if we've got any career counselors listed. If we do, I can get you their contact information. That way you'll at least have it if you want it.

Evan: Sure, can't hurt. And hey, thanks for helping me think through that. At least I have the start of a plan now. Can't let this keep me down.

IV. Caregiver's Compass Review

Write your ideas around the compass.

V. Looking Ahead

Confidentiality

Module 9 | Pre-Class Reading

CONTENTS

The Importance of Confidentiality

Have you ever told someone something that was private or embarrassing or that could otherwise cause problems if others found out about it—and then that person shared the information with someone else, who shared it with someone else, until it seemed everyone knew? Anyone who goes through that experience is likely to feel hurt that his or her trust in another person was broken like that.

It's easy to imagine why care receivers might feel reluctant to open up and tell someone about their painful experiences, distressing mistakes, and difficult feelings. Some may have shared personal information with someone in the past, only to have that trust broken. Others may not have had that experience themselves but are still uneasy about the possibility.

This is why confidentiality is a cornerstone of Stephen Ministry. Without it, few people would agree to receive care, and those who did would be more reluctant to talk about what they're really thinking and feeling.

For care receivers to feel safe sharing their painful feelings and talking about the difficulties they're experiencing, they need to trust their Stephen Ministers. Central to that trust is the assurance that Stephen Ministers will not reveal the identity of their care receivers or what's shared in their meetings. This assurance helps create a safe place where care receivers can openly share their most painful concerns—including those they may not discuss even with close friends or family.

Revisiting the Caregiver's Compass

Maintaining confidentiality is a crucial part of being a Stephen Minister. Think about the Caregiver's Compass—in addition to describing the characteristics of a Stephen Minister, the Caregiver's Compass is also a great guide for confidentiality within the Stephen Ministry relationship.

Confidentiality is an essential component of being *trustworthy*—of building and maintaining the trust necessary for any effective caregiving relationship. A Stephen Minister who is able and willing to keep caring visits confidential earns the care receiver's trust. Confidentiality is also a *skill* that Stephen Ministers learn to exercise. Protecting confidentiality is an expression of *compassion* as well, showing care and sensitivity in handling what is shared. Finally, maintaining confidentiality demonstrates the self-control that is part of the fruit of the Spirit (Galatians 5:22–23) in the lives of *Christ-centered* caregivers who are *full of faith*.

Why You Can Be Confident about Confidentiality

Maintaining confidentiality is a matter of knowing and following a few basic, largely commonsense guidelines. Occasionally, people imagine that maintaining confidentiality is more complicated and difficult than it really is. To avoid that trap, keep the following points in mind:

- There are clear, established guidelines for the different kinds of situations you may encounter connected with confidentiality. This Pre-Class Reading and the In-Class

Session will provide what you need to know to handle those situations.

- Although there are instances where the circle of confidentiality may need to be widened (as described on pages 182–188), they are very rare. It's not likely that you'll encounter them.

- In the unlikely event that this kind of situation should occur, your training will guide you in what to do. In addition, you won't have to handle it alone. Your pastor and Stephen Leaders are there to help, support, and guide you through it.

Hundreds of thousands of Stephen Ministers in millions of caring situations have demonstrated that keeping confidentiality is a manageable, achievable goal. Through this Pre-Class Reading and the In-Class Session, you'll be trained in the essential aspects of confidentiality and learn what to do in specific situations to honor your care receiver's trust. This training, combined with your commitment to being a trustworthy caregiver, will help you successfully maintain confidentiality in your caring relationships.

Understanding Confidentiality

Maintaining confidentiality is generally a straightforward task for Stephen Ministers once they know what confidentiality means in the context of Stephen Ministry and what is expected of them.

Confidentiality Is an Intentional Act

Many people think of confidentiality as a passive act—as *not* saying or doing something. For Stephen Ministers, however, maintaining confidentiality is an active,

intentional behavior. Stephen Ministers understand that those who purposefully decide to keep a confidence are much less likely to break that confidence.

When people intentionally maintain confidentiality, they're prepared with answers for others who might ask about the situation. They've thought through appropriate responses and can offer them promptly and assertively. They stay especially vigilant in situations that could compromise the trust others have placed in them. In short, people who make an intentional choice to maintain confidentiality don't simply avoid sharing the confidences they've been entrusted with—they actively work to preserve that trust. The rest of this module explores specific ways to do just that.

A Professional and Personal Commitment

Confidentiality plays an important role in many different professional and personal contexts. It's a key component of the professional commitments of physicians, nurses, other healthcare professionals, mental health professionals, attorneys, clergy, and many other caregivers and personal service providers. Although Stephen Ministers are not professional caregivers, their commitment to confidentiality is on a similar plane.

Confidentiality is more than a professional commitment, however; it's also a matter of personal ethics and integrity. When someone shares private information with us in confidence, we have a responsibility to honor that person's trust. This is an important part of daily living and relating, as illustrated by these situations:

- A friend who is struggling has recently vented some thoughts and feelings with you. Someone else who is friends with both of you asks you how the person is doing. You wonder how much you should say—or whether you should say anything at all.

- A church member texts you to say he is leaving town for a family emergency and won't be at worship this weekend. You think about posting a prayer request on your church's social media page, but then you wonder whether the person wants others, even people on the prayer chain, to know about the situation.

- A friend tells you that she's pregnant. That same day, you see a mutual friend and want to talk about the news, but you don't know whether this person has actually heard about it yet or whether you should say anything.

Questions about confidentiality regularly come up in friendships, family life, and other kinds of relationships. When people share personal information, they trust that those they share with will keep it to themselves. If others betray that trust, relationships can be seriously damaged.

STEPHEN MINISTER INSIGHT

"Confidentiality really isn't hard to do, but it's one of the most important aspects of Stephen Ministry. It's the key to a trusting relationship."

What a Stephen Minister Keeps Confidential

Stephen Ministers keep confidential the existence of the caring relationship and everything that happens in it, as summed up in Focus Note A and described in detail on the following page.

FOCUS NOTE A

Information That a Stephen Minister Keeps Confidential

A Stephen Minister protects confidentiality by not sharing any of the following:

- the *existence of the caring relationship*

- the *care receiver's name,* as well as the names of any of the care receiver's loved ones

- the *care receiver's specific situation or need*

- *communications* between the Stephen Minister and care receiver

- *observations or impressions* that the Stephen Minister has about the care receiver

- *written information* about the care receiver

When a Stephen Leader meets with a potential care receiver before assigning a Stephen Minister, the Stephen Leader will tell him or her about confidentiality.

The Existence of the Caring Relationship

Some care receivers would be embarrassed or perhaps even ashamed to let others know they are receiving help, so confidentiality begins with the caring relationship itself. Treat the fact that your care receiver has a Stephen Minister—and that you are that individual's Stephen Minister—as confidential. The relationship is built on trust, and not revealing the existence of your caring relationship is a key way to build and maintain that trust with your care receiver.

The Care Receiver's Name

Similarly, a Stephen Minister doesn't tell others the name of his or her care receiver or of any of the care receiver's loved ones. When asked whether he or she is caring for a specific person, the Stephen Minister explains that he or she is not at liberty to say whether that individual—or anyone else—is his or her care receiver.

The Care Receiver's Specific Situation or Need

A Stephen Minister doesn't say what specific situation or need his or her care receiver is dealing with. Even without identifying the care receiver by name, disclosing that information could lead some to guess the care receiver's identity or prod the Stephen Minister for more information, so it's safest not to bring it up at all.

Communications

As a Stephen Minister, you won't tell others what your care receiver says to you unless your care receiver gives you specific permission as to what, when, and with whom you can do so—and even then you would use careful judgment before sharing anything.

This confidentiality includes in-person conversations, phone conversations, and any other types of spoken or written communications your care receiver may give or send you.

Observations and Impressions

You will probably form impressions about your care receiver by observing him or her. You may pick up clues that indicate how your care receiver is feeling, how he or she is relating to others, how well he or she is keeping up with personal responsibilities, what he or she may be thinking of doing in the future, and other information. All your observations and impressions about your care receiver should be kept confidential.

Written Information

Confidentiality also applies to written information. Carefully guard any records, notes, or forms that refer to your care receiver. One such form is the Referral Form given to you when you're assigned to your care receiver. This is the one document where your care receiver's name, address, and phone number may appear. This highly sensitive document will be destroyed when the caring relationship concludes. While it's in your possession, keep it in a safe, secure place where no one else could stumble upon it, such as in a locked file drawer.

You also will record brief notes about each visit with your care receiver on the Contact Record Sheet. (You'll learn about that form in module 17, "How to Make a First Caring Visit.") Don't write the care receiver's name on this sheet, and don't include any identifying information or sensitive comments. As with the Referral Form, keep the Contact Record Sheet in a safe, secure location where others won't come across it.

Be especially careful about electronically recording any information about a care receiver, as electronic files carry additional risks in terms of confidentiality. Electronic files can be less secure than physical documents, and they have the potential to be shared rapidly and much more widely than intended through email, social media, or other means. Generally, it's safer to keep information about your care receiver in physical rather than electronic form.

Be sure to keep any written records related to the caring relationship in a secure place. When the caring relationship comes to a close, you will give all the forms to your Referrals Coordinator, who will destroy them.

What Isn't Confidential

While your care receiver's identity and anything the care receiver tells you are confidential, maintaining confidentiality *does not* mean hiding that you are a Stephen Minister. In fact, it's good for people in a congregation to know who all the Stephen Ministers are. It's perfectly appropriate to tell friends, relatives, coworkers, and others that you are a Stephen Minister, to share the basics about Stephen Ministry, and to talk about the personal and spiritual growth you're experiencing as a Stephen Minister. Confidentiality applies only to *your caring relationship* and the interactions between you and your care receiver.

Asking the Care Receiver for Permission to Share

At times your care receiver may benefit from your sharing confidential information about him or her. For example, your care receiver may need financial counseling, and you might know of a person who works in that area and could be of help to your care receiver. Before making such a connection, discuss the possibility with your Supervision Group and always ask your care receiver's permission first.

If your care receiver allows you to share something, don't share any more information than is necessary. For example, you wouldn't tell the financial counselor that the person you're referring is your Stephen Ministry care receiver. Instead, you would simply say he or she is a friend or acquaintance. Module 11, "Using Mental Health Professionals and Other Community Resources," says more about making these types of connections.

Even when you have your care receiver's permission, use careful judgment before divulging anything confidential. In some cases, it may still be better to refrain from sharing the information.

Your Care Receiver Is Not Bound by Confidentiality

Confidentiality applies only to the Stephen Minister, not to the care receiver. Although you will not tell anyone who your care receiver is or what the two of you talk about, your care receiver is free to share that information with others if he or she chooses. For instance, your care receiver may tell his or her spouse or other family members that you are his or her Stephen Minister, but even if they know, you would not share with them anything you and the care receiver discuss or give them any observations or updates.

It typically isn't an issue if the care receiver shares with a few family members or friends that you're his or her Stephen Minister, but occasionally it could cause some challenges for either you or the care receiver. For example, a family member who feels left out of the caring relationship may want to sit in on caring visits, or someone might press you or the care receiver for information about what was said during a visit.

If you think there's potential for a problem, talk with the care receiver about it and explain that, in order to minimize the chances of any issues, it might be best for now to limit the number of people who know about the caring relationship. In most situations, though, this sort of suggestion won't be necessary, as care receivers are unlikely to talk about the caring relationship that widely.

As a Stephen Minister, you are still bound to confidentiality, no matter how much the care receiver might have told others. The example in Focus Note B shows how to handle a request for confidential information.

FOCUS NOTE B

Responding to a Request for Confidential Information

Note: The Stephen Minister was not present when his care receiver, Matthew, told the inquirer the identity of his Stephen Minister.

Inquirer: Matthew mentioned that you're his Stephen Minister and that you've been helping him deal with the loss of his wife. I've talked to Matthew a little, but I just want to know how he's really doing.

Stephen Minister: I appreciate your concern for Matthew. I need to let you know that confidentiality is essential to Stephen Ministry. Anything a person tells his or her Stephen Minister is confidential. In fact, I can't even say whether or not I'm Matthew's Stephen Minister.

Inquirer: Well, I *know* you are, since Matthew told me. He and I are good friends, and I really care about him. So I'm sure he wouldn't mind you talking with me.

Stephen Minister: The person to speak to about this is Matthew, so I'd encourage you to ask him how he's doing. In Stephen Ministry, the Stephen Minister is bound by confidentiality. The person receiving care can talk freely about the caring relationship to anybody.

Inquirer: This is frustrating. I'm sure Matthew wouldn't mind.

Stephen Minister: It may be that a care receiver wouldn't mind other people knowing. Even so, it's best for the care receiver when the Stephen Minister maintains confidentiality. People need to be able to trust that anything they tell their Stephen Minister will be kept confidential. Again, if you're wondering how Matthew is, the best thing to do would be to talk with him.

It isn't often that a person would push you for information like this, but it's good to know in advance how you might respond just in case it happens.

Keep Confidentiality Even When Information Is Already Widely Known

Even when information about your care receiver is publicly known or available, you should still avoid discussing it. For example, suppose your care receiver has been diagnosed with cancer, and everyone in the congregation knows it because your care receiver's name and condition have been in the prayers during worship services the past few months. Although the care receiver's overall situation may be widely known, you most likely know additional details that aren't public knowledge about the situation. Because of this, it's best to avoid participating in any type of conversation about the care receiver's situation, as talking about it would risk divulging that confidential information, along with the existence of the Stephen Ministry relationship.

In short, treat *all* information about your care receiver as private information—and keep it confidential.

A Rare Exception: When Safety Is a Concern

In the strictest sense, confidentiality means that the Stephen Minister won't share with others anything a care receiver says. An exception, however, is when the safety of the care receiver or someone else may be at risk, as described in Focus Note C.

FOCUS NOTE C

Situations Where Safety Supersedes Strict Confidentiality

Preserving the safety of the care receiver or others supersedes the importance of main-taining strict confidentiality. This includes instances where:

1) the care receiver might harm him- or herself;

2) the care receiver might harm others; or

3) the care receiver may be in a situation involving abuse.

In these rare situations, the Stephen Minister needs to widen the circle of confidentiality to include other key individuals who are equipped to help the care receiver in very specific ways.

Most Stephen Ministers don't encounter any of these situations. Still, it's important to know that in these unique circumstances, the Stephen Minister's priorities shift from maintaining strict confidentiality to ensuring that the care receiver and others are safe. That kind of situation may mean the circle of confidentiality needs to be widened.

Before being assigned a Stephen Minister, each care receiver is told about these rare instances in which the circle of confidentiality may be widened to preserve the safety of the care receiver or others. The care receiver has already given permission for this possibility when he or she accepted a Stephen Minister assignment, so the Stephen Minister is not breaking confidentiality by taking the appropriate steps in such a critical situation.

Focus Note D shows how the circle of confidentiality may expand slightly to include a few key individuals who are uniquely equipped to help. The Stephen Minister still maintains confidentiality with all others.

Widening the Circle of Confidentiality

In the rare instances that a Stephen Minister suspects the care receiver may harm him- or herself or others or may be involved in an abusive situation, the Stephen Minister may need to include others within the circle of confidentiality to help ensure the safety and well-being of the care receiver and others.

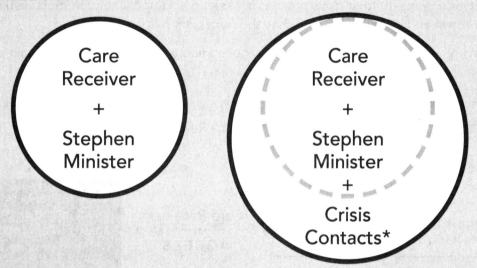

* Your Stephen Leader Team will let you know who your congregation's Stephen Ministry Crisis Contacts are. Most likely, those contacts will be a pastor and a Stephen Leader, who, in turn, might then include a professional whose area of expertise is specific to the situation (such as a mental health professional, local emergency services, or a medical professional).

If there's an imminent danger or threat of someone being harmed, the Stephen Minister should contact emergency services first and the Stephen Ministry Crisis Contacts after that.

As noted in Focus Note D, your Stephen Leaders will tell you who your congregation's Stephen Ministry Crisis Contacts are. These individuals will include a pastor and a Stephen Leader (most often the Referrals Coordinator), who will need to be contacted if you encounter one of these instances. However, in situations where someone is in imminent danger, you'll notify emergency services first and then let the pastor or Stephen Leader know as soon as possible. (In these situations, "imminent danger" means a person has expressed the intent of harming

him- or herself or someone else and has a plan and the means to carry it out.) The bottom line is that whenever someone's safety is a concern, you won't have to deal with the situation alone—nor should you.

A Process for Getting Additional Help

Most of the time, because of the trust you've built with your care receiver, he or she will most likely agree to contacting the necessary help. Only rarely would you ever need to seek additional help against your care receiver's wishes. Focus Note E describes the process for getting necessary help when the safety of your care receiver is a concern.

FOCUS NOTE E

A Process for Getting Additional Help When Safety Is a Concern

When safety is a concern, follow this process in seeking additional help. In most instances, your care receiver will end up agreeing to access the necessary help.

If there is an imminent danger to the care receiver or someone else, immediately contact emergency services instead of following this process.

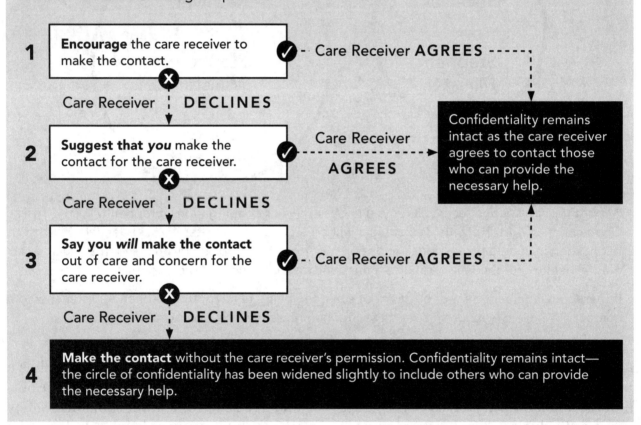

1 **Encourage** the care receiver to make the contact. ✓ - Care Receiver **AGREES**

Care Receiver **DECLINES**

2 **Suggest that _you_** make the contact for the care receiver. ✓ Care Receiver **AGREES**

Care Receiver **DECLINES**

3 **Say you _will_ make the contact** out of care and concern for the care receiver. ✓ - Care Receiver **AGREES**

Care Receiver **DECLINES**

Confidentiality remains intact as the care receiver agrees to contact those who can provide the necessary help.

4 **Make the contact** without the care receiver's permission. Confidentiality remains intact—the circle of confidentiality has been widened slightly to include others who can provide the necessary help.

Focus Note F goes into more detail on each part of the process.

Details on the Process for Getting Additional Help When Safety Is a Concern

1. Encourage the Care Receiver to Make the Contact

Encourage your care receiver to personally contact those who can provide the necessary help. Explain that you're very concerned about the well-being of the care receiver and any others involved and that you strongly believe there's a need for additional help. (Note: If there's an imminent danger to someone, skip this step and call your local emergency services for assistance.)

Often, the care receiver will agree and make the necessary contact. It's best to have the care receiver make that contact in your presence so you can confirm that it's taken place. Then, be sure to communicate with your Stephen Ministry Crisis Contacts yourself to tell them anything else they need to know about the situation.

When this happens, *confidentiality remains intact,* as the care receiver makes the contact him- or herself.

2. Suggest That *You* Make the Contact for the Care Receiver

If your care receiver refuses to make the contact personally, say that you could do so on his or her behalf. Clearly and directly state why you believe that additional help is necessary. Explain that you are insisting out of care and concern.

If your care receiver agrees, then *confidentiality remains intact,* as the care receiver gives you permission to make the contact on his or her behalf.

3. Say You *Will* Make the Contact

If your care receiver refuses to make the contact and doesn't want you to do so, state that you are going to make the contact. Say that you care deeply about the person and cannot stand by when the safety of the care receiver or others is at risk.

At this point, your care receiver may agree to make the contact him- or herself or may ask you to do so. In either case, *confidentiality remains intact.*

4. Make the Contact

If your care receiver still refuses, go ahead and make the contact yourself, explaining that it's because you care about him or her. As possible, stay with the care receiver, both to avoid leaving the person alone and to make sure he or she can hear what you're saying when you make the contact.

It's extremely rare to reach this fourth step. Even in these instances, though, *confidentiality remains intact as the circle of confidentiality is expanded slightly* to include others who can provide the necessary help. In addition, before being assigned a Stephen Minister, the care receiver has given permission for the Stephen Minister to consult with others in these critical situations.

When in doubt, err on the side of caution and consult with your Stephen Ministry crisis contacts about what to do. Should you have serious concern over imminent threats to the health and safety of your care receiver, others, or yourself, contact your local emergency services.

Following are additional details about responding to specific kinds of situations.

STEPHEN MINISTER INSIGHT

"When my care receiver takes the risk of sharing personal thoughts and feelings with me, I view that as a gift—and I guard that gift carefully and treat it with the utmost respect."

When the Care Receiver Might Harm Him- or Herself

Stephen Leaders do not knowingly assign people to Stephen Ministers when there's a risk of self-harm or suicide, because professional care is needed in such situations. However, it's possible that after being assigned a Stephen Minister, a care receiver could experience a new crisis or other unwelcome changes and then begin to contemplate harming him- or herself.

If you suspect that your care receiver is in imminent danger of harming him- or herself, get help right away by calling emergency services and then contacting your pastor or Stephen Leader. Stay with the person until help arrives. Unless your own personal safety is threatened in some way, do not leave the care receiver alone.

If the care receiver is not at immediate risk of harming him- or herself, you do not need to get help right then. Instead, talk with the care receiver about making a plan for getting the needed help, and follow the process in Focus Notes E and F.[1]

When the Care Receiver Might Harm Someone Else

When there's a threat, whether overt or implied, that a care receiver might physically harm another person, the process in Focus Notes E and F may or may not apply. Your first priority is to protect the threatened person and yourself, which may mean first contacting the police or other authorities to prevent potential harm.

For example, if a care receiver threatens bodily harm toward a neighbor, quickly assess how serious the threat is. If there doesn't seem to be an immediate risk of harm to yourself or others, follow the process in Focus Notes E and F to obtain the help the care receiver needs.

However, if the threat of the care receiver harming you or another person seems real and imminent, it's important *not* to first attempt to convince the care receiver to seek help. Don't try to be a hero—especially if your care receiver has access to a weapon and violence seems imminent. Instead, immediately leave the premises, call emergency services, and explain the situation; they will take over from there. If you believe the care receiver might harm someone before the authorities can respond, try to warn the person at risk of being harmed, if you can do so safely. Whatever the case, don't put yourself in harm's

---

1 For more information about helping care receivers at risk of self-harm, see modules 11, "Using Mental Health Professionals and Other Community Resources," 13, "Caring for Those with Depression: The Stephen Minister's Role," and 14, "Understanding Suicide: How to Help People Get the Care They Need."

way—consider your own safety, and involve the appropriate professionals to handle the situation. After you've involved the necessary authorities and have ensured your safety, let your Stephen Ministry Crisis Contacts know about the situation.

Fortunately, Stephen Ministers are highly unlikely to encounter a situation where a care receiver might harm others. For the safety of everyone involved, though, it's crucial to know what to do in such circumstances just in case.

STEPHEN MINISTER INSIGHT

"If one of the exceptions ever did arise, not only will you be well trained to respond, but you'll have the guidance and support of your Stephen Leaders."

When the Care Receiver May Be in a Situation Involving Abuse

Safety is also an issue if the care receiver may be involved in an abusive situation—whether it's child abuse, elder abuse, spousal abuse, or some other type, and whether the care receiver may be the one abusing or the one being abused. In any case, when abuse may be taking place, it's essential to get help for those involved.

If you suspect that your care receiver is involved in an abusive situation, even if the care receiver denies any abuse is taking place, immediately inform the Crisis Contacts for your Stephen Ministry. They can determine what to do next and provide consultation as necessary

to help you follow all applicable reporting laws. Note that it's not your responsibility to confirm for certain whether abuse is taking place—that's the job of the appropriate professionals. Your role is simply to report your suspicions for the sake of preserving safety and let the professionals take it from there.

A Higher Law

Different localities may have different reporting laws for a variety of situations involving potential violence or suspected abuse, and many professions have their own requirements and procedures. Stephen Leaders and Stephen Ministers need to be aware of and obey any laws or regulations that pertain to them. In addition to fulfilling these legal requirements, Stephen Leaders and Stephen Ministers also need to obey the law of Christian love and do what is right in God's sight in order to protect others from harm. This is true not only in Stephen Ministry caring relationships but in all your interactions.

Even if you're not entirely certain whether safety is a concern in a particular situation, it's always better to take action than to do nothing and risk the possibility of harm or tragedy. It may turn out to be a benign situation, but responding to it regardless is the right thing to do for the sake of your care receiver and others who may be involved. Consult with your Crisis Contacts about your uncertainties; they will most likely involve an expert professional and then take the appropriate actions. Again, if you believe the threat is so imminent that someone might be harmed in the time it takes to get help from your Crisis Contacts, inform emergency services immediately. Then, as soon as you're able, let your Crisis Contacts know what's going on.

Whatever the circumstances, do what you can to protect and preserve life—your care receiver's, that of anyone else involved, and your own.

Confidentiality and Supervision

Once you've been commissioned as a Stephen Minister, you will participate in twice-monthly Small Group Peer Supervision. You will share certain details about your caring relationship with the others in your Supervision Group and receive their support in helping you provide the best care possible.

Confidentiality in supervision sessions is covered in depth in module 16, "Supervision: A Key to Quality Christian Care," but Focus Note G contains a number of key points.

FOCUS NOTE G

General Guidelines for Maintaining Confidentiality in Supervision

1. Don't share your care receiver's name or the names of his or her loved ones.

2. Offer enough information for your group to understand your care receiver's situation and provide you with effective supervision, but beware of adding details that aren't essential and only serve to increase interest or satisfy curiosity.

3. If you're unsure whether it's appropriate to share something, ask a Stephen Leader privately beforehand, or just don't share it.

4. Focus your discussion on *process* goals, which relate to what the Stephen Minister can do to care for and support the care receiver. Avoid discussion of *results* goals, which deal with desired outcomes or changes for the care receiver.

5. Follow the supervision process—it's been designed to provide thorough guidance and support while maintaining confidentiality. You will learn the supervision process in detail in module 16.

6. Remember that everyone in your Supervision Group is bound by confidentiality, so if any confidential information is inadvertently revealed, it won't leave the group.

Practicing these guidelines ensures that you can participate fully in supervision while maintaining confidentiality. You'll have an opportunity to explore these points more thoroughly in module 16.

Before being assigned a Stephen Minister, your care receiver also will have been told about Small Group Peer Supervision and will have given his or her permission for you to participate in supervision. Because of that permission, and because you'll take care with any details that might identify the care receiver, you can participate fully in supervision without needing to worry about compromising confidentiality. In addition, as the last item in Focus Note G points out, all of the other Stephen Ministers in your Supervision Group are bound by confidentiality, so if any information does slip out during supervision, it doesn't leave the group.

Building a Safe House

Maintaining confidentiality is one of the keys to building a safe house of trust for your care receiver, as described in module 2, "Feelings: Yours, Mine, and Ours." You can do an effective job of listening, empathizing, and offering grace-based acceptance, but without the shelter provided by confidentiality—the assurance that everything shared will remain between the two of you—the care receiver isn't likely to share openly or deeply.

THE SAFE HOUSE

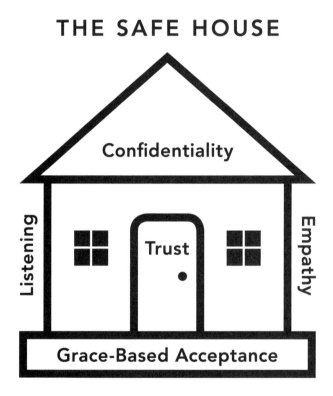

By offering confidentiality to your care receiver, you are providing a real gift: the opportunity to talk freely and work through a painful situation without fear of private thoughts and feelings being shared with others.

Above All, Prevent Harm

Confidentiality is a way to protect your care receiver and build trust in the caring relationship. Care receivers share personal, sensitive information with their Stephen Ministers and may be hurt if such information becomes known outside the caring relationship. If confidentiality is broken, the caring relationship will be damaged, and the care receiver may refuse to continue in the relationship.

Even if your care receiver gives you permission to share something, prevent harm by using your own good judgment and sharing only what you believe is absolutely necessary and appropriate.

Widening the circle of confidentiality, an uncommon but important exception to strict confidentiality, serves to protect the care receiver and others from harm. If someone is in danger, preserving his or her life and well-being *always* takes precedence.

Getting Ready for the In-Class Session

In your In-Class Session, you'll share your own experiences with confidentiality, and you'll have the opportunity to practice the skills of communicating about confidentiality and protecting it.

stephenministries.org/library

See the *Stephen Minister Online Library* for additional resources and downloads related to this Stephen Minister training topic.

Confidentiality

Module 9 | Presentation Outline

Reckless words pierce like a sword, but the tongue of the wise brings healing.
Proverbs 12:18

 Devotion: The Power of Words

I. When Confidentiality Was Important to Me

II. How to Communicate about Confidentiality

A. Simple Guidelines for Maintaining Confidentiality

FOCUS NOTE 1

Guidelines for Maintaining Confidentiality

1. Do not share with anyone—including your spouse and close friends—the name of your care receiver, any information about him or her, or anything that happens in your caring visits.

2. Neither confirm nor deny that you are someone's Stephen Minister.

3. If you're considering sharing potentially confidential information in order to help your care receiver, such as seeking an outside resource to provide additional care and support for him or her, always ask your care receiver for permission first.

4. Even if information about your care receiver is public knowledge, treat it confidentially and exercise great care if others bring up the topic.

5. Remember that safety supersedes confidentiality—if there's a risk that the care receiver or someone else may be harmed, you will widen the circle of confidentiality.

B. Telling Your Care Receiver about Confidentiality

FOCUS NOTE 2

Explaining Confidentiality to Your Care Receiver

"I know that *[name of pastor or Stephen Leader]* told you about confidentiality, and I just want to emphasize that whatever we discuss is just between the two of us. So feel free to share whatever you're thinking and feeling—what you say to me will remain confidential. Even the fact that I'm your Stephen Minister will be confidential."

1. Telling Your Care Receiver about Supervision

FOCUS NOTE 3

Describing Supervision to Your Care Receiver

"*[Name of pastor or Stephen Leader]* mentioned to you that Stephen Ministers participate in supervision. Twice a month, I meet with a small group of Stephen Ministers, and we discuss how we can provide the best care for our care receivers. Everyone in the group protects confidentiality, and we don't share the care receiver's name or any information that might reveal the care receiver's identity."

FOCUS NOTE 4

What to Say If Your Care Receiver Does Not Want You to Participate in Supervision

"Thank you for letting me know about your concerns—I wouldn't want anything to keep you from receiving care that would be helpful for you. I can assure you that we are very careful to protect confidentiality in our supervision sessions.

"Supervision is an essential part of Stephen Ministry, and I've made a commitment to participate in it so I can provide you with the best possible care. In order for me to be your Stephen Minister, I will need to receive supervision. *[Listen to the care receiver's response.]*

[If the care receiver still doesn't want you to participate:] "Would you like me to mention your concerns to *[name of pastor or Stephen Leader]* so we can talk about how we might work this out?" *[Listen to the care receiver's response.]*

2. Always Be Ready to Discuss Confidentiality

FOCUS NOTE 5

Possible Ways to Reassure Care Receivers about Confidentiality

- "I want to assure you that I will keep everything that we talk about confidential."

- "Let me remind you that everything we say here is strictly confidential. I will not share it unless you give me permission and it's appropriate for me to do so."

- "I won't let anyone else know what we say. You can feel free to say whatever is on your mind."

- "You seem uneasy about sharing some very sensitive matters with me, and I understand that. I want to remind you about what I said before about confidentiality, though, and I encourage you to feel free to talk about anything with me."

C. Communicating to Others Who Ask about Confidential Information

1. If Someone Asks Whether an Individual Is Your Care Receiver

FOCUS NOTE 6

What to Say If Someone Asks the Identity of Your Care Receiver

- "Since Stephen Ministry is confidential, I can't confirm that I'm anyone's Stephen Minister. That information is confidential."

- "I can't say one way or the other, because my work as a Stephen Minister is confidential."

- "As a Stephen Minister, I'm not at liberty to share who is or is not a care receiver, since Stephen Ministry is a confidential ministry."

2. Questions from a Relative or Close Friend of the Care Receiver

FOCUS NOTE 7

How to Respond to Questions from a Care Receiver's Relative or Close Friend

- "I appreciate your concern, but because Stephen Ministry is confidential, I'm not able to talk about a caring relationship. I hope you understand."

- "As a Stephen Minister, I am bound by confidentiality. I appreciate your concern for *[name of care receiver]*, but I don't have any information I can share about *[him/her]*."

- "Since Stephen Ministry is a confidential caring ministry, I wouldn't be able to provide any information about any care receiver. The best thing is probably to talk to *[name of care receiver]*."

3. In the Unlikely Event That an Inquirer Pressures You

FOCUS NOTE 8

If the Inquirer Pressures You

"Stephen Ministers' relationships with their care receivers are strictly confidential, and we're simply not able to discuss them. I hope you understand."

4. Don't Apologize for Maintaining Confidentiality

D. Communicating to Others about Your Ministry More Generally

III. Widening the Circle of Confidentiality for Safety Reasons

FOCUS NOTE 9

Stephen Ministry Crisis Contacts at Our Congregation

Name: *PASTOR ERICA*

Phone Number: 650-283-0444

Name: *PASTOR DAVE*

Phone Number: (408)755-9496 408-455-9416

Special Instructions:

IV. Confidentiality Challenges: Skill Builder Sets

Skill Builder Set 1: Explaining Confidentiality

FOCUS NOTE 10

Situation and Roles for Skill Builder 1-A

Note: Read only the part about your role. The care receiver will begin the skill builder.

Stephen Minister: You and your care receiver are meeting for the first time. You will be offering your care receiver a simple explanation of the basics of confidentiality, without getting into supervision.

Care Receiver: You're meeting with your Stephen Minister for the first time. You don't have any specific concerns about confidentiality, but you do want to know what it means in the context of Stephen Ministry. Begin the skill builder by saying: "The pastor told me Stephen Ministry is confidential. Can you tell me more about that?" Ask clarifying questions as necessary to learn more.

FOCUS NOTE 11

Situation and Roles for Skill Builder 1-B

Note: Read only the part about your role. The care receiver will begin the skill builder.

Stephen Minister: It's your first caring visit, and you've just given your care receiver an overview of the basics of supervision and why it's important to the caring relationship. Now respond to any questions from your care receiver about how confidentiality is maintained in supervision, sharing briefly and using the points in the "Confidentiality and Supervision" section of your Pre-Class Reading as needed.

Care Receiver: It's your first caring visit, and your Stephen Minister has briefly explained supervision. It makes sense to you that your Stephen Minister would be in supervision, but you're interested in how the process works and how it can be confidential. Begin the skill builder by saying, "I understand the need for supervision, but how do you keep things confidential?" Ask any clarifying questions to learn more about how confidentiality is maintained in Supervision Groups.

FOCUS NOTE 12

Discussion Questions for Skill Builders 1-A and 1-B

1. What words or phrases were helpful for describing confidentiality or hearing it described?

2. What other words or phrases might you use the next time you explain confidentiality?

3. What else did you learn from these two skill builders that you can share with the group?

Skill Builder Set 2: Addressing Concerns about Supervision

FOCUS NOTE 13

Situation for Skill Builder 2-A

Note: Read only the part about your role. The care receiver will begin the skill builder.

Stephen Minister: It's your first caring visit, and you've just explained to your care receiver that Stephen Ministers meet twice a month for supervision. You can tell by your care receiver's reaction that he/she is a little uneasy about it. Reassure him/her that Stephen Ministers protect confidentiality in supervision, and explain how supervision benefits the care receiver.

Care Receiver: It's your first caring visit, and your Stephen Minister has just told you that Stephen Ministers meet twice a month for supervision. You trust your Stephen Minister, but you're unsure about the Supervision Group. Begin by saying, "I'm not sure about this supervision stuff. It makes me feel a little uneasy." Allow your Stephen Minister to respond. In your follow-up questions, reveal your concern about embarrassing personal details possibly leaking to others in the group. See how your Stephen Minister responds.

FOCUS NOTE 14

Situation for Skill Builder 2-B

Note: Read only the part about your role. The church member will begin the skill builder.

Stephen Minister: After worship, a church member you know approaches you with questions about Stephen Ministry. Answer his/her questions.

Church Member: You've been going through a difficult time and are interested in possibly having a Stephen Minister. However, you don't know much about Stephen Ministry, and you've heard that Stephen Ministers meet regularly to talk about their caring relationships, which you're uneasy about. Begin the conversation by saying, "You're a Stephen Minister, right? What exactly do Stephen Ministers do?" After that ask, "Is it true that Stephen Ministers have meetings where they talk about the people they're helping? That would worry me if I were one of those people being helped." Don't immediately mention your possible need for care; instead, reveal that information gradually as you ask follow-up questions.

FOCUS NOTE 15

Discussion Questions for Skill Builders 2-A and 2-B

1. What went well in your explanations of confidentiality?

2. What was difficult about explaining confidentiality in these situations?

3. What did you learn from these two skill builders that you can share with the group?

Skill Builder Set 3: Reassuring a Care Receiver about Confidentiality

FOCUS NOTE 16

Situation for Skill Builder 3-A

Note: Read only the part about your role. The care receiver will begin the skill builder.

Stephen Minister: You're meeting with your care receiver. During the visit, your care receiver has been sharing vulnerably for a while, but he/she stops abruptly, apparently uncomfortable about having shared too much. Reassure your care receiver that anything he/she shares with you is confidential and encourage him or her to continue sharing.

Care Receiver: You're meeting with your Stephen Minister and have been sharing more than you thought you would about what you're thinking and feeling. Suddenly, you feel uncomfortable about the depth and amount of what you've shared, and you begin to worry that it might somehow reach others. So you stop abruptly and change the subject. Start the conversation by saying, "I'm sorry, I've probably said way too much about that. Why don't we talk about something else? Have you seen any good movies lately?" Be hesitant to share more, fearful that you've said too much and it might somehow leak out.

FOCUS NOTE 17

Situation for Skill Builder 3-B

Note: Read only the part about your role. The care receiver will begin the skill builder.

Stephen Minister: Your care receiver lost a loved one. You've been meeting for several months and just had a bit of a breakthrough as your care receiver shared some very deep, difficult, private feelings about the loss. Affirm your care receiver for sharing his/her thoughts and feelings. Remind him/her about confidentiality and reassure him/her that it's safe to share such things with you.

Care Receiver: You are grieving the loss of a loved one and have been meeting with your Stephen Minister for several months. You've had a lot of difficult, private thoughts and feelings buried deep inside, and you've just shared some of them. You pause afterward, wondering whether you should have shared something so sensitive and personal. Begin by saying, "I've never told anyone that before. Please forget what I just said." Then stop and look away from the Stephen Minister, ashamed of what you shared.

FOCUS NOTE 18

Discussion Questions for Skill Builders 3-A and 3-B

1. What feelings did you have as a Stephen Minister when the care receiver suddenly wanted to stop sharing?

2. What was helpful in explaining confidentiality or hearing it explained?

3. What did you learn from these two skill builders that you can share with the group?

Skill Builder Set 4: Responding to Someone Asking about Your Care Receiver

FOCUS NOTE 19

Situation for Skill Builder 4-A

Note: Read only the part about your role. The acquaintance will begin the skill builder.

Stephen Minister: Someone you know at church starts asking questions about your care receiver, Chris. Respond in a way that maintains confidentiality about your caring relationship.

Acquaintance: You've been concerned about your friend, Chris, who has been going through some tough times lately. You don't know anything about Stephen Ministry or that Chris is a Stephen Ministry care receiver, but over the weekend, you saw Chris talking with the person in front of you. Begin the conversation by saying, "Hey, the other day I saw you talking with Chris in the coffee shop. I didn't know you were acquainted. I've been really concerned about him/her. How's he/she doing?"

FOCUS NOTE 20

Situation for Skill Builder 4-B

Note: Read only the part about your role. The friend will begin the skill builder.

Stephen Minister: A good friend of your care receiver, Jordan, knows you're Jordan's Stephen Minister and begins asking you questions about him/her. Respond in a way that maintains confidentiality about your caring relationship and avoids even confirming that you are Jordan's Stephen Minister.

Friend: Your good friend, Jordan, has told you who his/her Stephen Minister is. You're not aware of the Stephen Minister's need to maintain confidentiality, and you'd like to learn more about how Jordan is doing and exchange information in order to help Jordan. Begin by saying, "I'm a really good friend of Jordan, and he/she mentioned to me that you're his/her Stephen Minister. I just wanted to know how Jordan's doing and see if there's anything I can help with."

FOCUS NOTE 21

Discussion Questions for Skill Builders 4-A and 4-B

1. How did you feel as the Stephen Minister explaining confidentiality in these situations?

2. How did you feel as the inquirer when the Stephen Minister answered your questions?

3. What did you learn from these two skill builders that you can share with the group?

Skill Builder Set 5: Responding to a Relative of a Care Receiver Wanting to Know More

FOCUS NOTE 22

Situation for Skill Builder 5-A

Note: Read only the part about your role. The family member will begin the skill builder.

Stephen Minister: You arrive at the home of your care receiver, Jamie, for your weekly visit. A family member of Jamie's opens the door and tells you that Jamie will be about ten minutes late. Respond to his/her questions while preserving confidentiality.

Family Member: You live in the same home as Jamie, a close family member of yours. Jamie just called you to say that he/she is running late and his/her Stephen Minister will be arriving shortly. Start the conversation by saying, "Jamie's running about ten minutes late and asked me to let you in and keep you company. I'm glad, actually, because this gives us a chance to talk. Jamie seems to really appreciate your weekly visits. So I'm curious, how's Jamie doing—and what exactly do the two of you talk about?" Be somewhat persistent in trying to find out what the Stephen Minister and Jamie talk about. You're interested mainly because you care about Jamie, and Jamie always seems to feel a little better after those caring visits. At the same time, you're curious what Jamie might have told the Stephen Minister about you.

FOCUS NOTE 23

Situation for Skill Builder 5-B

Note: Read only the part about your role. The sibling will begin the skill builder.

Stephen Minister: Your care receiver, Drew, recently got divorced. His/her spouse initiated the divorce, leaving your care receiver devastated. Drew has a sibling in town who knows about the divorce, but Drew has told you that, even though the two of them have always been close, he/she just feels too broken and humiliated to talk with his/her sibling right now. One day, Drew's sibling sees you at the grocery store and approaches you, deeply concerned. Respond assertively to preserve confidentiality.

Sibling: Your sibling Drew recently divorced. You've always been close to Drew, but Drew doesn't seem to want to talk with you about it, which leaves you deeply concerned. You did find out, however, who Drew's Stephen Minister is, and you catch sight of the Stephen Minister at the grocery store. Start by saying, "You're Drew's Stephen Minister, right? He/she won't tell me anything about the divorce, so I need you to tell me what's going on." Somewhere in the conversation, suggest that the Stephen Minister let you take part in the caring visits so you can know what's going on and offer support. You really want to help Drew, so be persistent and push back with lots of follow-up questions and statements.

FOCUS NOTE 24

Discussion Questions for Skill Builders 5-A and 5-B

1. What did you find most challenging about responding in these situations?

2. What might you say or do differently if you had to respond to these challenges again?

3. What did you learn from these two skill builders that you can share with the group?

V. Caregiver's Compass Review

Write your ideas around the compass.

COMPASSIONATE · FULL OF FAITH · SKILLED · TRUSTWORTHY ·

VI. Looking Ahead

Caring between Visits: Caregiving and Communications Technology

Module 10 | Pre-Class Reading

CONTENTS

A Ministry of Presence

As you learned in module 3, "The Art of Listening," in order to be effective caregivers, Stephen Ministers need to be *fully present* with their care receivers—physically, mentally, emotionally, and spiritually. Stephen Ministry is a ministry of presence, so the Stephen Minister's care needs to be primarily in person. That's the kind of care that Stephen Ministers are equipped to provide, and it's by far the most beneficial for care receivers.

The Apostle Paul knew about the ministry of presence. It wasn't always possible for him to be there in person with those under his care, but that was his desire and preference, as shown in the verses in Focus Note A.

Paul and the Ministry of Presence

- "I long to see you so that I may impart to you some spiritual gift to make you strong" (Romans 1:11).

- "After I go through Macedonia, I will come to you" (1 Corinthians 16:5a).

- "My dear children, for whom I am again in the pains of childbirth until Christ is formed in you, how I wish I could be with you now" (Galatians 4:19–20a).

- "God can testify how I long for all of you with the affection of Christ Jesus. . . . And I am confident in the Lord that I myself will come soon" (Philippians 1:8; 2:24).

- "Recalling your tears, I long to see you" (2 Timothy 1:4a).

Although this module addresses caring for your care receiver through other means than in-person communication, it's important to keep in mind the reasons in-person care is the best approach.

- In-person care facilitates the clearest, fullest, most effective communication.

- In-person care involves your physical presence, which communicates in a powerful way, "You are not alone. I'm here. I care about you."

- In-person care makes possible the appropriate use of touch—such as a pat on the back or clasped hands during prayer—to meet the care receiver's needs.

- In-person care enables the Stephen Minister to use all his or her senses to perceive how the care receiver may be feeling, including feelings the care receiver may be trying to avoid.

- In-person care makes it easier for the Stephen Minister to notice cues suggesting the care receiver's immediate needs, such as receiving affirmation and validation or having an opportunity to continue sharing.

- In-person care helps the Stephen Minister be fully present with the care receiver and assures the care receiver that he or she has the Stephen Minister's undivided attention.

- In-person care enables the Stephen Minister to engage in incarnational ministry, providing the opportunity to communicate the care and compassion of Christ through his or her expressions and actions, such as offering a warm smile or a brief hug.

In short, Stephen Ministry is a ministry of *presence*—because that's the way to provide the best care for the care receiver.

Other Means of Communication Can Play a Supporting Role

While Stephen Ministry is in-person care by nature, at times you may need to communicate with your care receiver in other ways. There may be times when it simply isn't possible for you to see your care receiver in person, such as when one of you is out of town. In such situations, you might consider using another means of communication until you're able to meet again.

It's important to think carefully before using other means of communication to ensure that they support and supplement your in-person care rather than harm or interfere with it. When used with discernment and care, those other means can play a supporting role in your ministry, as in the examples in Focus Note B.

Examples of How Other Means of Communication Can Support a Caring Relationship

- During a caring visit, your care receiver mentions that he or she has a promising job interview on Tuesday at 10 A.M. On Tuesday morning, you might text your care receiver a supportive message like, "I'm praying for you this morning. Call me afterward if you need to talk."

- Your care receiver sends you a message saying he or she had an especially difficult day. In response, you might call to say, "I'm sorry to hear about your day. Would you like to get together tomorrow so we can talk about it, or do you want to wait until our regular visit?"

- Your care receiver says he or she will be out of town on a business trip in two weeks and will miss your regularly scheduled caring visit. The two of you might set up a time to talk by phone instead.

Keep in mind that these means of communication can be helpful in a *supporting* role, not as your primary means of caring or as a replacement for in-person visits. In particular, text-based communication like email, texting, and other types of messaging are not effective for providing high-quality care to your care receiver. They can be useful for brief, factual messages (such as confirmation of a scheduled visit) or affirmation (such as a prayer or Scripture verse). When care is needed and in-person communication is not feasible, though, voice-based communication works best.

This Pre-Class Reading provides a number of guidelines for discerning when it may be appropriate to use various means of communication. These other means, however, can never replace the high-quality care Stephen Ministers provide in person with a care receiver.

Using the Phone in a Caring Relationship

Although the most effective care happens in person, you sometimes may need to communicate with your care receiver between visits or during those times when you are unable to meet in person. In these situations, often a phone call is the most effective. Here are some considerations for using the phone in a caring relationship.

When to Call

Focus Note C lists the three main times when Stephen Ministers and care receivers will communicate by phone.

When to Use the Phone in a Caring Relationship

1. *Making an appointment for the first caring visit.* In most cases, you'll set up your first caring visit via phone call, since it may require some conversation. After that, you'll likely schedule a regular

weekly meeting time or set up future meetings toward the end of each caring visit.

2. *When the care receiver needs to talk between visits.* Let your care receiver know that if something important comes up that can't wait until the next visit, he or she can feel free to call. These situations might include when there is an emergency or when the care receiver would like to briefly check in after a significant event such as a job interview or test results from a physician.

3. *Maintaining long-distance contact.* If you or your care receiver will be out of town, you might plan to have one or more caring contacts by phone call. Doing so may not always be necessary, especially if the trip is a shorter one, but in some situations, long-distance care by phone may be preferable to missing a caring visit.

To ensure that phone calls don't become a replacement for in-person meetings or cause boundary issues, it's generally best for Stephen Ministers to stick to using the phone primarily in limited situations like those in Focus Note C.

STEPHEN MINISTER INSIGHT

"Technology works well for touching base in between visits, but be careful how much you use it. You don't want to quench the need to meet in person—that's where the real caring happens."

How to Care Effectively over the Phone

When you're caring over the phone, you'll need to be very intentional about paying full attention to your care receiver, avoiding distractions, and using your voice to communicate warmth, attention, and presence. Here are several ways to do that.

Listen Carefully to Your Care Receiver's Voice

Pay very close attention to any vocal cues that can fill in what you cannot see. Focus Note D lists a number of characteristics to listen for.

FOCUS NOTE D

Vocal Cues to Listen For

1. *Tone.* The care receiver may sound friendly, upset, sincere, intense, worried, or distracted.

2. *Pitch.* If your care receiver's voice is higher-pitched than normal, it could indicate that he or she is feeling excited or afraid. If your care receiver speaks in a monotone, that can be a sign of sadness or boredom.

3. *Volume.* Speaking loudly might point to anger or intense feelings. A soft voice may mean that the care receiver is feeling insecure or unsure of how to proceed.

4. *Pace.* If the care receiver is speaking unusually fast, that may indicate he or she is upset or agitated. A very slow pace may show deep sadness or resignation.

5. *Trembling or Cracking.* If you hear your care receiver's voice tremble or crack, that could be a sign that he or she is crying or struggling with strong emotions.

6. *Sighing.* Deep sighs may indicate that your care receiver is feeling stressed, overwhelmed, or down. Sharp sighs can signal frustration or exasperation.

7. *Hesitation.* If your care receiver hesitates before talking about a particular topic, it may indicate that he or she has strong feelings about that subject. A very long pause may mean that your care receiver is having great difficulty talking about a topic.

Listen especially for differences from how your care receiver typically talks. For example, if your care receiver normally sounds calm and relaxed, but during a particular phone call he or she speaks in an intense, loud voice, something is probably troubling him or her. Similarly, if your care receiver has been speaking at a normal pace for a while but suddenly hesitates, he or she may have come to a topic that raises strong feelings.

Check Your Impressions

Since your impressions about what your care receiver is feeling during a phone call are based only on what you can hear, you'll need to confirm those impressions more frequently than you might in person. Focus Note E contains examples of what you can say to verify your impressions.

FOCUS NOTE E

Statements for Checking Impressions

- "It sounds as if you're disappointed about that."

- "You seemed a little more intense than usual talking about that. I'm wondering how you're feeling about it."

- "It's difficult for me to tell whether you're happy or unhappy."

- "You sound as if you're feeling down. How are you feeling right now?"

- "You seem excited."

- "It sounds as if others are in the room with you. Are you comfortable talking right now?"

Confirm Your Presence by Voice

Use simple words or phrases to show that you're listening and following the other person. Examples include "Yes," "I see," "Sure," and "Okay." You can also use verbal cues such as "mm-hmm," "uh-huh," or "ah" to provide confirmation of your presence and attention without interrupting the care receiver.

During a phone call, use these responses more than you would in person. Your voice needs to communicate what is normally expressed through facial expressions, body language, and touch.

Pay Attention to What Your Own Voice Communicates

Pay careful attention to what your care receiver might perceive through your voice. You'll want to sound warm, caring, calm, and attentive so that the care receiver feels comfortable sharing and knows you're there for him or her.

Sometimes we need to watch out for outside factors that affect how our voice sounds. Suppose, for example, your care receiver calls right after you've had a humorous conversation with someone else. In that situation, you'd need to guard against letting a light-hearted tone carry over into your conversation with your care receiver; otherwise, the care receiver might think you aren't taking him or her seriously and might become hesitant to communicate openly. Or, if you have a cold or allergies and sound congested, it's good to let your care receiver know so he or she doesn't think you're crying or unhappy and decide not to burden you with what he or she is feeling.

All the vocal cues listed in Focus Note D are also important to manage in your own communication. Pay careful attention to how you're using your voice and what it might be communicating, and adjust accordingly.

Be Aware of Background Sounds and Other Distractions

Pay attention to the ambient noise where you are, especially any noise your care receiver may hear over the phone. Some kinds of background sounds—like music, a TV, shuffling papers, doing dishes, or traffic—can lead care receivers to think, "My Stephen Minister doesn't care enough about me to concentrate on this conversation." These same noises are likely to distract you as well.

It's important to find a place where others aren't around. If the care receiver hears other voices in the background, he or she may become concerned about others overhearing the conversation—or even wonder how mindful you are about confidentiality. As a result, the care receiver may become less willing to share openly about his or her thoughts and feelings. If others come into the room while you're talking with your care receiver, find another place to carry on the

conversation. If you don't have any privacy at the time, arrange a time to call your care receiver back when you can be alone.

STEPHEN MINISTER INSIGHT

"No matter how fast and effective you are with these other forms of communication, they just don't have the same caring impact as reflective listening."

Four Areas of Consideration for Using Any Technology in a Caring Relationship

Beyond phone calls, people have many other technologies that can be used for communicating—including email, texting, online chat, video calls, and social media—with new ones added on a regular basis. Each of these means of communication may be helpful for specific purposes. If used in a caring relationship without careful consideration, however, they could hinder the high-quality, confidential, distinctively Christian care that Stephen Ministers provide.

Below are four areas to consider before using technology to communicate with a care receiver. Regardless of the tool you may be using, your concern as a Stephen Minister remains the same: determining whether, when, and how your use of that option can best support and enhance the in-person caring that is essential to Stephen Ministry. (Note that these guidelines apply specifically to Stephen Ministry caring relationships and may be less relevant outside that context.)

Confidentiality Concerns

Because confidentiality is a key part of a Stephen Ministry caring relationship, it's important to think through any confidentiality concerns that could arise with the technology you're considering using. Focus Note F contains questions to consider with any means of communication.

FOCUS NOTE F

Questions Related to Confidentiality Concerns

- Might someone be able to see or hear my care receiver's name or in some way learn his or her identity through our use of this technology?

- Might someone other than my care receiver be able to read, hear, retrieve, or otherwise learn the content of our communications through our use of this technology?

- How might these communications be inadvertently misrouted or made available to others?

- If these communications are saved or stored, how secure are they, and who else might be able to access them now or in the future?

- What safeguards or practices are necessary for my care receiver and me to maintain confidentiality when using this technology?

- For the sake of confidentiality, what kinds of communication should this technology not be used for?

Before using a new means of communication with your care receiver, be aware of any potential confidentiality issues or risks and talk with your care receiver about them. If either of you has concerns—even if the other doesn't—err on the side of caution and avoid using that communication tool within the caring relationship.

Caregiving Limitations

Every means of communication has its own advantages and limitations, and some of those limitations can directly affect your ability to offer quality care. In particular, because many communications technologies reduce the amount of visual and nonverbal information you get from your care receiver, it would be more difficult for Stephen Ministers and care receivers to be fully engaged in the conversation. The questions in Focus Note G focus on possible caregiving limitations of any communications technology.

FOCUS NOTE G

Questions Related to Caregiving Limitations

- How might using this technology affect my ability to discern my care receiver's true feelings?

- How might using this technology affect my ability to clarify, reflect, and validate my care receiver's feelings?

- How might this technology make it more difficult to converse on a deep level?

- How might this technology affect my care receiver's level of comfort in sharing difficult emotions?

- What limitations, glitches, or other issues inherent in this technology might make it harder for my care receiver and me to connect emotionally?

- How might using this technology reduce the desire or perceived need for in-person caring visits?

- What kinds of caregiving would this technology not be effective for?

Keep in mind that the goal of Stephen Ministry is to provide the highest-quality care for the care receiver, and make sure that any technology you use supports that goal.

STEPHEN MINISTER INSIGHT

"Text messages are just words or symbols. There may be emotions behind them or expressed through them, but you really can't determine what they are the way you can when you're actually with the person, listening."

Risks of Miscommunication

The potential for miscommunication and misunderstanding exists with any communication, but sometimes the use of technology increases the risk of miscommunication. Focus Note H contains questions to help you think through miscommunications that may occur with any specific communications technology.

FOCUS NOTE H

Questions Related to Risks of Miscommunication

- What limitations does this technology have for communicating tone of voice?

- What limitations does this technology have for communicating emotion?

- What limitations does this technology have for communicating facial expressions or body language?

- How might this technology affect the pace of the conversation? For instance, what kinds of issues might we experience with lag time or delays in receiving and replying to communications?

- How likely is it that technical difficulties will impede communication?

- What kinds of mistakes, misspellings, misunderstandings, or misinterpretations can arise with the use of this technology?

- How might it affect my caring relationship if my care receiver or I experienced such issues?

Think through any potential miscommunications that may occur with specific technologies. If there is any uncertainty, it is best to stick with a means of communication that you know will allow for maximum understanding.

Boundary Issues

Different means of communication can raise a variety of boundary issues, possibly blurring the lines of the relationship and giving the care receiver expectations that go beyond a Stephen Ministry relationship.

Before using a particular tool, device, or service, think through the questions in Focus Note I to consider how it might affect the boundaries of the caring relationship.

Questions Related to Boundary Issues

- How might using this technology affect the frequency with which my care receiver contacts me?

- How likely is it that my care receiver would use this technology to contact me unnecessarily at inappropriate or inconvenient times?

- What expectations might this technology set about how quickly I'll respond to communications from my care receiver?

- How might this technology affect my care receiver's expectations about my availability to communicate?

- How might using this technology blur the lines between a formal caring relationship and a friendship?

- How likely is it that using this technology would bring me into my care receiver's social circles—or bring the care receiver into mine?

- What kinds of boundaries might I need to establish around the use of this technology? How difficult would it be to establish those boundaries?

- If I later needed to change the boundaries related to using this technology, how likely would that be to cause upset or disappointment?

The Challenges of Using Communications Technologies in a Caring Relationship

Using means of communication other than in-person visits can introduce new challenges into a caring relationship. Focus Note J contains a number of scenarios Stephen Ministers have shared from their own experience, illustrating the difficulties of using various communications technologies in a caring relationship. As you read each example, keep in mind the four sets of questions in Focus Notes F, G, H, and I and how they apply to these scenarios.

FOCUS NOTE J

Challenges of Using Various Communications Technologies

Phone: A Stephen Minister is riding in his car with his wife and two friends when he receives a phone call. The Stephen Minister has been expecting a call, so he instinctively answers, and his phone immediately routes the call to the car's speakers. It's not the call he expected, though—it's his care receiver, who immediately identifies himself and starts sharing private details about something distressing that happened earlier that day.

Texting: A care receiver regularly texts his Stephen Minister with updates about his situation throughout the week, and the Stephen Minister texts back with encouraging words. On the evening when they're supposed to meet, the care receiver texts, "Let's just cancel our meeting since you're already caught up on everything."

Email: A Stephen Minister writes a thoughtful, encouraging email to his care receiver who is grieving the loss of his wife. The care receiver finds the words so helpful, he forwards them to his adult children. His children then forward the message to even more people. One of the care receiver's children even posts the message on social media, saying, "My dad's Stephen Minister shared these kind words." When the Stephen Minister's Supervision Group meets the next week, nearly all his fellow Stephen Ministers know who his care receiver is.

Video Call: During a video call, a care receiver is sharing some deep feelings with her Stephen Minister when the video freezes and the audio starts cutting in and out. The Stephen Minister can hear bits and pieces of what the care receiver is saying, but can't understand most of it. She tells the care receiver, "I can't hear you," but the care receiver doesn't seem to realize it's a bad connection. After several moments of frustration, the Stephen Minister finally ends the call and tries calling back—three times before the connection goes through. The Stephen Minister says, "I missed most of what you said just now. Can you tell me again?" The care receiver gives a quick, dispassionate recap, but the Stephen Minister can't help but think she missed a significant moment of sharing.

Social Media: A Stephen Minister accepts her care receiver's friend request on social media. A few days later, the care receiver publically posts details about the caring relationship, including the name of the Stephen Minister. The Stephen Minister then begins to get friend requests from family members of the care receiver.

Make Sure Any Technology Is Supporting—Not Impairing—In-Person Care

Many different ways of communicating, each with its unique benefits and challenges, can potentially play some role in your caring relationship. When used appropriately, these means can supplement the in-person relating the care receiver needs.

When considering other means of communication, ask, "How can I use this so it will truly support my regular in-person caring visits and not interfere with those visits?" It's essential that any use of these communication tools preserve confidentiality, facilitate effective caring, guard against miscommunication, and avoid any boundary issues. They need to support—not detract from or attempt to replace—the in-person caring visits that most benefit your care receiver.

Getting Ready for the In-Class Session

In preparation for the In-Class Session, refer back to the questions in Focus Notes, F, G, H, and I, and think about how those considerations apply to the use of a phone to make or receive calls with a care receiver. On page 215, write any possible issues to consider with phone calls, along with possible good uses and misuses.

stephenministries.org/library

See the ***Stephen Minister Online Library*** for additional resources and downloads related to this Stephen Minister training topic.

- Confidentiality concerns

- Caregiving limitations

- Risks of miscommunication

- Boundary issues

What are some possible good uses of phones in a caring relationship?

What are some possible misuses of phones in a caring relationship?

Caring between Visits: Caregiving and Communications Technology

Module 10 | Presentation Outline

When we were torn away from you for a short time (in person, not in thought), out of our intense longing we made every effort to see you. For we wanted to come to you—certainly I, Paul, did, again and again.

1 Thessalonians 2:17–18a

 Devotion: Ministry from Afar

I. Using Phone Calls in a Caring Relationship

FOCUS NOTE 1

Considerations for Using Phone Calls in a Caring Relationship

• Confidentiality concerns

• Caregiving limitations

• Risks for miscommunication

• Boundary issues

FOCUS NOTE 2

Good Uses and Misuses of Phone Calls in a Caring Relationship

In the space provided, write down thoughts shared by the group about good uses and misuses of phone calls in a caring relationship, based on the considerations from Focus Note 1.

Good uses:

Misuses:

II. Ministry of Presence

FOCUS NOTE 3

Discussion Questions for Communicating Care

Part 1: Communicating by Notes

1. Person A: How fully did you understand the annoyance or disappointment that was communicated?

2. Person B: How fully did you feel understood and cared for?

Part 2: Communicating Face to Face

1. Person B: How fully did you understand the annoyance or disappointment that was communicated?

2. Person A: How fully did you feel understood and cared for?

III. Using Communications Technology in a Caring Relationship

FOCUS NOTE 4

Considerations for Using a Specific Means of Communication in a Caring Relationship

Means of Communication: _Text,_____

Confidentiality concerns:

Calling —

Caregiving limitations:

Risks for miscommunication:

Boundary issues:

FOCUS NOTE 5

Good Uses and Misuses of a Specific Means of Communication in a Caring Relationship

Means of Communication: _Meeting_

Good uses: A

Misuses:

Notes on Other Means of Communication

IV. Caring over the Phone

A. Seven Skills for Caring over the Phone

FOCUS NOTE 6

Seven Skills for Caring over the Phone

Phone Skill 1: Making Any Time Limitations Known

Example 1: *"I'm glad you called. Right now, I have about ten minutes to talk. Is that enough time? If not, we can schedule another time. I just wanted to let you know."*

Phone Skill 2: Finding Out the Reason Your Care Receiver Called

Example 2: *"It's good to talk to you. I was wondering, was there anything in particular you wanted to talk about at this time?"*

Phone Skill 3: Keeping the Conversation on Track

Example 3: *"It sounds like you're worried. Tell me more about what you're thinking."*

Phone Skill 4: Responding to Silences

Example 4: *"I'm wondering whether some difficult thoughts or feelings have surfaced that you might find hard to talk about."*

Phone Skill 5: Responding to Crying

Example 5: *"I'm still here. Take your time."*

Phone Skill 6: Knowing When to End the Call

Example 6: *"Is there anything else it would be good for us to talk about now? We can also talk more about this when we meet later this week."*

Phone Skill 7: Assertively Suggesting to Meet in Person

Example 7: *"This seems important for us to talk about, and I'm thinking it would be most helpful for us to discuss it in person. We're scheduled to meet on Thursday, but would it be good for us to get together sooner?"*

B. Leaving a Voicemail for Your Care Receiver

Principles for Leaving a Voicemail for Your Care Receiver

1. Speak in a calm, caring, clear, and confident voice.

2. Keep your message brief.

3. Avoid sharing confidential information in case someone else receives or overhears the message.

   • Don't mention Stephen Ministry.

   • Don't mention the care receiver's situation or need to receive care.

   • Don't mention any upcoming visits or meetings.

4. Leave a simple, straightforward message asking the care receiver to return your call. Here are a couple of examples:

   • "Hi, this is *[name]*. Please call me when you can at *[phone number]*. That's *[name]* at *[phone number]*. Thank you."

   • "Hello, this is *[name]* from church. If you could call me when you're available, that would be great. Thanks."

Questions to Ask Your Care Receiver about Voicemail

• "Is it okay if I leave a message at this number?"

• "If I leave a message, is it likely or possible that anyone else would hear it?"

• "Is there anything you would or wouldn't want me to say if I leave a message?"

V. Establishing and Maintaining Boundaries on Communicating between Visits

Discussion Question

What types of boundaries might we need to set with our care receivers regarding communications between caring visits?

Skill Practice 1: Stephen Minister's Instructions

Your care receiver has been through a difficult breakup that has shaken him/her badly. You sense that your caring visits with him/her have been very meaningful, and you feel good about the caring relationship you're building.

However, there has been a significant increase in contacts from your care receiver between visits in the last few weeks—sometimes a phone call, other times a text. There seems to be a reason each time, but you wouldn't describe them as urgent needs. You've talked with your Supervision Group about the increase in contacts, and you've decided it's time to establish some boundaries on these types of communications.

Begin the skill practice by saying, "Hey, before we wrap up, there's something I wanted to mention to you." Be affirming and positive, but firmly set a clear boundary about the amount and nature of contact between caring visits.

FOCUS NOTE 11

Skill Practice 1: Care Receiver's Instructions

You have just been through a difficult breakup. In the aftermath, you've felt very lonely, and your self-esteem has suffered. Your friends don't seem to understand; they just offer platitudes and try to cheer you up. With your Stephen Minister, though, you feel valued and validated, and each time a caring visit ends, you wish it could have gone on just a little longer.

Recently, you've been contacting your Stephen Minister more and more in between visits, just to check in or share something you've been dealing with. You know you're probably stretching the limits of what Stephen Ministry is for, but you've been glad to have someone responding so quickly whenever you initiate communication.

Now, your latest caring visit is about to end. Your Stephen Minister will start the skill practice.

FOCUS NOTE 12

Discussion Questions

1. What went well and what could have gone better in the conversation?
2. What insights or principles did you gain from this skill practice?

FOCUS NOTE 13

Skill Practice 2: Stephen Minister's Instructions

Your care receiver was initially uneasy during your caring visits but seems to be getting more and more comfortable with the caring relationship. He/she is doing well at recognizing and accepting his/her feelings and is learning to express them.

Earlier this week, when your care receiver was really struggling, he/she sent a few long texts to tell you about what was going on. Rather than texting back, you called him/her right away. The conversation went well, but you decided to talk with your care receiver about texting at your next caring visit.

Begin the skill practice by saying, "Hey, before we wrap up, there's something I wanted to mention to you." Be affirming and positive, but firmly set boundaries around the use of texting in your caring relationship.

FOCUS NOTE 14

Skill Practice 2: Care Receiver's Instructions

Your preferred form of communication in just about any situation is texting. However, you understand the importance of meeting in person with your Stephen Minister, and even though it's a little outside your comfort zone, you find that it really does work and help. You've started to look forward to your Stephen Minister's visits.

Earlier this week, when you were dealing with especially difficult feelings, you sent a couple of long texts to your Stephen Minister to explain what was going on. Rather than returning your text, he/she called you on the phone to talk.

Now, your latest caring visit is about to end. Your Stephen Minister will start the skill practice.

FOCUS NOTE 15

Discussion Questions

1. What went well and what could have gone better in the conversation?

2. What insights or principles did you gain from this skill practice?

VI. Caregiver's Compass Review

Write your ideas around the compass.

VII. Looking Ahead

Using Mental Health Professionals and Other Community Resources

Module 11 | Pre-Class Reading

CONTENTS

Needs beyond the Care a Stephen Minister Can Provide

A Stephen Minister seeks to care for the whole person of the care receiver. Most often, a Stephen Minister can provide all the help a hurting person needs by offering emotional and spiritual support, trusting God to provide healing.

At times, however, care receivers have needs that go beyond the care a Stephen Minister is intended or able to provide.

229

- A care receiver may need a *type* of help that is outside of Stephen Ministry, such as transportation, shopping, childcare, or medical assistance.

- A care receiver may need a *volume* of help that is beyond what a Stephen Minister should provide. For instance, a grieving care receiver may benefit from participating in a grief support group in addition to the one-to-one care of a Stephen Minister.

- A care receiver may need a different *level* of help than a Stephen Minister is qualified to provide, such as psychological care from a mental health professional or spiritual guidance from a pastor.

In such cases, rather than trying to meet those specific needs personally, the best way that a Stephen Minister can help is by connecting the care receiver with an individual, agency, ministry, or other organization that can meet those specific needs. Depending on the situation, the Stephen Minister might continue to provide care after such a referral takes place. Appropriate boundaries would remain in place, with the Stephen Minister offering emotional and spiritual care while other persons or organizations provide care and support in areas where they're best equipped to do so.

For instance, if a care receiver is dealing with losing a job, the Stephen Minister can certainly help with the care receiver's feelings about the job loss, but trying to help the care receiver find a new job falls outside what a Stephen Minister does. Instead, the Stephen Minister might help connect the care receiver with a social worker or career assistance service while focusing personally on the care receiver's emotional and spiritual challenges connected with the job loss.

There's no need for the Stephen Minister to feel bad about not providing for every need him- or herself. In fact, knowing one's limits and drawing on outside resources appropriately, rather than trying to do everything independently, makes a Stephen Minister a more effective caregiver. Stephen Ministers provide the emotional and spiritual care they're equipped to provide, and they turn to others to help care receivers obtain the additional support they need.

Making Referrals to Mental Health Professionals

In *When and How to Use Mental Health Resources: A Stephen Ministry Guide,* you read about how to recognize and respond to situations where a care receiver might need to be referred to a mental health professional. You also read about the importance of seeking consultation in those circumstances to help ensure that care receivers are connected with the most appropriate type, volume, and level of care for their needs. Depending on the specific situation, the role of the Stephen Minister after the referral may vary.

During the In-Class Session, you'll learn more about how Stephen Ministers function in areas connected to care receivers' mental health, as well as how mental health referrals are handled in your congregation.

Making Referrals When Other Types of Care or Support May Be Needed

Besides mental health care, there are a number of other needs where a Stephen Minister may refer his or her care receiver to another type of community resource. Focus Note A describes some of these areas where care receivers may need additional care or support.

Areas Where Care Receivers May Need Additional Care or Support

Medical or Physical Care

Care receivers may have or develop physical symptoms or experience an injury that requires medical care. If the care receiver does not have a primary care physician to offer care or make a referral, he or she may need help finding appropriate medical care. Also, a care receiver may have other physical needs that are not medical, such as transportation, nutritious meals, or help with maintaining a home or car.

Legal or Criminal Justice Needs

Many different needs could require an attorney's help, such as a family member who has been arrested or a lawsuit filed against the care receiver. A care receiver may need help finding legal assistance, especially if he or she is unable to afford an attorney and needs *pro bono* legal representation.

Financial or Housing Assistance

Financial or housing needs, such as debt, bankruptcy, or eviction, may require the help of an attorney, consumer credit counseling service, ombudsperson, or other consumer advocate, government agency (such as a state public assistance agency), or private institution.

Educational or Vocational Assistance

If a care receiver loses a job, shifts careers, or is returning to the workforce, he or she may need help from school or vocational counselors, government agencies, or vocational therapists.

Religious or Spiritual Guidance

Care receivers may have questions about life, death, and meaning that ultimately have to do with their relationship with God. Although Stephen Ministers can certainly care for spiritual needs, sometimes care receivers may need the insights and guidance of a pastor or other spiritual leader.

These types of needs go beyond what a Stephen Minister can or should provide for a care receiver. If a care receiver needs and wants additional help, however, a Stephen Minister can assist in connecting him or her with an appropriate organization, agency, or individual.

In addition, a care receiver who is dealing with a specific situation may also benefit from other kinds of help. For example, a person caring for a parent with Alzheimer's may benefit from being connected with an agency that provides support for family members of Alzheimer's patients. Or, a person with a cancer diagnosis might benefit from being in a cancer support group in addition to receiving one-to-one care from a Stephen Minister.

As part of this module, you'll learn more about organizations, agencies, groups, and individuals that may be able to assist care receivers with these needs for additional care and support. You will also contribute to a directory of these services in your community, which you can use to support future care receivers as effectively as possible.

What If You Have Professional or Personal Expertise in a Particular Area?

A number of Stephen Ministers are professionals specially trained to offer particular kinds of help or care. Or Stephen Ministers may have skills or experience in certain areas in which the care receiver might need assistance. Sometimes Stephen Ministers with this kind of background wonder whether it's appropriate for them to draw on that expertise to provide specific kinds of help their care receivers might need.

Even if you have expertise in one of these areas and could possibly assist your care receiver using those skills, it's best to refrain from providing dedicated, recurring support in that area. Your role in this caring relationship is as a Stephen Minister, so you can help your care receiver the most by focusing on what you provide as a Stephen Minister—listening, caring, and offering empathetic support. Adding other kinds of assistance would detract from that essential ministry and blur the boundaries of the caring relationship.

Instead of fulfilling other types of needs yourself, you can best help by identifying and referring your care receiver to an outside source that could provide additional support. That way, your care receiver will benefit both from the referral and from the ongoing care you are providing as a Stephen Minister.

Signs That Additional Help Might Be Needed

The following lists of behaviors, symptoms, and other signs might indicate a need for additional help in one of the five areas listed in Focus Note A. For signs that may indicate a need for mental health care, see chapter 6 in *When and How to Use Mental Health Resources.*

You can use these lists to help determine whether your care receiver may need additional support beyond what you as a Stephen Minister can or should provide. If your care receiver exhibits a sign on one of these lists, you can suggest that he or she connect with an organization, agency, or individual that can provide support in that area. If he or she needs help making an initial contact, you could assist with that as well. These lists are not exhaustive, so be aware of possible needs for additional care even if the care receiver is not displaying one of these signs.

1. Signs of a Possible Need for Medical or Physical Care

Be alert for the possible need for medical or physical care if your care receiver:

- is on medication and seems confused or disoriented;

- talks about a sudden change in vision, hearing, touch, taste, or smell;

- describes an unexplained acute or chronic physical ailment and has not sought medical help;

- mentions dizziness, disorientation, passing out, fainting, poor balance, or falling as a result of these symptoms;

- has physical problems that are chronic or severe enough to warrant a home health care service;

- is ill or incapacitated to the point that 24-hour nursing care is necessary;

- is not interested in eating;

- suddenly loses or gains weight;

- is experiencing a high-risk pregnancy;

- lacks adequate medical equipment or supplies to treat a physical ailment;

- appears malnourished or emaciated;

- requires ongoing therapy for chronic physical problems resulting from an earlier event, such as an illness, stroke, accident, or surgery;

- qualifies for government nutritional assistance but doesn't apply for or use it;

- needs regular transportation to and from a clinic or hospital for therapy or medical treatment; or

- is living in conditions that are unsanitary, unhealthy, or hazardous.

2. Signs of a Possible Need for Legal or Criminal Justice Assistance

Be alert for the possible need for legal or criminal justice assistance if your care receiver:

- has a family member in jail or prison or sees this as a realistic possibility;

- has a family member currently in detention or on probation;

- is in jail or prison or sees this as a realistic possibility;

- is separated or divorced and is being harassed by his or her spouse or ex-spouse;

- is being sued for divorce by his or her spouse but is unsure of the legal procedure;

- has been the victim of sexual assault;

- has been the victim of violent crime;

- has been a victim of fraud;

- needs to defend him- or herself in a lawsuit;

- is being evicted from his or her home;

- has experienced a burglary or other theft;

- is having difficulty collecting money from an insurance company;

- qualifies for particular governmental assistance benefits but is not receiving them;

- wants to make or amend a will or living trust;

- has a serious, valid complaint about a product or service but has not gotten a satisfactory response from the provider;

- has bruises, scars, or other possible signs of abuse;*

- has family members with bruises, scars, or other possible signs of abuse;*

- has been threatened with physical violence;*

- has family members who have been threatened with physical violence;*

- wants to become a naturalized citizen;

* See pages 182–188 of the Pre-Class Reading for module 9, "Confidentiality," for how to respond when the safety of the care receiver or others is a concern.

- has experienced discrimination by an employer or in obtaining housing or other accommodations, products, or services;

- expresses concern about threats to his or her health or safety at work; or

- has filed a grievance against his or her employer or union.

3. Signs of a Possible Need for Financial or Housing Assistance

Be alert for the possible need for financial or housing assistance if your care receiver:

- is unable to pay rent or utility bills;

- does not have enough food;

- has serious credit problems;

- needs help filing a tax return;

- has difficulty developing or sticking to a personal budget;

- needs to make a major, long-term financial decision;

- is deeply in debt;

- faces bankruptcy;

- needs to secure a loan and doesn't know how;

- is unable to maintain his or her home;

- doesn't have a place to live;

- is about to be evicted; or

- cannot get the landlord to make needed repairs.

4. Signs of a Possible Need for Educational or Vocational Assistance

Be alert for the possible need for educational or vocational assistance if your care receiver:

- believes that his or her child is not receiving necessary educational services or is being treated unfairly in school;

- wants to obtain a general equivalency diploma or other certificate;

- wants to return to school to complete a degree program;

- has a child who requires special educational services;

- needs job counseling, aptitude testing, or vocational placement;

- has a disability and needs vocational evaluation, training, or counseling; or

- is unemployed.

5. Signs of a Possible Need for Spiritual Guidance

Be alert for the possible need for spiritual guidance if your care receiver:

- is faced with a difficult and complex decision involving moral, ethical, and spiritual issues;

- wants to be baptized, become a member of a congregation, or take a more active role in church life;

- becomes inactive or less active in the church, transfers to another church, or asks to be removed from the church roll;

- asks specifically to see an ordained minister or one of the church staff;

- expresses deep inner conflicts or doubts about God; or

- expresses the desire to participate in a sacrament or rite of the church requiring the ministry of ordained clergy.

How to Find Community Resources for Referrals

In some situations, you may already be familiar with an organization, agency, or individual that could help your care receiver. If you aren't, you can do an online search or check with your Supervision Group. You can also consult with your Community Resource Contact, a Stephen Leader who can help identify which resources might be most helpful for your care receiver.

Another good starting point is appendix A, "Finding Resources to Provide Additional Help," which provides guidance for how and where to find reliable community resources for different needs a care receiver may have. Your Stephen Leader Team may also have put together a *Community Resources Handbook* with information about a variety of local resources.

From time to time, your Stephen Leader Team may request your help in finding and evaluating community resources that can be used for referrals. Appendix B, the "Community Resource Assessment Questionnaire," is a tool you can use to research, evaluate, and organize information about community resources you encounter. Each time you fill out one of these questionnaires, pass it along to a Stephen Leader to be included in the *Community Resources Handbook.*

The *Community Resources Handbook* also may include information your Stephen Leaders have gathered about local mental health professionals.

Getting Ready for the In-Class Session

Your Stephen Leader gave you an assignment to research a community resource, along with a copy of the Community Resource Assessment Questionnaire to fill out. Use appendix A to help you find a resource. Bring your completed questionnaire to the next In-Class Session.

stephenministries.org/library

See the *Stephen Minister Online Library* for additional resources and downloads related to this Stephen Minister training topic.

Appendix A

Module 11

Finding Resources to Provide Additional Help

PURPOSE

To provide guidance to Stephen Ministers for identifying community resources they can use when referring care receivers for additional help. As Stephen Leaders and Stephen Ministers learn about various helping resources in the community, they can add them to the congregation's *Community Resources Handbook.*

It's important to know what resources for additional help may be helpful to a care receiver and are available in your area. This appendix provides guidelines to help you identify caring resources to include in your congregation's *Community Resources Handbook,* whether you're helping create a new handbook or adding to an existing one.

Categories and Examples of Resources

Below are several categories of community resources, along with some ideas for the types of resources you might connect a care receiver with, depending on his or her needs. These are not exhaustive lists—just some examples to get you started thinking about the possibilities.

Medical Care

- hospitals, clinics, and medical centers
- hospices

- physicians
- public health nurses
- medical supply and equipment services

Practical Assistance

- social workers (who might connect people with many different kinds of care and support)
- transportation services or ministries
- food and meal services
- thrift stores or clothing assistance organizations
- caregiver assistance programs

Legal or Criminal Justice Needs

- attorneys
- state-sponsored legal assistance services
- legal aid societies

Financial or Housing Assistance

- public assistance agencies
- community assistance clearinghouses and hotlines
- credit counseling services
- consumer advocates
- emergency housing programs or shelters

Educational or Vocational Assistance

- vocational counselors
- employment assistance programs
- adult education programs
- area community colleges and trade schools

Religious or Spiritual Guidance

- local pastors
- deacons
- elders
- chaplains
- religious bookstores
- spiritual directors

Mental Health Care

- professional counselors
- mental health clinics
- hospitals with inpatient mental health facilities
- mental health referral hotlines
- twelve-step programs
- support groups

Situation-Specific Support

It can be good to seek out resources that offer support for specific needs that Stephen Ministry care receivers frequently have, such as:

- grief
- chronic or terminal illness
- job loss
- divorce
- challenges related to pregnancy and childbirth
- military deployment of a loved one
- aging
- being a long-term caregiver for a loved one

Resources That May Already Be in Your Congregation's Handbook

If your congregation already has an established Stephen Ministry, you'll most likely have a good number of existing resources in your *Community Resources Handbook.*

- Your Stephen Leaders will have received a variety of recommendations from the pastor and incorporated those resources.

- Other church staff may have contributed to the handbook based on their experience and expertise in particular areas.

- Earlier classes of Stephen Ministers will have researched caring resources and added them to the handbook as part of their training.

These prior entries can give you ideas of where to look for other possibilities and show you what resources your Stephen Ministry already knows about. In addition, it's important to periodically give the older resources another look to update your information on them and reassess them, which your Stephen Leaders may ask you to do on occasion.

Suggestions for Finding Resources

Following are some thoughts about where to locate resources for your handbook.

Seek Out Resources within Your Congregation

There may be a number of potential resources within your own congregation. Perhaps your congregation includes physicians, nurses, counselors, lawyers, employees of government agencies, and the like. Others may not work in those areas themselves but have connections with people who do. In addition, other ministries in your congregation could be of help to care receivers. Whatever the case, don't be reluctant to ask people in your congregation what caring or helping resources they know of. You may turn up possibilities you didn't expect.

Denominational Resources

Your denomination may have information or guidance about faith-based or other organizations that exist to meet various needs. Check to see what resources are offered or recommended by your denomination.

Look into City, County, or Other Local Services

You might also look into what services are offered by your city or county. In many areas, community resource directories are available, often for a nominal fee. There are also clearinghouses that have already identified and evaluated local resources. One such organization is United Way; in the United States, calling them at 211 will connect you with a community resource specialist who can help identify what's available in your area.

Of course, you'll still want to evaluate these resources yourself to make sure they'll meet the needs of the people your Stephen Ministry serves, but drawing on others' research can give you a head start.

Search Online

You can quickly find many different possibilities by searching on the internet, but be careful in evaluating the usefulness and reliability of the information you see online. Here are some ideas for determining the quality of resources you find.

- Ask people you know with knowledge in relevant areas. Their insights are often the most important filter for determining what to trust.

- Look into what others are saying about the resource. If the organization or individual has a positive reputation elsewhere, such as on third-party review websites or in newspaper articles, that's usually a good sign.

- Check the website's "About Us" page and ask yourself: What is the mission of this website and its sponsor? What are the sponsor's values? How well known and respected is the sponsor? What is this website trying to accomplish?

- If the resource has a phone number listed on their website, make a call and ask some basic questions, possibly using the Community Resource Assessment Questionnaire as a guide. Just a short conversation can give you an idea of how the organization operates, how friendly the staff is, and other impressions about its general quality.

Evaluating Resources You've Identified

Once you've identified a possible resource, you'll want to give it a thorough evaluation. Try to get a variety of perspectives on the resource in order to put together the most complete picture possible. Here are some suggestions.

Complete the Community Resource Assessment Questionnaire

First, fill out a Community Resource Assessment Questionnaire (see appendix B) for the resource, filling in the information and answering the questions as best you can. The more details you provide, the better the Stephen Leader team can determine how beneficial the resource will be.

Check with Other Organizations

As noted earlier, various local, national, and international organizations, such as United Way, keep track of and evaluate community resources of different types. If you haven't already, it's good to check what they have to say about the resource you're looking at. In addition, you might check with some of the trusted organizations already in your handbook to see whether they can offer insights about a resource you're considering.

Seek Insights and Opinions from Appropriate Professionals

Specific professionals in your congregation or community may be familiar with the resource in question and share their thoughts about its usefulness. For example, you might check with a nurse about a support group for cancer patients, an attorney about a legal resource, or a social worker about a financial assistance organization. With their expertise, they can give you a greater understanding of the advantages and disadvantages of a particular resource.

Whatever the current state of your congregation's *Community Resources Handbook,* you can always update, add to, and strengthen it. Your *Community Resources Handbook* will be a constantly growing reference, and it will become an indispensable tool for your Stephen Ministry and congregation. In those situations where a care receiver would benefit from support outside of Stephen Ministry, you can use the handbook to be confident that you're referring the person to just the kind of help he or she needs.

Appendix B

Module 11

Community Resource Assessment Questionnaire

_____

Name of resource

_____

Website

_____

Address

_____

Phone

_____

Fax

_____

Contact person at resource

_____

Contact phone or extension

_____

Contact email

_____

Report submitted by

_____

Date

1. What services does the resource provide? (List as many as you can identify.)

2. What hours are these services typically available?

3. How much do these services cost?

241

4. Where are these services available?

5. Who is eligible for these services?

6. How does one access these services?

7. What, if any, information, identification, or paperwork does the care receiver need to provide to use these services?

8. Describe the reputation of this resource and the experiences of other church members with it. How consistent is it in providing quality service to its clients?

9. Other information:

Using Mental Health Professionals and Other Community Resources

Module 11 | Presentation Outline

For by the grace given me I say to every one of you: Do not think of yourself more highly than you ought, but rather think of yourself with sober judgment, in accordance with the measure of faith God has given you. Just as each of us has one body with many members, and these members do not all have the same function, so in Christ we who are many form one body, and each member belongs to all the others. We have different gifts, according to the grace given us.
Romans 12:3–6a

Devotion: Entrusting Your Care Receiver to God

I. *Navigating Mental Health Issues in Stephen Ministry*

I. *Navigating Mental Health Issues in Stephen Ministry*
(continued)

II. Making Referrals to Mental Health Professionals

II. Making Referrals to Mental Health Professionals
(continued)

III. Making Referrals to Other Community Resources

A. Steps in Making a Referral to a Community Resource

FOCUS NOTE 1

Steps in Making a Referral to a Community Resource

1. Identify a possible need with your care receiver.
2. Explore the need with your Supervision Group.
3. Put together a list of possible resources to meet that need.
4. Share the list of resources with your care receiver.
5. Follow up.

1. Identify a Possible Need with Your Care Receiver

2. Explore the Need with Your Supervision Group

3. Put Together a List of Possible Resources to Meet That Need

4. *Share the List of Resources with Your Care Receiver*

5. *Follow Up*

B. Identifying Additional Needs for Care

FOCUS NOTE 2

Descriptions of Possible Care Receiver Situations

For each of these seven situations, identify any *non–Stephen Ministry needs* the care receiver might have.

Situation 1

Your care receiver lost his/her spouse. During a caring visit, you learn that the spouse who died had managed all the family finances during their 40 years of marriage.

Example: Legal help with estate issues

Situation 2

Your care receiver has experienced a debilitating arm injury that has left him/her unable to continue in his/her previous line of work. Your care receiver's spouse now works full time to support them, and the care receiver is home alone much of the day.

Situation 3

During a caring visit, you learn that your care receiver's teenage son had been involved in an automobile accident the previous night. Nobody was injured, but the son had been drinking and was arrested.

Situation 4

Your care receiver's spouse has been diagnosed with early-onset Alzheimer's.

Situation 5

Your care receiver's spouse left abruptly, moved out of state, and filed for divorce. Your care receiver is now a single parent, working full time, managing the household, and taking care of three young children.

Situation 6

Your care receiver is self-employed and recovering from a serious illness. He/she is expected to make a full recovery and resume work eventually, but right now he/she is overwhelmed by medical bills.

Situation 7

Your care receiver has lost his/her job due to company closure. Other job opportunities in the same field would require moving across the country, which just isn't feasible for your care receiver right now.

C. Talking with a Care Receiver about a Possible Community Resource Referral

FOCUS NOTE 3

Three Care Receiver Scenarios

Scenario 1

Care Receiver: You have just been laid off after twenty years of service. You don't have enough money saved up to retire. You've told your Stephen Minister that other companies in your line of work are also in the process of laying off employees.

Begin the scenario by saying, "I'm just at a loss. Nobody's hiring for what I do, and there's nothing else I can do. It's extremely frustrating."

Stephen Minister: It's clear to you that your care receiver needs to start thinking about how his/her skills and experience might transfer to a new field. You've decided to suggest that your care receiver contact a vocational counselor for help in working through the transition.

Scenario 2

Care Receiver: Your spouse recently died unexpectedly. Not only are you grieving the loss of your spouse, but you also are feeling overwhelmed by new responsibilities. Your spouse was the one who took care of many home upkeep activities that you've never had to do—and now those tasks have fallen onto you.

Begin the scenario by saying, "I've never done any of these things before. I don't even know where to start."

Stephen Minister: After talking with your Supervision Group, you've identified a few organizations that provide home upkeep services. You also know of some congregation members who regularly volunteer to assist others in the activities your care receiver needs help with.

Scenario 3

Care Receiver: Your family has experienced multiple medical crises, leaving the family with massive debt. During a recent caring visit, you told your Stephen Minister that you're not sure how you will even cover the utility bills next month, much less pay off the debt.

Begin the scenario by saying, "I just feel so hopeless and weighed down. I don't know what to do or where to turn."

Stephen Minister: After talking with your Supervision Group, you decide to suggest a couple of options to your care receiver. One possibility is a local government program that assists with paying utilities for people in need. Another is a social worker that can help your care receiver develop a long-term plan for paying off the debt.

IV. Caregiver's Compass Review

Write your ideas around the compass.

V. Looking Ahead

Ministering to Those Experiencing Grief

Module 12 | Pre-Class Reading

CONTENTS

Grief Is a Journey

The death of a loved one can be one of the most devastating experiences many people encounter. It often turns their world upside down, shattering the life they knew into pieces. Mourning that loss and putting together the fragments takes time. Compounding these difficulties are the many misconceptions about grief. All too often, people feel pressured to stuff away difficult feelings and move on with their lives. The death of a loved one can stir up faith struggles too—people may feel angry at God or even question God's existence, and then feel guilty for having such thoughts. Those who have lost a loved one often assume they need to hide their grief or move through it quickly.

Caring for someone experiencing grief is one of the more frequent situations in which Stephen Ministers serve. It's a place where you can make a big difference in a care receiver's life.

The Three *Ns* of Grief

Grief is a healthy, human process that helps people work through their difficult feelings and eventually adjust to the changes in their lives. Focus Note A includes an excerpt from *Journeying through Grief*, in which Dr. Kenneth Haugk describes the "three *Ns*" of grief.

FOCUS NOTE A

The Three *Ns* of Grief

Grief is a very normal, natural, and necessary process. I like to call these the three *Ns* of grief.

- Grief is *normal* because it is how people respond to a significant personal loss. It's normal to expect people who've lost someone they love to be deeply affected by their loss.

- Grief is *natural* in that it's a completely human thing to do. We can't avoid grief—it's built into us. We're created to grieve, just as we're created to love. We love, and when we lose someone we love, we grieve.

- Grief is *necessary.* Grief provides a healthy way to cope with the loss and everything it means to us. Trying to ignore or avoid grief won't work. It will only make the grief last longer and possibly cause even more pain.

Over the years I've talked with many people who've apologized for expressing their emotions about losing a loved one. I've always told them something like this: "You've got nothing to apologize for. Showing your feelings is absolutely the best thing you can do right now. It's healthy, and it shows you're human."[1]

People typically experience some level of grief after any loss—certainly including the death of a loved one, but also losses such as the loss of a job, a broken relationship, the loss of being single due to marriage, or a future dream becoming unattainable. When people encounter the painful feelings associated with

---

1 Kenneth C. Haugk, *Journeying through Grief, Book 1: A Time to Grieve* (St. Louis: Stephen Ministries, 2004), 3–4.

a loss, it's normal, natural, and necessary to grieve. Grieving is the ongoing process of working through the difficult feelings following the loss and of adjusting to a new normal in life.

This Pre-Class Reading describes the grief process and the feelings and issues people commonly experience throughout the journey. Your In-Class Session will then discuss ways to minister to care receivers at each point. Although this module focuses on grief after the death of a loved one, most of the principles in it will apply to grief after any type of loss.

Grief Affects the Entire Self

The loss of a loved one can affect people in many different ways. This can include:

- **Psychologically or emotionally.** Losing a loved one often stirs up deep, difficult feelings, including emotions a person may not be accustomed to feeling.

- **Socially.** The loss of a significant relationship can affect other relationships. The grieving person may withdraw from others, and others may withdraw from him or her as well. Some social groups may no longer feel like a good fit.

- **Spiritually.** Sometimes people feel closer to God after a loss. Other times they feel as if God is far away or may even question God's existence.

- **Physically.** Grieving can affect a person's eating and sleeping habits and can contribute to various physical symptoms.

- **Mentally.** During grief, many people don't feel as sharp as they do at other times.

Their thoughts may be muddled or hard to communicate.

Every grief experience is unique; the same person may grieve different losses in very different ways. Factors that influence how someone grieves include:

- the person's background, personality, and past experiences;

- the type and quality of his or her relationship with the one who died; and

- the circumstances surrounding the death.

STEPHEN MINISTER INSIGHT

"There's nothing you can do or say to take away your care receiver's grief. Just allow them to talk, to cry, to be sad or mad, to share their pain over and over, whatever they need to do. Work the process and let God work the healing."

The Three Phases of Grief

Although every grief journey is different, there are commonalities in the way most people grieve. A person typically goes through three general phases while adjusting to the loss of a loved one.

1) *Shock.* The grieving person experiences a sense of disbelief and denial in response to the loss.

2) *Recoil.* The shock gives way, the reality of the loss sets in, and the person struggles to make emotional adjustments.

3) *Rebuilding.* The person begins to adapt to his or her new situation and becomes ready to move forward in life.

People typically experience a lot of back-and-forth movement as they make their way through these phases—they don't cleanly finish one phase and move on to the next. Challenges from one phase may reappear in a later phase. However, thinking in terms of these phases can help clarify the most common progression of feelings and challenges as someone gradually readjusts to life after losing a loved one.

1. Shock

Just as people go into physical shock when they suffer a severe injury, they experience emotional shock when they learn that a loved one has died. With the loss, their life turns upside down, and their world changes forever.

Following is what people often experience during Shock. All these reactions are normal and natural after a loved one has died.

Disbelief or Denial

Shock typically begins with denial. For many people, the realization that a loved one has died is so painful and overwhelming that they have difficulty accepting it. That's why you'll sometimes hear people say things like, "I can't believe it," "You must be mistaken," or "No, it's not true!"

When people are in denial, they may go for hours or even days without having any strong emotional reaction to the loss, unable or unwilling to accept that the loss is real. This temporary rejection of reality may be surprising or confusing for the grieving person and for people around the grieving person.

Denial is an immediate way of dealing with a painful reality. The grieving person knows on one level that the loss is real, but on another level he or she can't fully accept it yet. As one woman said, "My head knew, but my heart denied!"

In the immediate period after a loss, denial can be a blessing. It's like an emotional anesthesia that blocks much of the deep pain until the grieving person is more prepared to handle it. This is also why some people may appear to be calm and composed at the funeral of a loved one—they might be experiencing Shock.

For some, denial may last only a few minutes or hours; for others, it may last a few days or longer. This temporary reaction is healthy because it gives people time to build up the inner resources to deal with a potentially overwhelming situation.

STEPHEN MINISTER INSIGHT

"Walking alongside a care receiver who is grieving is your gift to them. Their allowing you to walk alongside is their gift to you. But the biggest gift is God working through the caring relationship to heal the person's heart. That's a gift to both of you."

The Fog of Grief

Another common experience is the fog of grief, described in Focus Note B.

FOCUS NOTE B

The Fog of Grief

Grief causes a fog to roll into our lives. The fog of grief can affect our ability to think or concentrate. This fog often sets in right after a loved one has died. But even after the shock wears off the fog can linger or come and go for a long time . . . . What happens is that our grief gets so heavy that it surrounds us, clouds our minds, and interferes with our ability to think clearly.[2]

Here are some ways people have described the fog of grief:

- "I was in a daze. It just didn't seem real."

- "I felt totally detached."

- "The situation was so surreal. It felt like it just couldn't be happening."

- "My world was spinning out of control. I was completely disoriented."

- "I was just numb—I couldn't think or feel anything."

The fog of grief is a natural response to the shock of a loss and can continue or recur for a long time afterward.

Physical Symptoms

People can experience a wide range of physical symptoms during Shock. Some may seem to have a lot of excess energy—wringing their

---

2 Haugk, *Journeying through Grief, Book 1: A Time to Grieve*, 27.

hands, pacing around the room, or shaking uncontrollably. Others may seem drained, becoming withdrawn or nearly motionless, like they're temporarily shutting down.

2. Recoil

Eventually, the grieving person's shock fades, and the reality of the loss begins to set in. The Recoil phase usually happens after the rest of the world seems to have moved on:

- After the out-of-town relatives have gone home.

- After people have stopped visiting so frequently.

- After the phone calls and cards have tapered off.

For the grieving person, it can feel as if everyone else has gone back to life as normal—while the painful reality is just sinking in that his or her life will never be the same.

Intense Feelings

Recoil is a tumultuous time filled with a lot of back-and-forth, up-and-down movement. It's typically when grieving people experience many intense, difficult feelings. Emotions that may have been bottled up during the Shock phase start flooding out as the person comes to grips with the reality of the loss.

The psalmist's words in Focus Note C show some of the strong feelings that care receivers might experience during Recoil.

FOCUS NOTE C

The Cry of a Grieving Heart

I am bowed down and brought very low;
    all day long I go about mourning.

My back is filled with searing pain;
    there is no health in my body.

I am feeble and utterly crushed;
    I groan in anguish of heart.

All my longings lie open before you,
O Lord;
    my sighing is not hidden from you.

My heart pounds, my strength fails me;
    even the light has gone from my eyes.

My friends and companions avoid me
because of my wounds;
    my neighbors stay far away. . . .

I have become like a man who does not hear,
    whose mouth can offer no reply.

Psalm 38:6–11, 14

The shock wears off, the floodgates open, and the feelings come gushing out. Care receivers may groan or wail to give voice to their anguish. At times they may sob uncontrollably.

Remember, though, that everyone's grief journey is different. Which specific emotions a person may experience—as well as the depth of the emotions, how long they last, and how the person expresses them—will vary. Here are a few of the more common emotions people encounter during grief.

Loneliness

People often feel incredibly lonely in the midst of their grief. Not only is the loved one gone, but the grieving person may withdraw emotionally from others, thinking that no one understands or is interested in his or her pain. On top of that, other people may pull away from the grieving person because they don't know what to say or do, leaving the person feeling even more isolated.

Guilt

For many grieving people, guilt is a real struggle. Focus Note D contains some words about guilt from *Journeying through Grief.*

FOCUS NOTE D

Feelings of Guilt Are Common

Some [grieving people] blamed themselves for somehow having caused or not prevented the death. Many deeply regretted words they'd said or deeds they'd done while the person was still alive. Those who had to make difficult medical choices for their loved one sometimes second-guessed their decisions. Many felt guilty about certain feelings, such as anger, relief, apathy, or even moments of happiness or laughter.[3]

Journeying through Grief goes on to describe five challenges in dealing with guilt.

1. *Guilt can be irrational.* The grieving person may feel guilty when he or she didn't do anything wrong or when what happened was outside the person's control.

2. *Guilt is often buried deep inside.* The grieving person may not be fully aware of any feelings of guilt.

3. *Guilt often arises out of unrealistic expectations.* The grieving person may have an unrealistic perspective on what he or she should have done or avoided doing.

4. *Guilt can distort the facts.* The grieving person may become so focused on particular aspects of what happened that they become magnified out of proportion in his or her mind.

5. *Guilt is usually over something we cannot change.* The causes of a grieving person's feelings of guilt are in the past. Although we can change our future actions based on the past, we can't change the past itself.

Guilt is a useful feeling for helping us identify when we may need to address some wrong. However, it's meant to be temporary, fading after we resolve the situation. Guilt that continues long after an issue has been resolved—or guilt that's irrational and not based on any actual wrong—can be debilitating for a grieving person.

Anger

People frequently experience anger after a loss. Someone precious has been taken away, so it's understandable people would feel angry about it. Many times, anger is buried or hidden. The person might not know the anger is there or might be surprised at its intensity when it does come out.

People can have a variety of targets for their anger, but four of the most common are:

- whoever or whatever the grieving person believes is responsible for the death;

- the loved one who died;

- the grieving person him- or herself; and

- God.

---

3 Kenneth C. Haugk, *Journeying through Grief, Book 3: Finding Hope and Healing* (St. Louis: Stephen Ministries, 2004), 19.

Be aware that in dealing with angry feelings, a care receiver occasionally may direct some of that anger toward a caregiver, even when the caregiver has done nothing to justify it. These expressions of anger are part of the normal process of releasing pent-up feelings. Focus Note E contains a story of how a Stephen Minister supported a care receiver who was dealing with anger.

FOCUS NOTE E

Listening to Anger

"My care receiver had lost her daughter in a car crash. Early in our first visit, she made one point very clear to me: 'I don't want to talk about God. I'm just too angry.'

"So I honored that, and I didn't bring up God—but she did. She told me she was angry at God for letting her daughter die while the others in the accident were barely injured. She was angry at God for not preventing the crash, and she was angry with me for believing in God. She had a lot of venting to do, and I was often right in the line of fire. So were her friends, most of whom stopped coming to see her, because they didn't know how to deal with her anger.

"But I was able to stick with it, thanks to my Supervision Group. They reminded me that her anger was normal for a person who had lost someone so precious to her, and they supported, encouraged, and prayed for me all along the way. I kept meeting with my care receiver, week after week, month after month, listening to her, validating her feelings, and accepting her right where she was. And, as she let those feelings out and allowed the tears to flow, her anger began to lessen and the healing was able to begin.

"Later on, she said to me, 'I can't thank you enough for sticking with me through all my venting. You were there for me, with God working through you, and that helped get me through this.'"

Helping people find healthy ways to release their anger keeps it from building up inside, becoming even more intense, and causing serious problems.

Sudden Upsurges of Grief

From time to time a person may experience sudden upsurges of grief—waves of painful feelings when the loss feels especially acute. Sometimes these upsurges can be anticipated, such as the anniversary of the loss, a birthday, a wedding anniversary, a holiday, or another significant day. People may be able to prepare for the difficult feelings they may have on these days, although the intensity of the pain may still be surprising.

Other times, the person may be blindsided by these waves of intense grief. A photograph, a location, a song, a scent, or something else can stir up memories of the loved one and trigger a sudden upsurge of grief.

When your care receiver experiences a sudden upsurge of grief, you can help in a couple of ways. First, encourage your care receiver to let the feelings out, while you offer a caring, listening presence. Second, let him or her know such upsurges are a normal part of the grief process.

Faith Crises

The loss of a loved one can often have an effect on people's faith. Sometimes people draw closer to God than they've ever felt before; other times they experience a crisis of faith, wondering how a loving God could allow the loss to happen or questioning whether God really cares.

Anyone, no matter what his or her faith was like before the loss, can experience doubts about God's goodness or love during a time of grief. The grieving person may find it difficult to pray or come to worship. He or she may even question God's existence—and then feel guilty for thinking that.

Experiencing a faith crisis doesn't mean someone has weak faith or something is wrong with him or her. Any of us might go through such a crisis. We're all human, and we all can have a hard time reconciling our beliefs with a painful reality. Often, these faith struggles are temporary, and God's faithfulness in the crisis can bring the person through it with an even stronger faith.

Preoccupation with Thoughts of the Loved One

During the Recoil phase, people can become preoccupied with their loss and think constantly about it. When a person loses someone important in his or her life, it's natural to become fixated on thoughts about that lost loved one. Many grieving people experience difficulty focusing or become forgetful as a result. If the loss was especially traumatic, they might play it over and over again in their mind.

In the midst of this preoccupation, sometimes grieving people wonder, "Am I going crazy?" It can be reassuring to let them know that their difficulty concentrating does not mean there's something wrong with them—it's a natural part of grief. As one hospice bereavement counselor put it, "Crazy feelings are *normal* during grief."

STEPHEN MINISTER INSIGHT

"It's an honor and privilege to be a part of someone's grief journey and getting to watch God bring the hope and healing your care receiver needs."

Depression

Depression occurs when sadness settles around a grieving person like a thick cloud, cutting off his or her ability to perceive anything as happy or hopeful. When depressed, a person may have low energy, a short attention span, and little enthusiasm. The depression may come and go and can last for weeks, leaving the grieving person wondering whether he or she will ever feel happy again.

Some depression is normal during grief, but it's important to consider the different levels of depression.

- As a lay caregiver, you can appropriately care for a person experiencing *mild* to *moderate* depression—when the person feels ongoing sadness but is still able to carry on with life fairly normally.

- However, if someone is experiencing *severe* depression—if the person isn't eating or sleeping, if he or she loses all interest in the outside world, or if his or her life seems to be falling apart—the person needs care from a mental health professional.

In module 13, "Caring for Those with Depression: The Stephen Minister's Role," you'll learn more about depression, including how to recognize depression you can care for and depression that requires professional care. For the latter, the best way to care for someone is to refer the person to the appropriate outside support.

Physical Symptoms

After a loss, people may find that their feelings surface in physical symptoms, including headaches, backaches, upset stomachs, or other ailments. It's best not to assume, however, that a physical problem is being caused by grief, so if your care receiver is experiencing any type of physical symptoms, encourage him or her to go to a physician. However, if the doctor can't find any physical explanation, the symptoms may be connected to the person's difficult feelings.

How Long Does Grief Last?

As people move through Recoil, some periods may seem better, while others may hurt worse. Although this is a normal part of the grieving process, these unpredictable ups and downs can raise the question, "How long will my grief last?"

The short answer is, "As long as it takes." Focus Note F shows a more detailed answer from *Journeying through Grief.*

FOCUS NOTE F

How Long Grief Lasts

In one sense your grief will always be with you. . . . In another sense, grief does end. Eventually the intense pain subsides, memories bring more smiles than tears, and the future appears more hopeful than foreboding. How long does it take to get there? Many people will take two to three years

to do the grieving they need to do—some may take less, some

may take more. There's no one-size-fits-all time frame for grief. There's only your unique and personal time frame. That's the only one that really matters for you.

Many people describe grief as waves from a storm crashing onto the shore. At first the waves are very large, coming at you one right after another. Each wave knocks you flat. Often you don't even have time to get back on your feet after one wave before the next one knocks you down. But gradually the waves get smaller and come farther apart. In time an occasional wave may still batter you, but more often you're able to keep your balance and stay on your feet.[4]

The progression and duration of Recoil and the specific feelings and issues the person encounters vary for each individual and each loss. At certain times, a grieving person may feel as if he or she is making progress, but other times, the person may feel stuck or even like he or she is moving backwards.

The deep pain of Recoil almost always outlasts the period during which others provide care for the bereaved person. This is why the care you offer as a Stephen Minister is so valuable. You may be the only person who will consistently be there to listen nonjudgmentally, offer care and empathy, and show your care receiver that he or she is not alone. While others might be minimizing the person's pain and pressuring him or her to get over it, you are letting your care receiver know it's okay to grieve for as long as necessary.

---

4 Haugk, *Journeying through Grief, Book 3: Finding Hope and Healing,* 3–4.

3. Rebuilding

There eventually comes a time in people's grief when they find themselves spending less energy on simply surviving the loss and instead focus more on rebuilding their life and looking forward to the future. They begin adjusting to a "new normal"—piecing together a life that may be very different from what they had before. Focus Note G shows how *Journeying through Grief* describes Rebuilding.

FOCUS NOTE G

Rebuilding Your Life

In one sense we begin rebuilding our lives the moment our loved one dies. But rebuilding doesn't begin in earnest until we've sifted through the majority of the feelings, memories, and issues that resulted from our loss. Only then do we have the strength and footing to begin putting our whole self back into daily life and looking to the future.

Rebuilding doesn't mean your life goes back to exactly what it was before—life can never be the same because of the loss you've experienced. Rebuilding means picking up the pieces and putting them together again, but probably in a very different way because a significant piece of your life is missing and cannot be replaced.[5]

Although Rebuilding is a time when a grieving person begins to move past grief, it still contains a number of possible challenges.

---

5 Kenneth C. Haugk, *Journeying through Grief, Book 4: Rebuilding and Remembering* (St. Louis: Stephen Ministries, 2004), 16–17.

Putting Together a New Life

After the death of a loved one, a grieving person loses not only that loved one but also the parts of life that involved that person. Depending on the relationship, they may have spent a lot of time together, shared responsibilities, enjoyed common interests and activities, and made various plans. They relied on each other in many ways and made each other's lives better. The loss of the loved one leaves a void in the grieving person's life.

It isn't possible to fill the void completely or in exactly the same way, but over time the person can put together a new life. Doing so might involve reconnecting with old friends and finding new friends. It may mean finding new interests, hobbies, or volunteer activities. It may include learning to go to restaurants or the movies alone. A new life may mean a new love, another spouse, or a deepened relationship with a different family member. The person gradually finds a new normal, whatever it might look like, and goes on living.

Reconnecting with the Loved One in a New Way

Another part of rebuilding involves reconnecting with the lost loved one in a new and different way. As the care receiver lets go of the loved one in a physical sense, he or she learns how to hold the person close in thoughts, memories, and feelings. Here are some ways grieving people have done so:

- Sharing stories about their lost loved one and reliving fond memories

- Seeing how the loved one has affected the lives of others who were close to him or her

- Beginning or continuing traditions connected to the loved one, such as using

About *Journeying through Grief*

Journeying through Grief is a set of four short books to send to people at four crucial times during the first year after the loss of a loved one.

Book 1: *A Time to Grieve* . . . . sent 3 weeks after the loss

Book 2: *Experiencing Grief*. . . . . sent 3 months after the loss

Book 3: *Finding Hope and Healing* . . . . sent 6 months after the loss

Book 4: *Rebuilding and Remembering* . . . sent 11 months after the loss

Each book focuses on what the person is likely to be experiencing at that point in grief—offering understanding, empathy, compassion, and hope.

To learn more, visit **stephenministries.org/JTG**.

beloved recipes or rewatching favorite holiday movies

- Drawing on and passing along wisdom and guidance shared by the loved one

As they rebuild, grieving persons can come to understand that their connection with the loved one doesn't end after he or she dies. Rather, it continues in a new, meaningful way.

Letting Go of Grief

A significant challenge people face during Rebuilding is simply letting go of their grief. Because the grief has been a part of their life for so long, moving forward can present a number of challenges.

Part of this challenge is feeling guilty about experiencing moments of joy or going for a period of time without thinking of their loved one. Grieving people sometimes worry that if they become happy again or resume living a normal life, it means they've abandoned or forgotten their loved one. But

letting go of grief does not mean the grieving person has abandoned the lost loved one—the person can move forward while always treasuring the loved one in his or her heart. It's important to help your care receiver understand that.

Another reason letting go of grief is challenging is that people may feel as if continuing to grieve helps keep their loved one's memory alive. Letting go of grief can become one more way of saying goodbye to the loved one. As a Stephen Minister, you may need to offer a care receiver an opportunity to mourn the end of that time of sorrow—in a way, grieving the loss of grief.

Finally, people may resist letting go of their grief because it can seem painful or frightening to return to normal life, with decisions to make and challenges to face—sometimes without a loved one who had always been by their side before. It takes courage to step out and take on a life beyond grief. Your caring, supportive presence can help your care receiver find that courage.

Experiencing Growth through Loss

Over time, people often find that their experience of grief has helped them grow, mature, and find greater depth and understanding of life. They might feel greater compassion toward others who have experienced loss. They may also come to trust Jesus more fully, thanking God for his care and love through each phase and even finding that God has transformed their life and relationship with him. The pain of the loss may always be there, but this kind of growth demonstrates how greater wholeness can come out of a crisis.

Other Types of Loss Can Also Cause Grief

As mentioned previously, any loss has the potential to cause difficult feelings, even if that loss might not seem significant to some. For instance, grief can occur after the loss of a personal possession, a broken relationship, or a major transition in life.

Focus Note H lists several examples of the types of losses a person might grieve.

FOCUS NOTE H

Types of Losses That May Cause People to Grieve

- Death of a loved one
- Divorce
- Broken relationship with a family member or significant other
- Loss of job

- Military deployment for oneself or a loved one
- Retirement
- Illness
- Illness of a loved one
- Amputation
- Loss of independence or a move into assisted living
- Diagnosis of Alzheimer's or dementia
- Having a loved one diagnosed with Alzheimer's or dementia
- Being in a hospital or rehabilitation facility
- Being a victim of crime or violence
- A child moving away for school or a job
- Death or loss of a pet
- Moving and losing friends and familiar surroundings
- Being incarcerated or having a loved one incarcerated
- Losing a hero—discovering a weakness or failing in someone you idolize
- Losing contact with God
- Losing a treasured object or memento
- Losing a friend
- Losing an opportunity to spend time with a friend
- Being apart from one's family for a time
- Getting married—adjusting to the loss of being single
- Having a child—losing the way life was before the child was born

The intensity and length of the grief will vary depending on the loss and the individual. One person may feel a particular loss deeply, while another person might be barely affected by the same type of loss. A loss that may seem minor to us could be major to another person. Also, a series of relatively small losses can add up into what feels like a major loss.

Part of your role as a Stephen Minister is to pay attention to any loss experienced by a care receiver and to how the person reacts; those reactions could give glimpses of feelings that the person may not have fully addressed. If a person has a disproportionate response to a minor loss, it could indicate some unresolved grief related to other losses.

Getting Ready for the In-Class Session

In the In-Class Session, you will explore how best to care for others who are grieving. To prepare:

- Review your Pre-Class Reading and notes for module 2, "Feelings: Yours, Mine, and Ours," on pages 19–43, and module 8, "Crisis Theory and Practice," on pages 153–174. You will apply insights from those modules during class.

- Develop a personal grief timeline as described in the instructions on the following page. During the In-Class Session, you'll share parts of your grief experiences with one other person.

stephenministries.org/library

See the *Stephen Minister Online Library* for additional resources and downloads related to this Stephen Minister training topic.

Instructions for Developing Your Personal Grief Timeline

1. Think back on times when you have suffered any type of loss and what it was like to grieve those losses.

2. Using the example in Focus Note I as a model, create a timeline in Focus Note J to chart your own experiences with grief, starting from birth and continuing on to the present.

3. Mark an X on the timeline to indicate each loss.

4. Draw a horizontal line above each X to estimate the combined length of time for the Shock and Recoil phases after each loss.

5. Write a brief description of each loss next to it on the timeline. You don't need to go into detail—just say what kind of loss it was.

FOCUS NOTE I

Personal Grief Timeline (Sample)

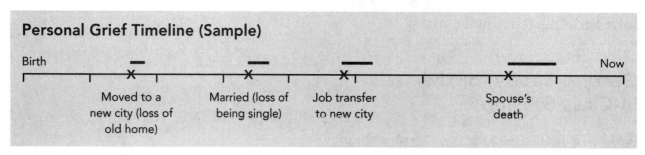

FOCUS NOTE J

Personal Grief Timeline

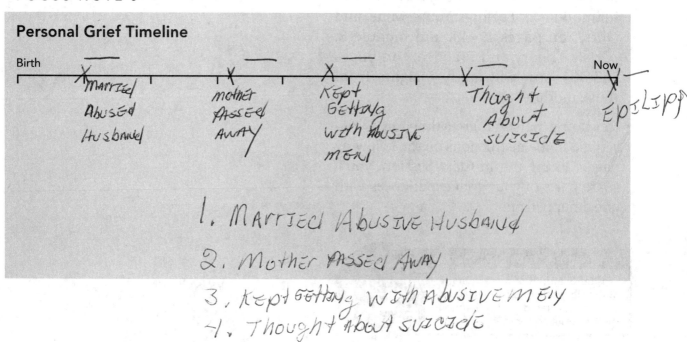

1. Married Abusive Husband

2. Mother Passed Away

3. Kept Getting with Abusive men

4. Thought About suicide

5. Epilispy

Ministering to Those Experiencing Grief

Module 12 | Presentation Outline

Jesus wept.
John 11:35

 Devotion: Real Christians Really Can Grieve

FOCUS NOTE 1

Jesus Grieves

Narrator: On his arrival, Jesus found that Lazarus had already been in the tomb for four days. Bethany was less than two miles from Jerusalem, and many people had come to Martha and Mary to comfort them in the loss of their brother.

When Martha heard that Jesus was coming, she went out to meet him, but Mary stayed at home.

Martha: Lord, if you had been here, my brother would not have died. But I know that even now God will give you whatever you ask.

Jesus: Your brother will rise again.

Martha: I know he will rise again in the resurrection on the last day.

Jesus: I am the resurrection and the life. He who believes in me will live, even though he dies; and whoever lives and believes in me will never die. Do you believe this?

Martha: Yes, Lord, I believe that you are the Christ, the Son of God, who was to come into the world.

Narrator: And after she had said this, Martha went back and called her sister Mary aside.

Martha: The Teacher is here and is asking for you.

I felt eye opening, stuff. I'm having been holding in.

No to Judge, water body

Narrator: When Mary heard this, she got up quickly and went to him.

Now Jesus had not yet entered the village, but was still at the place where Martha had met him. When those who had been with Mary in the house, comforting her, noticed how quickly she got up and went out, they followed her, supposing she was going to the tomb to mourn there.

When Mary reached the place where Jesus was and saw him, she fell at his feet.

Mary: Lord, if you had been here, my brother would not have died.

Narrator: When Jesus saw her weeping, and the crowd who had come along with her also weeping, he was deeply moved in spirit and troubled.

Jesus: Where have you laid him?

Crowd: Come and see, Lord.

Narrator: Jesus wept.

Crowd: See how he loved him!

Adapted from John 11:17–36

I. Three Quick Points about Grief

A. Grief Is Normal, Natural, and Necessary

B. Christians Can and Should Grieve

C. Caregivers Need to Focus on the Grieving Person's Frame of Reference

II. Applying Key Caring Concepts to Grief

A. The Safe House

FOCUS NOTE 2

The Safe House

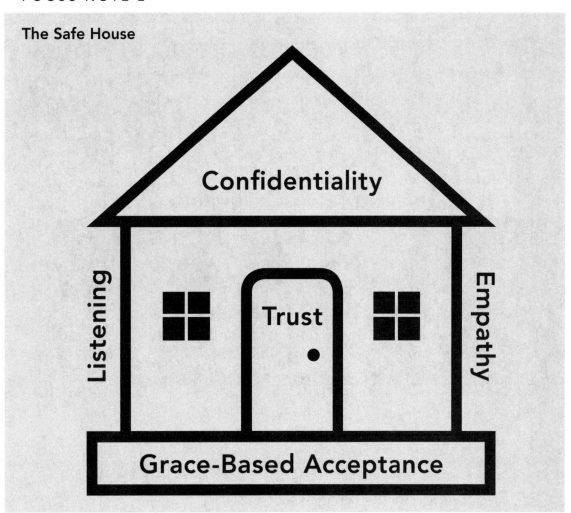

B. The Mudhole

FOCUS NOTE 3

The Mudhole

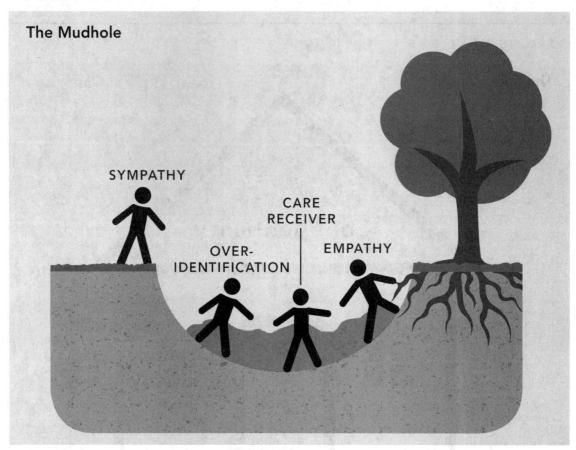

C. Focusing on the Process of Caring

D. Course of a Crisis

FOCUS NOTE 4

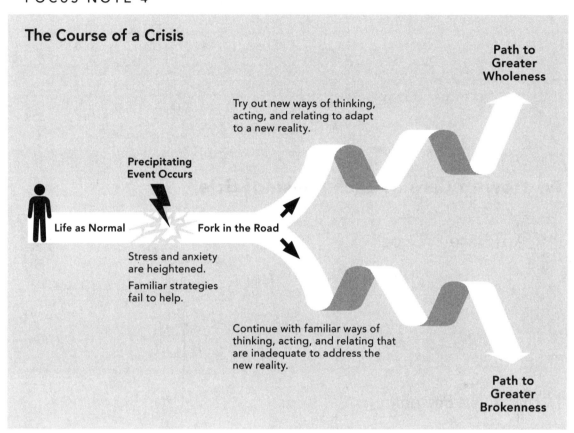

The Course of a Crisis

Path to Greater Wholeness

Try out new ways of thinking, acting, and relating to adapt to a new reality.

Precipitating Event Occurs

Life as Normal

Fork in the Road

Stress and anxiety are heightened.

Familiar strategies fail to help.

Continue with familiar ways of thinking, acting, and relating that are inadequate to address the new reality.

Path to Greater Brokenness

They are the taught to be strong not to cry.

III. Our Own Grief Experiences

IV. How to Care at Each Phase of Grief

A. Phase 1: Shock

1. Be Present

FOCUS NOTE 5

Expressing Your Presence

"I'm with you."

[or]

"I'm here, and I care."

2. Accept the Care Receiver

where they are.

3. Listen — *Key of showing ACCEPTANCE*

FOCUS NOTE 6

Reflecting Feelings

Care receiver: I can't bear the thought of my son being gone.

Stephen Minister: It's difficult even to imagine it.

Care receiver: How can I go on?

Stephen Minister: It seems overwhelming to you.

FOCUS NOTE 7

Validating Feelings

Care receiver: I'm almost embarrassed to say it, but while I'm sad my mother died, there's also a sense of relief. She's no longer in pain—and it feels like a burden has been lifted off my shoulders too.

Stephen Minister: Tell me more about that.

[after further conversation]

Care receiver: . . . So that's what I mean. You don't think I'm a bad person?

Stephen Minister: Of course not. People often feel that way in situations like this. There's no need to be embarrassed about what you're feeling.

4. Don't Challenge Denial — *Early point of grief, care receiver may not can't believe it (person has died).*

FOCUS NOTE 8

Letting the Denial Be

Care receiver: I can't believe she's dead.

Don't say: You'll get used to it. It just takes time.

Do say: It doesn't seem possible, does it?

[or]

Care receiver: He can't be dead—he just can't. I know I'm going to turn around and find him here again.

Don't say: You have to accept the fact that he's dead.

Do say: I'm so sorry!

5. Expressing Your Own Grief

B. Phase 2: Recoil

1. Be Available

Long period of Adjusting to the lost of A loveone

2. Be Aware of Special Dates or Events *- Recent Events*

FOCUS NOTE 9

Special Dates

- Anniversary of the death
- Anniversary of the death of another loved one
- Birthday of the person who died
- Birthday of the grieving person
- Wedding anniversary
- Mother's Day or Father's Day
- Valentine's Day
- Holidays
- First day of school or other life stage event
- Special events that the grieving person usually shared with the deceased loved one, such as family reunions, fairs, and festivals

3. Encourage Emotional Expression

FOCUS NOTE 10

The Three Steps in Dealing with Feelings

- Recognize
- Accept
- Express

Difficult feelings

FOCUS NOTE 11

Encouraging the Release of Feelings

"You haven't said much about all that has happened. I want to let you know that it's all right to cry if you want to."

FOCUS NOTE 12

Questions for Evoking Feelings

- "What are you remembering today about *[name of deceased]*?"
- "Tell me about how you and *[name of deceased]* met."
- "What were your happiest times together?"
- "What were some sad or difficult times you spent together?"
- "Tell me some stories about *[name of deceased]*."
- "May I see pictures of *[name of deceased]*?"
- "What were some of the important events in your life together?"
- "What do you wish had been different in your life with *[name of deceased]*?"
- "Are there any memories of *[name of deceased]* that bring up difficult feelings for you now?"

FOCUS NOTE 13

How One Stephen Minister Used a Question to Draw Out Feelings

"My care receiver had lost his wife of 50 years. We had been meeting weekly for several months, but he still was having a difficult time opening up. The turning point came one day when I asked if he had a favorite picture of him and his wife. He got out the family photo albums, and we began looking through all the pictures together. As we did, he shared story after story about his wife and their marriage—and the grief and loneliness he was feeling. The feelings began to flow, and our relationship moved to a deeper level."

4. *Offer Distinctively Christian Resources*

1. Prayer
2. Scripture
3. Forgiveness

5. Guard against Platitudes, Clichés, and Other Hurtful Expressions

FOCUS NOTE 14

Examples of Platitudes

- "I know just how you feel."
- "You need to start looking to the future and quit holding on to the past."
- "Every cloud has a silver lining."
- "Everything will be all right."
- "Time heals all wounds."
- "It's time for you to get on with your life."
- "She/he lived a good, long life."

FOCUS NOTE 15

Talking about a Platitude

Stephen Minister: I noticed when your friend told you everything would turn out all right, it seemed that wasn't what you wanted to hear.

Care receiver: No, it wasn't. That's so easy for her to say, but she didn't lose her husband.

Stephen Minister: It sounds like you're thinking she doesn't really understand what you're going through.

Care receiver: No! If she knew what it was like, she wouldn't have said that.

Stephen Minister: And it hurt you that she said that?

Care receiver: It did, even though I know she was trying to be helpful.

FOCUS NOTE 16

Inviting a Care Receiver to Examine a Platitude

Care receiver: I guess God needed him in heaven.

Stephen Minister: Could you tell me more about that?

Care receiver: *(pause)* I don't know. It's just so hard to understand why it happened.

Stephen Minister: It must be difficult to wrap your mind around it.

6. *Mobilize Support*

Looking for help to the care receiver to find some support to help.

C. Phase 3: Rebuilding

1. Continue Your Caregiving

2. Encourage New and Renewed Social Relationships

3. Continue Paying Attention to Feelings

FOCUS NOTE 17

Continue to Encourage Expression of Feelings

"We're coming up on the anniversary of when Chris died. How are you feeling about that?"

[or]

"We haven't talked about Chris for a while. Tell me how you're feeling."

FOCUS NOTE 18

How Mentioning the Lost Loved One by Name Helped

"After my son Matthew died, most people avoided mentioning his name, thinking it might make me sad. But my Stephen Minister would ask me about Matthew regularly, and every time I was glad for the chance to talk about him. I would sometimes shed some tears while doing so, but that was important to me because it helped me feel connected to Matthew."

V. Practicing Grief Care

Care Receiver's Situation for Skill Practice 1

The funeral is over, and you are with the Stephen Minister at your home. React with denial and disbelief. Voice thoughts such as, "It can't be. He was perfectly healthy," and "I just feel like if I turn around, he will be right there." Then be mostly silent for the rest of the skill practice, only responding briefly to anything the Stephen Minister says to you.

Begin the skill practice by saying, "I just can't believe he's dead."

Discussion Questions

1. **Stephen Minister:** How did it feel to be a caregiver in this situation?

2. **Care receiver:** How did it feel to receive the care that the Stephen Minister offered?

3. **All:** What did you learn that will help you minister in this kind of situation in the future?

FOCUS NOTE 21

Care Receiver's Situation for Skill Practice 2

It has been three months since your mother died. You're still angry with the emergency responders for not showing up sooner and with the hospital staff for not saving your mother, although you realize they did everything they could. Tell your Stephen Minister about those feelings. Then talk about the guilt you feel because your mother had been under the weather the entire day she died, and you didn't take her to the doctor sooner.

Begin the skill practice by telling the Stephen Minister, "I know you've heard this before, but I'm still so angry with the ambulance crew and the hospital staff."

FOCUS NOTE 22

Care Receiver's Situation for Skill Practice 3

It has been a year and a half since your spouse died. Although you still feel sad, the worst of it seems to be over, and now you're thinking about your future. You feel very lonely, but the thought of resuming a social life is frightening to you. You've been alone for so long that you aren't sure you'll be able to handle social situations well.

Begin the skill practice by saying, "I've been thinking about what the rest of my life is going to be like. If I'll always feel this lonely, it'll be really tough."

VI. Caregiver's Compass Review

Write your ideas around the compass.

VII. Looking Ahead

Caring for Those with Depression: The Stephen Minister's Role

Module 13 | Pre-Class Reading

CONTENTS

Depression is a common reaction to life crises; people grieving the loss of a loved one, going through a divorce, dealing with an illness, or facing other serious life challenges often experience depression to some degree. Because you as a Stephen Minister may at times have a care receiver who is feeling depressed, it's important to be able to recognize the signs of depression so you can offer the appropriate care or, when necessary, refer your care receiver to a mental health professional.[1]

Depression is not a feeling people can just "snap out of." In some individuals, depression is a short-term or long-term response to a life situation. In others, it is a mental disorder that needs to be diagnosed and treated by a professional caregiver. Focus Note A describes three types or severities of depression.

---

1 The process for referring a care receiver to a mental health professional, in consultation with the Community Resource Contacts, is described in module 11, "Using Mental Health Professionals and Other Community Resources."

FOCUS NOTE A

Types of Depression[2]

- *Mild depression* is the most common type of depression. It can be brought on by sad events or by happy but stressful ones. Mild depression does not usually interfere with a person's ability to function, but it may make daily life and managing stress feel more difficult.

- *Moderate depression* is longer-lasting and often more intense than mild depression. It frequently follows a major, unhappy event, such as a loved one's death or a divorce. Moderate depression typically does not significantly interfere with a person's ability to go about daily life, but it may make regular activities and responsibilities more challenging. In some instances, moderate depression may become severe.

- *Severe depression*[3] occurs when a person exhibits characteristics of depression for most of the day, nearly every day for at least two weeks, and is unable to adequately function in daily life. A person with severe depression generally experiences more characteristics of depression and in greater intensity than someone with mild or moderate depression. Severe depression always requires professional help.

Stephen Ministers can care effectively for care receivers who are mildly or moderately depressed, although it's crucial to stay alert for signs that a care receiver's depression is becoming severe.

---

2 "Depression," Missouri Department of Mental Health, Division of Behavioral Health, accessed November 15, 2019, https://dmh.mo.gov/media/pdf/depression-facts.

3 Severe depression is also known as *major depressive disorder* or *clinical depression*.

Stephen Ministers are *not* equipped or intentionally assigned to care for people who are severely depressed. Those experiencing severe depression need professional care, so the Stephen Minister's role in such situations is to recognize signs that a care receiver has such a need and then, in consultation with the Community Resource Contacts, to help get him or her the appropriate care.

STEPHEN MINISTER INSIGHT

"We can't fix care receivers' depression, cure them, or talk them out of being depressed. What we can do, though, is show up and walk with them through it."

Signs of Depression

Not everyone who is depressed will feel or act the same way, nor will the same signs of depression always be present in the same way for every individual. Even the length of time people are depressed can vary greatly. For some, depression lasts for multiple days in a row; for others, it comes in waves, with the person feeling good for a while but depressed the next day or later the same day. Sometimes individuals may not even realize when they're experiencing depression.

However, there are a number of recognizable traits and behaviors people frequently exhibit during depression. The emotional, mental, relational, and physical characteristics described in this reading can appear during any type of depression—mild, moderate, or severe. If a care receiver has "symptoms of depression most of the day, nearly every day for at least two weeks that interfere with [his or her] ability to work, sleep, study, eat, and enjoy life,"[4] it may be a sign that the person is severely depressed and needs professional help.

Emotional Characteristics

People who are depressed tend to experience negative emotions, although the specific feelings can vary.

Lowered Mood

One of the most common emotional signs of depression is lowered mood—a mixture of sadness, gloom, apathy, despair, or general unhappiness that is usually noticeable to those around the person. This lowered mood is sometimes referred to as "depressed feelings." When a care receiver talks about "feeling depressed," this lowered mood is often what he or she is referring to.

Although the specifics of depression vary greatly between individuals, the vast majority of people with depression experience a lowered mood. On its own, this sign does not mean someone is depressed, but in combination with other characteristics, it can be an indicator of depression.

Loneliness

People who are depressed may feel lonely. Some people with depression experience loneliness because they have isolated them-selves; others may feel alone even when surrounded by loved ones. It can also be difficult for people with depression to find someone who offers the kind of care and support they need, so they might feel as if they're facing their challenges alone, which can compound their other difficult feelings.

Low Self-Esteem

Those who are depressed may struggle with low self-esteem. It may be that they already had low self-esteem, which contributed to the depression in the first place, or they may come to see themselves in a more negative light after becoming depressed. Some may think that the depression is somehow their fault or that they should be able to handle it on their own. They may also believe that their depression diminishes their worth as a person or even see it as evidence of their worthlessness. Compounding these issues, the social stigma around depression can reinforce people's low self-esteem and make it more difficult for them to reach out for help.

Hopelessness

A general sense of hopelessness sometimes accompanies depression, leaving people unable to see an end to their suffering or feeling helpless to change their situation. This feeling can be closely tied to other emotional characteristics, such as low self-esteem or a long-lasting lowered mood. Statements like those in Focus Note B may be signs that someone is feeling hopeless.

---

4 "Depression Basics," National Institute of Mental Health, accessed November 15, 2019, https://www.nimh.nih.gov/health/publications/depression/index.shtml.

Statements That May Show Hopelessness

- "There's no end to this feeling."

- "This isn't going to get better, no matter what I try."

- "I guess I'm always going to feel this way."

- "There's nothing I can do about it."

Hopelessness can lead a care receiver deeper into depression. It diminishes people's motivation to take action. In the face of such feelings, it may seem useless to a person to take steps toward getting better. Feelings of hopelessness are often a sign that a person's depression may have become severe.

Emotional Numbness

Struggling with depression can be mentally, emotionally, and physically exhausting. As depression wears on a person, he or she may experience emotional numbness—a lack of any feelings, positive or negative. This characteristic most often appears in individuals who are severely depressed, although those who are mildly or moderately depressed may experience some degree of emotional numbness as well.

Mental Characteristics

Depression also often affects people's cognitive skills and thinking in various ways.

Mental Fog

Some people describe their experience of depression as being in a mental fog. They may become less able to concentrate, find their thoughts wandering, and have trouble remembering things. This fog often leads to indecisiveness, uncertainty, or a lack of motivation, which can make even simple decisions or tasks more difficult.

Someone experiencing a mental fog might also take longer than they normally do to respond to auditory and visual stimuli. For instance, a care receiver may take an unusually long time to react to a comment or question.

Repetitious or Cyclical Thinking

Those dealing with depression may repeat certain phrases, statements, or stories without even realizing they're doing so. These patterns often indicate what is important to care receivers, so it's helpful for Stephen Ministers to focus on what's being repeated, asking questions to explore the feelings associated with it.

It's also common for people with depression to exhibit cyclical patterns of thinking. They may make the same decisions repeatedly without recognizing the consequences, or they may fall into a downward spiral of negative or self-disparaging thoughts. For example, a care receiver might express frustration at his or her ongoing depression and blame him- or herself for it, becoming increasingly depressed and frustrated as a result. Without outside support, it can be difficult for someone to break out of this kind of cycle.

Emphasis on the Negative

When people are depressed, their negative perspective and thoughts can seem to take over their lives. Negativity colors their view of the world around them, and they may find that activities such as pursuing hobbies or spending time with friends no longer bring them happiness. This inability to find joy in life can be discouraging and contribute to their negativity as efforts to experience positive emotions are met with failure.

When people with depression think negatively about themselves and what they experience, they might also begin to believe that others think negatively about them, interpreting people's words or actions in ways that validate their negative perspective. As a result, they may communicate less and less with others.

Relational Characteristics

Depression can affect people's relationships, both with other people and with God.

Difficulty with Relationships

Many people who are depressed turn inward and avoid contact with others. Some may want to devote their mental energy to dealing with depression or simply lack the energy to maintain their relationships, while others may want connections with people but don't feel comfortable initiating or maintaining interactions. Still others may push people away due to feelings of low self-esteem or worthlessness. Whatever the reason, people who are depressed tend to withdraw and exclude others from their lives.

Another possibility is that people who are feeling depressed may reach out to others seeking love, care, and concern, but drive them away by relating in ways that are perceived as overbearing, clingy, or needy. This can become a vicious cycle, leading them to feel even more depressed and unintentionally continue to push others away through the same behaviors.

Expressions of Anger

Those who are depressed may express varying amounts of anger. Even though people's anger in the midst of depression is often directed inward at themselves, it may also manifest in expressions of anger toward others. Those with depression may seem irritable, touchy, or easily offended. Circumstances that wouldn't usually bother them may spark angry outbursts toward a family member, a friend, their Stephen Minister, or God, which can add to relational difficulties.

Feeling Abandoned by God

In addition to isolation from other people, those who are depressed can also feel distant from and abandoned by God. Job expressed such thoughts in the passage in Focus Note C.

FOCUS NOTE C

Feeling Abandoned by God

"If I go forward, [God] is not there;
　or backward, I cannot perceive him;
on the left he hides, and I cannot
　behold him;
I turn to the right, but I cannot see him."

Job 23:8–9 (NRSV)

Those dealing with depression may feel as if God has left them and wonder what they've done to deserve that. This, in turn, may lead to feelings of guilt or anger with themselves, further feeding their negativity and depression.

Physical Characteristics

Depression can affect people physically, draining their energy and making normal activities more difficult to complete or enjoy.

Low Energy Levels

People who are depressed may feel sluggish, lethargic, or physically unable to move quickly. As a result, they might do various activities more slowly, such as walking and talking at a slower rate than normal. Those with mild or moderate depression are typically still able to complete necessary tasks, but often with reduced efficiency or effectiveness. Someone with severe depression, on the other hand, may not have enough energy to function normally or even get out of bed.

Fatigue

Fatigue resulting from depression is a feeling of complete physical exhaustion. People with this kind of fatigue see particular tasks as "too much work" or "too difficult" and leave them undone, even when they would normally find such tasks easy to do. For example, someone who usually keeps a well-maintained front yard might neglect it entirely. A person experiencing ongoing fatigue that hinders everyday functioning may require care from a physician as well as a mental health professional.

Sleep Problems

At times, low energy levels or fatigue are compounded by difficulty sleeping. Even when people with depression feel physically tired, they may have trouble falling asleep or sleeping through the night. They might also wake up at early hours or consistently feel tired after sleeping. All this can contribute to a general lack of energy and worsen depression.

Others, on the other hand, may find themselves constantly tired and needing to sleep far more than they normally would. They may nap throughout the day, sleep at odd hours, or sleep longer than usual through the night and into the morning.

Other Physical Issues

People who are depressed may suffer from various aches, pains, or other physical issues. Common ailments include headaches, backaches, constipation, and neck pains. Some people experience weight loss because they have little or no interest in eating, whereas others may eat more than usual and gain weight. Sometimes it's difficult to determine whether depression is causing physical ailments or the reverse—or whether the physical issues are entirely separate from the depression. It's best in these situations for a care receiver to consult with a physician to help determine the underlying issues.

STEPHEN MINISTER INSIGHT

"When my care receiver was depressed, allowing her to talk about how she felt was so key. More than anything else, what she needed was a non-judgmental, caring presence to accompany her on that journey as she developed coping strategies."

Situations That Can Lead to Depression

There are a wide variety of possible causes and contributing influences for depression. For many people, depression arises not because of any one precipitating event but instead due to multiple factors. In some instances, depression is triggered by a specific life crisis; in others, a person becomes depressed following a number of smaller crises or even for reasons not connected to any specific event.

Following are some kinds of situations that may contribute to depression. Being aware of these situations can help Stephen Ministers recognize when their care receivers may be depressed.

Taking the Path toward Greater Brokenness after a Crisis

As you learned in module 8, "Crisis Theory and Practice," a person in a state of crisis might take one of two paths:

1) the path toward greater wholeness, where the person finds new ways of thinking and acting to adapt to a new reality; or

2) the path toward greater brokenness, where the person clings to familiar but inadequate ways of dealing with the current circumstances.

A person on the path toward greater brokenness may experience depression as normal coping mechanisms continue to fail. Whatever the circumstances that led to the crisis and to the person's being on the path of greater brokenness, the resulting depression may sap the person's motivation to make the necessary changes and get back on the path to greater wholeness.

Loss

Depression often involves some kind of loss—whether actual, perceived, anticipated, or remembered.

Actual Loss

Actual losses include events such as the death of a loved one, divorce, losing a job, illness, or moving to a new city. Depression might stem from a single major loss or an accumulation of several smaller losses. In some situations, a loss that seems relatively inconsequential to an outside observer—such as finding out that a planned weekend trip won't be possible—can hit a person hard and lead to some degree of depression, especially if it comes after a string of other losses.

Perceived Loss

People can become depressed when they perceive that a loss has occurred even though it hasn't. For example, a person who lost a job may believe that he or she has lost the respect of friends and family, even if that isn't the case at all. Such a perceived loss can hurt badly, so it's important to understand it from the care receiver's point of view and avoid trivializing it or trying to convince the care receiver that there was no loss.

Anticipated Loss

Sometimes people get depressed thinking about losses that have not yet occurred but are likely to happen. Examples might be when a person dwells on the eventual death of his or her aging parents or a terminally ill spouse, even before the death has occurred. Although the loss has yet to take place, the pain, anxiety, and sadness of an anticipated loss are real, tangible, and current to the person.

Days or Events Connected to Past Loss

Remembering a past loss can contribute to depression, especially in connection with particular days or events associated with loss. For instance, for a person who has lost a loved one, reminders might include the anniversary of the loss, the loved one's birthday, or a wedding anniversary, any of which may bring up new or renewed difficult feelings and lead someone to become depressed.

Guilt

Feelings of guilt may lead to depression, particularly if those feelings are especially intense. Sometimes a person's guilt is specific: "If I hadn't lost my temper, my girlfriend wouldn't have broken up with me," or "It's my fault for messing up the contract and losing the account." Other times the guilt is more general, such as when a person feels unable to live up to personal expectations or those set by others. Depression is a possibility in circumstances like these, whether the person's feelings of guilt are a result of a perceived failure or something he or she has actually done wrong.

Unresolved Conflict or Uncertainty

When a person is having ongoing problems or is unable to make an important decision, the difficult feelings over that unresolved conflict can fester, possibly leading the person to feel depressed. This conflict may be external, such as issues in a relationship with a loved one or with colleagues at work. It can also be internal, such as uncertainty about what to expect or do in a particular area of life—like one's vocation or education—producing worry or fear about the future and bringing on depression.

Loss of Purpose

Depression may come when a person can no longer see meaning in his or her life, often tied to feelings of worthlessness or uncertainty. For example, someone who dedicates his or her entire life to a career may feel great uncertainty about his or her purpose in life upon retirement and the loss of that career. The mental and emotional struggle brought on by this situation can contribute to depression.

Burnout

Becoming physically and mentally overwhelmed by a situation—commonly known as burnout—can lead to depression. Often, a person experiencing burnout is also dealing with other issues, such as feelings of failure or guilt, which can increase the chances of becoming depressed. In addition, depression can make it more difficult for a person to recover from burnout and resume his or her activities as normal. If this happens, the combination of depression and burnout can become a spiral that is very difficult to break.

Holidays

Holidays are a time of joy and comfort for many people. However, for a variety of reasons, days like Christmas, Thanksgiving, Easter, Valentine's Day, and others can stir up difficult feelings and potentially depression for someone. This can be especially true for those who have recently experienced a significant loss or who frequently deal with stress, anxiety, or interpersonal conflict during the holidays.

Other Situations

Many other difficult circumstances have the potential to contribute to depression. Focus Note D lists a number of examples. In the course of your care for people who are dealing with these or other painful events or changes, be aware of the possibility that they are feeling depressed as well.

FOCUS NOTE D

Some Situations That May Contribute to Depression

- Traumatic injury or illness
- Death of a loved one
- Challenges related to childbirth
- Being a single parent
- Empty nest
- Separation and divorce
- Job loss or transition
- Retirement
- Moving
- Loneliness or social isolation
- Military deployment
- Faith struggles
- Unresolved anger
- Being arrested or convicted of a crime
- Natural disasters
- Stress over a long period of time

Helping Care Receivers Experiencing Depression

As stated at the beginning of this Pre-Class Reading, Stephen Ministers can provide effective care for care receivers who are experiencing mild and moderate depression. All

the skills you've learned in prior modules apply when caring for someone who is depressed, but when depression is a factor, the process may require a little extra time and attentiveness.

People experiencing depression often struggle to take the steps necessary to help themselves. Many of the characteristics of depression reinforce or contribute to each other, and it's possible for people to fall into a negative cycle that pulls them deeper into depression. As a Stephen Minister, your presence and care can be key for people who are depressed, providing them with the solid foundation of support they need.

Whatever factors are involved in a care receiver's depression, Stephen Ministers should offer the care and support needed. That support includes talking to their Community Resource Contacts when a referral to a mental health professional may be necessary.

Getting Ready for the In-Class Session

Be very familiar with the characteristics of depression discussed in this Pre-Class Reading for the In-Class Session. During class, you will learn how to care for those who are mildly to moderately depressed, as well as how to recognize when a person with depression may need care beyond what you can provide as a Stephen Minister, requiring a referral to a mental health professional.

stephenministries.org/library

See the **Stephen Minister Online Library** for additional resources and downloads related to this Stephen Minister training topic.

Caring for Those with Depression: The Stephen Minister's Role

Module 13 | Presentation Outline

But he himself went a day's journey into the wilderness, and came and sat down under a solitary broom tree. He asked that he might die: "It is enough; now, O LORD, take away my life, for I am no better than my ancestors."

1 Kings 19:4 (NRSV)

 Devotion: A Steady, Caring Hand

I. When to Refer a Care Receiver Experiencing Depression to a Mental Health Professional

FOCUS NOTE 1

Types of Depression[1]

- *Mild depression* is the most common type of depression. It can be brought on by sad events or by happy but stressful ones. Mild depression does not usually interfere with a person's ability to function, but it may make daily life and managing stress feel more difficult.

- *Moderate depression* is longer-lasting and often more intense than mild depression. It frequently follows a major, unhappy event, such as a loved one's death or a divorce. Moderate depression typically does not significantly interfere with a person's ability to go about daily life, but it may make regular activities and responsibilities more challenging. In some instances, moderate depression may become severe.

- *Severe depression* occurs when a person exhibits characteristics of depression for most of the day, nearly every day for at least two weeks, and is unable to adequately function in daily life. A person with severe depression generally experiences more characteristics of depression and in greater intensity than someone with mild or moderate depression. Severe depression always requires professional help.

1 "Depression," Missouri Department of Mental Health, Division of Behavioral Health, accessed November 15, 2019, https://dmh.mo.gov/media/pdf/depression-facts.

FOCUS NOTE 2

Likelihood That a Care Receiver Needs to Be Referred to a Mental Health Professional

Remain Alert	Consider Referral	Referral Needed
MILD	MODERATE	SEVERE

◄──────── TYPES OF DEPRESSION ────────►

FOCUS NOTE 3

Signs That a Care Receiver's Depression May Be beyond a Stephen Minister's Ability to Care

Particularly Intense Characteristics of Depression: Care receivers who are experiencing severe depression will often experience the common characteristics of depression very intensely. For example, someone may experience a lowered mood so intense that the person is unable to find happiness or joy in anything, rather than just being unhappy sometimes.

Pervasive Negative Effects: The care receiver's depression may be causing significant problems in almost all areas of his or her life. Regardless of any other factors, if a person seems to have lost control of life due to depression, he or she needs professional help.

Giving Up Hope of Improvement: A person who has been depressed for a while or who has experienced a particularly difficult event in life may give up on overcoming depression. The person may believe that he or she will always be depressed and seem to lack the motivation to take steps toward healing.

Distorted Perception of Reality: A person who is severely depressed may express unreasonable or irrational thoughts or impressions. For instance, the person may assume that everyone is making fun of his or her situation, or a downward spiral of negative thoughts may leave the person unable to see the situation objectively or believe that it will change for the better.

Suicidal Thoughts: A person who is depressed may begin to have suicidal thoughts. Module 14 will cover in depth how to recognize the signs that a care receiver may be considering suicide and how to refer him or her to professional help.

FOCUS NOTE 4

When to Make a Referral to a Mental Health Professional for a Care Receiver Who May Be Depressed

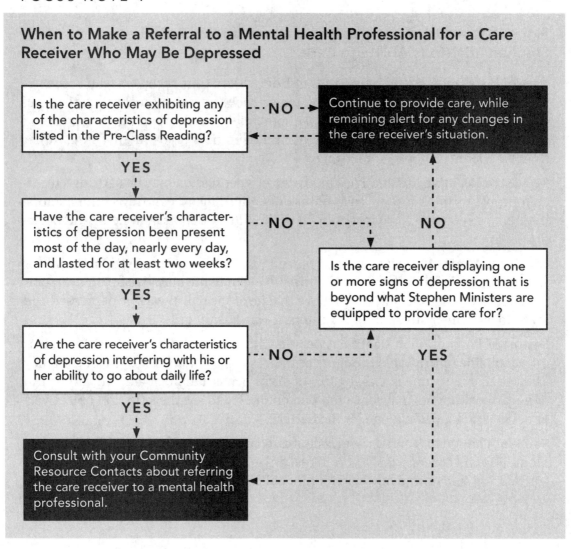

FOCUS NOTE 5

Deciding Whether or Not to Refer in Specific Situations

Read over the following situations one at a time. Discuss with the entire class whether each situation calls for a possible referral to a mental health professional, using the flow chart in Focus Note 4 as a reference. If the answer to any of the questions from the flow chart isn't given in the situation, you can assume the answer is no.

1. Your care receiver says, "I've been feeling so sad every day since Al died. It's been a couple of weeks already, and even though I'm keeping up with everything all right, I just don't know when this sadness is going to go away."

    _____✓ Refer   _____ Don't Refer

2. Your care receiver has been feeling more and more down every week. He or she finds it difficult to talk about feelings and has stopped going out with friends. During your caring visits, he or she frequently just sits quietly with a downcast expression. When you ask your care receiver about his or her feelings, the care receiver just shrugs.

    _____✓ Refer   _____ Don't Refer

3. Your care receiver has been exhibiting some emotional characteristics of depression. In addition, the care receiver complains that every day for the past two months he or she has had headaches and felt constantly exhausted. A doctor's appointment last week did not find any physical reason for the headaches.

    _____✓ Refer   _____ Don't Refer

4. It has been six months since your care receiver moved to the city. After the initial thrill of being in a new place, the care receiver has started to feel lonely and down. Recently, the care receiver has talked a lot about friends at home and has mentioned having some trouble sleeping over the past week.

    _____✓ Refer   _____ Don't Refer

5. Your care receiver, who lost his or her spouse months ago, says, "I've been feel-ing so bad for so long. Anything would be better than this. I've been thinking a lot recently about Chris. Sometimes, I just think about how much I wish I could go to heaven soon too. I've been collecting sleeping pills. I know I should throw them away, but I've been hanging on to them just in case."

_____ Refer   _____ Don't Refer

6. Your care receiver says, "I used to think I was a good parent, but I haven't thought that for a while now. I've been so tired since the baby was born. I don't even have the energy to play in the backyard with my other son even though I love doing that. Life feels just so exhausting right now. I know I'll bounce back eventually, but it's really frustrating."

_____ Refer   _____ Don't Refer

7. Your care receiver says, "It feels like this has gone on forever. It's been six months since we broke up, and I still can't think about it without feeling miserable. Mean-while, where's God? I used to pray and believe God heard me. Now I think he's deserted me. I guess I'm just going to have to get used to feeling like this forever."

_____ Refer   _____ Don't Refer

8. Your care receiver has been feeling upset and depressed about losing his or her job a week and a half ago. The care receiver hasn't gone grocery shopping since then, didn't show up for the church committee meeting he or she chairs, and has told you he or she isn't going to apply for any other jobs.

_____ Refer   _____ Don't Refer

9. While meeting, your care receiver whispers to you, "I think my family has been meeting without me and talking about what to do with me. I'm sure they're thinking about having me put away in a mental institution or kicking me out of the house and making me live on the streets."

   ___✓___ Refer   _____ Don't Refer

10. Your care receiver says, "I've been feeling sad and wanting to cry ever since Kyle left for college. I call him once a week and feel better for a while, but whenever I walk past his room, I really miss him. I'm able to forget about these feelings when I'm at work or when I'm working in the yard, but there always seems to be a time every day when I remember Kyle and start feeling sad again."

   ___✓___ Refer   _____ Don't Refer

II. Twelve Guidelines for Caring for People with Mild or Moderate Depression

1. Be Accepting

FOCUS NOTE 6

Communicating Acceptance

- "I know you've been struggling with feeling down. I just want to say that when people go through what you've been through, feeling down is natural. I'll be with you while you work through this."

- "You said earlier that you felt bad for being depressed and not acting like yourself. I just want you to know that no matter what you're going through or how you're feeling, I'll walk with you through it."

2. Take Your Care Receiver's Feelings of Depression Seriously

3. Be Patient

4. Initiate Conversation as Needed

FOCUS NOTE 7

Giving Permission to Continue Sharing

"Please feel free to talk. I'm here to listen."

FOCUS NOTE 8

Decreasing Anxiety over Silences

- "Take your time."
- "It's all right just to be silent if you need to."

FOCUS NOTE 9

Breaking Silences

- "You've been quiet for a while. I'm wondering what you're thinking."
- "You're not saying much, which is perfectly okay, but I imagine there's a lot going on inside."

5. Encourage Expression of Feelings

FOCUS NOTE 10

Giving Encouragement for Expression of Feelings

"Thanks; I'd been wondering what you were feeling about that."

FOCUS NOTE 11

Inviting Tears or Expressions of Anger

- "If you feel like crying, go right ahead."
- "It's all right to cry."
- "It's perfectly okay to cry to let out what you're feeling."
- "It seems like you're angry about _____. I wonder if you can tell me more about that."
- "If you're feeling angry, you can let it out. I'm willing to listen."
- "If you have some anger to let out, I can handle it."

FOCUS NOTE 12

Encouraging Further Reflection on Feelings

- "There must have been some pretty strong emotions behind those tears. Could you tell me more about it?"
- "It's really good that you were able to recognize and express those feelings. I'm wondering what else you're feeling right now."
- "Those are some strong feelings you've shared. Tell me more about them."

6. Help Your Care Receiver Work through Negative Thoughts

FOCUS NOTE 13

Responding to Negative Thoughts

Care Receiver: I hate feeling like this. I just want to feel normal again, but nothing seems to help. If I wasn't such a failure, I wouldn't be so depressed. I'm sick of this.

Stephen Minister: It's hard not being able to shake off those feelings.

Care Receiver: It is! I really just want to be over this already. I feel like I *should* be over it, but I'm not, and it's my fault. I wish I could just snap out of this.

> **Stephen Minister:** I'd like to know more about what you mean when you say it's your fault.
>
> *[The Stephen Minister continues to listen and talk to the care receiver until the end of the caring visit.]*
>
> **Stephen Minister:** Thanks for sharing with me. I know you've been feeling pretty down on yourself lately, but I want to say that I don't see you as a failure at all. I've got a lot of confidence in you and I'm going to be here for you through all this.

7. Follow the Care Receiver's Lead in Using the Word *Depression*

8. Discourage Self-Defeating Behavior

FOCUS NOTE 14

Delaying Harmful Decisions

> **Care Receiver:** I've decided to quit my job.
>
> **Stephen Minister:** That's a big change to make. Tell me about how you came to that decision.
>
> *[Stephen Minister listens to the care receiver for a good while, asking clarifying questions and using reflective listening to understand the care receiver's decision.]*
>
> **Care Receiver:** So I just don't feel like working in this field anymore.
>
> **Stephen Minister:** I see. You're really feeling unfulfilled by your job right now. I'm wondering, though, if you really need to quit immediately. It might be a good idea to wait a little. You can always quit your job. But if you quit it now and want to go back later, you might not be able to.
>
> **Care Receiver:** Well . . . I suppose it wouldn't hurt to wait a while.
>
> **Stephen Minister:** You can take that time to think through your situation before doing anything.

9. Help Your Care Receiver Think through Positive Steps

FOCUS NOTE 15

Brainstorming Positive Steps to Take

Care Receiver: I just feel so bad about everything right now. It's not just the breakup, either. I'm not keeping up with some of the stuff around my apartment, and lately I haven't felt like going out with my friends. I'm sick of this, but I don't know where to start.

Stephen Minister: It sounds like you want to make some changes, but you're having a hard time getting yourself to take action.

Care Receiver: Yeah, exactly.

Stephen Minister: Tell me about some of the chores or errands you feel you're not keeping up with at home.

Care Receiver: I don't know. . . . It's been a while since I've cleaned my apartment, and I feel like I've been just living off microwaved food for the last few days.

Stephen Minister: Maybe you can just start with something small. What's one errand you think you could handle right now?

Care Receiver: I guess I could maybe go to the store today to get some groceries. Maybe I'd feel better if I actually had something good to eat.

Stephen Minister: That sounds like a good idea to me.

Care Receiver: Yeah. I'll give it a shot later today.

10. Help Identify the Source of the Depression

FOCUS NOTE 16

Helping to Identify the Source of the Depression

Care Receiver: I'm so depressed.

Stephen Minister: What's led to you feeling depressed?

Care Receiver: *(sighs)* I don't know.

Stephen Minister: That's okay. *(pause)* When did you start feeling depressed?

Care Receiver: I guess . . . sometime last week.

Stephen Minister: Can you remember anything in particular that happened last week that might have brought this on?

Care Receiver: Nothing really. Just, now that I think about it, I guess I started feeling bad after meeting a friend for lunch on Wednesday.

Stephen Minister: Tell me more about that.

Care Receiver: Well, we spent some time catching up and we talked for a while about my friend's new job. And I remember that I couldn't stop thinking about how I haven't been able to find work since I was laid off.

11. Recognize and Affirm Small Improvements

12. Share Christian Resources When Appropriate

III. Skill Practice: Caring for People Who Are Mildly or Moderately Depressed

FOCUS NOTE 17

Stephen Minister's Situation Description for Skill Practice 1

You have been meeting with your care receiver for about a year and a half since his or her spouse died. He or she had been feeling happier recently and talking hopefully about the future. Suddenly, however, he or she seems very depressed.

Your care receiver will begin the skill practice.

FOCUS NOTE 18

Care Receiver's Situation Description for Skill Practice 1

Your spouse passed away about 18 months ago, and you started meeting with your Stephen Minister shortly afterward. Your close friend, who happens to live next door, has been an important support after your spouse's death and helped you feel less alone. You just found out that this friend is moving to another part of the country, and you feel depressed over the news. You thought that you were getting over your sadness at your spouse's death, but now the coming loss of your friend has set you back. You find it hard to talk about the difficult feelings resulting from this loss because you're sure you'll break down if you try.

Begin the skill practice by saying, "I can't believe this is happening," and give single-sentence answers to any questions your Stephen Minister asks. As your Stephen Minister encourages you to talk about your feelings, slowly open up and tell him or her what has happened. Be hesitant to use the word *depression* to describe how you feel, although you might use the word if it feels appropriate.

FOCUS NOTE 19

Discussion Questions

1. What characteristics of depression did the care receiver show?

2. What caring skills did the Stephen Minister use to care for the care receiver?

3. What did the Stephen Minister do that worked well? What could the Stephen Minister do differently next time?

4. What did you learn from this skill practice that you will try to remember or do when you care for a care receiver who is mildly or moderately depressed? Write your answers below.

Skill Practice 1

Skill Practice 2

Skill Practice 3

FOCUS NOTE 20

Stephen Minister's Situation Description for Skill Practice 2

Several months ago, you began meeting with a care receiver who had just lost a long-time job. Since then, the care receiver has found a new job but has struggled to adjust to the new workplace. He or she has shared about feeling unhappy and missing the old job. This week when you arrive, the care receiver seems even more down than in past weeks.

Your care receiver will begin the skill practice.

FOCUS NOTE 21

Care Receiver's Situation Description for Skill Practice 2

You have been feeling down for several months since you lost your job. You managed to find a new job, but it has been difficult to adjust to the new workplace. You miss your old job and have not been getting along very well with your new coworkers.

Earlier this week, you made a major mistake on an important project and got severely reprimanded by your supervisor in front of several coworkers. In the days since, you have felt very upset at yourself, both for the mistake and for being depressed. You feel stuck in a mental rut. You keep thinking about how everything is your fault and that feeling depressed caused you to make the mistake, and the more you think about it, the worse you feel.

Begin the skill practice by telling your Stephen Minister about what happened at work. Then start talking about how upset you are at yourself and keep repeating how it is your fault for being depressed and messing up at work. Use the word *depressed* to describe how you're feeling.

FOCUS NOTE 22

Stephen Minister's Situation Description for Skill Practice 3

Your care receiver has been the primary caregiver for his or her elderly mother for the past three years. You began your caring relationship about six months ago during a particularly stressful period when the care receiver's mother seemed about to pass away. She recovered but has gradually declined in health since then. Although your care receiver has generally coped well with this situation, lately he or she has been down and hasn't seemed like him- or herself.

Your care receiver will begin the skill practice.

FOCUS NOTE 23

Care Receiver's Situation Description for Skill Practice 3

You have been the primary caregiver for your aging mother for the last three years. You first began meeting with your Stephen Minister six months ago, when it seemed that your mother was going to pass away. She recovered, but her health has been slowly declining since.

Although you have coped well with the situation in the past, recently it's struck you that you are going to lose your mother in the near future, and you have begun to feel depressed. You feel bad for being so sad while your mother is still alive; you wish you could feel hopeful about the future like you have in the past. You have always relied on your faith to get you through tough times, but right now God feels far away, and you would really like some spiritual support.

Begin the skill practice by telling your Stephen Minister your realization about your mother's coming death and how you feel like you shouldn't be so down since she's still alive. Then share about your spiritual struggles. Do not use the word *depression* to talk about how you are feeling. If the Stephen Minister uses the word to describe your feelings, say that you aren't depressed.

IV. Caregiver's Compass Review

Write your ideas around the compass.

V. Looking Ahead

Understanding Suicide: How to Help People Get the Care They Need

Module 14 | Pre-Class Reading

CONTENTS

The Stephen Minister's Role in Helping Persons Who Are Considering Suicide

As a Stephen Minister, you will never knowingly be assigned a care receiver who is experiencing suicidal thoughts or exhibiting suicidal behavior. If a potential care receiver is identified as being at risk for suicide, your Stephen Leaders will refer him or her to a mental health professional. It is possible, however, that a care receiver may begin thinking about suicide during the course of a caring relationship. For this reason, it's important to know the signs that someone may be considering suicide and how to help a person at risk get the necessary care.

Stephen Ministers are not equipped to be the primary caregiver for someone considering suicide; a professional caregiver is needed in those situations. Focus Note A spells out the Stephen Minister's role when a care receiver may be considering suicide.

FOCUS NOTE A

The Stephen Minister's Role

If you suspect that your care receiver may be suicidal, your role is to 1) determine the current level of suicide risk[1] to the best of your ability, and 2) work with Stephen Ministry Crisis Contacts to help your care receiver obtain professional care.

To help people receive the care they need in these situations, you need an awareness of the basic facts about suicide, the risk factors and signs to watch for, and the steps to take if you believe someone is considering suicide. It's unlikely you'll have a care receiver who becomes suicidal, but a solid understanding of this topic is essential so you can help your care receiver get the necessary care if such a situation arises.

Suicide Information: A True/False Questionnaire

This questionnaire is designed to help you assess your knowledge about suicide and learn key facts to serve as background for this module. Read through the following statements and mark each one true or false. The answers are on pages 320–322.

---

1 For this module, the term *suicide risk* is used to mean "the current danger that a person will attempt suicide." Suicide risk is a determination, to the best of your ability, of the likelihood that a particular person will try to end his or her own life at a particular moment in time.

1. Depression, mental disorders, and substance use disorders are three of the most common suicide risk factors.

    True False

2. People may turn to suicide because it seems like the only way to stop intense physical pain.

    True False

3. Sometimes people decide to die by suicide because they feel like a burden on others.

   True False

4. People may turn to suicide because it seems the only way to stop unbearable emotional pain.

    True False

5. Most people who die by suicide haven't really thought through their decision or plan.

   True False

6. Once a person begins having suicidal thoughts, he or she will always be suicidal.

   True False

7. People thinking about suicide never provide clues as to their thoughts and intentions.

   True False

8. Someone who attempted suicide in the past but survived is at a lower risk of attempting suicide again.

   True False

9. If a person jokes about suicide, it's not a cause for concern.

True (False)

10. If a person has been depressed or in severe emotional pain but suddenly becomes calm or upbeat, he or she has probably gotten better.

True (False)

11. Once a person has decided to attempt suicide, nothing can change his or her mind.

True (False)

12. Someone who's part of a demographic group that is statistically at a lower risk for suicide won't attempt suicide.

True (False)

13. Drug overdose is the most common method of suicide.

True (False)

14. Most people who die by suicide leave a note.

True (False)

15. If you think someone may be contemplating suicide but you aren't sure, it's best not to bring it up because that might encourage the person to attempt suicide.

True (False)

16. If you tell a person thinking about suicide that you don't want him or her to die, that will only upset the person and make him or her more likely to go through with it.

(True) False

17. Asking a person about his or her suicide plan will make him or her more likely to go through with it.

True (False)

18. If you believe someone is at immediate risk of suicide, you should not leave the person alone.

(True) False

19. Due to confidentiality, you should not tell anyone when you believe a care receiver might be considering suicide.

True (False)

20. A mental health professional's care is essential for helping a person who is having suicidal thoughts or exhibiting suicidal behavior.

(True) False

21. A Stephen Minister must always refer a care receiver to a mental health professional if the care receiver is struggling with suicidal thoughts.

(True) False

22. Stephen Ministers should be 100-percent certain that a care receiver is suicidal before acting to get him or her professional help.

True (False)

Suicide Information: Answers to the True/False Questionnaire

1. **Depression, mental disorders, and substance use disorders are three of the most common suicide risk factors.**

   True. Although there are many possible risk factors for suicide, these three are among the most frequent.

2. **People may turn to suicide because it seems like the only way to stop intense physical pain.**

   True. When people find the intensity of their physical pain intolerable and see no hope of it ending, they may turn to suicide.

3. **Sometimes people decide to die by suicide because they feel like a burden on others.**

   True. Among the possible causes for suicidal impulses are feelings of worthlessness and of being a burden.

4. **People may turn to suicide because it seems the only way to stop unbearable emotional pain.**

   True. People who attempt suicide often do so because they're suffering from extreme feelings of hopelessness, helplessness, or worthlessness.

5. **Most people who die by suicide haven't really thought through their decision or plan.**

   False. Although some suicides occur without prior consideration, the vast majority take place after a long period of internal struggle with the decision.

6. **Once a person begins having suicidal thoughts, he or she will always be suicidal.**

   False. Although suicidal urges may be intense, they typically come and go in waves, fading after an initial impulse.

7. **People thinking about suicide never provide clues as to their thoughts and intentions.**

   False. The majority of individuals considering suicide provide some indication through direct or indirect statements, uncharacteristic actions, or other signs.

8. **Someone who attempted suicide in the past but survived is at a lower risk of attempting suicide again.**

   False. A previous suicide attempt is a risk factor that indicates a person may be more likely to attempt suicide in the future.

9. **If a person jokes about suicide, it's not a cause for concern.**

   False. Any mention of suicide, even one seemingly intended to be humorous, is a cause for concern as it may be a sign that a person is considering suicide.

10. **If a person has been depressed or in severe emotional pain but suddenly becomes calm or upbeat, he or she has probably gotten better.**

    False. A sudden improvement in mood, particularly a dramatic change, may be a sign that a person has decided to end his or her life and is no longer struggling with the issue.

11. **Once a person has decided to attempt suicide, nothing can change his or her mind.**

    False. Almost all those who are suicidal experience a conflict between their desire to live and the impulse to die, so a decision to attempt suicide is not absolute. The key to helping them is to stay with the person or remain on the phone with them until they are connected with professional help.

12. **Someone who's part of a demographic group that is statistically at a lower risk for suicide won't attempt suicide.**

    False. Although some demographic groups may statistically be at higher risk than others, anyone can be at risk for suicide depending on the situation.

13. **Drug overdose is the most common method of suicide.**

    False. Firearms are the most common method of suicide.

14. **Most people who die by suicide leave a note.**

    False. The majority of those who die by suicide do not leave a note.

15. **If you think someone may be contemplating suicide but you aren't sure, it's best not to bring it up because that might encourage the person to attempt suicide.**

    False. Bringing up the issue of suicide is not enough to make someone decide to attempt suicide. In fact, by addressing the topic, you provide an important opportunity for the person to talk about any difficult feelings.

16. **If you tell a person thinking about suicide that you don't want him or her to die, that will only upset the person and make him or her more likely to go through with it.**

    False. By conveying to a person who is thinking about suicide that you want him or her to live, you communicate your care for him or her and may be able to connect with the person's own desire to live. This can help alleviate a person's immediate suicidal impulses long enough to help him or her get professional care.

17. **Asking a person about his or her suicide plan will make him or her more likely to go through with it.**

    False. Giving a person a chance to talk about suicidal feelings and plans can help alleviate his or her immediate suicidal impulses and open the door to professional help.

18. **If you believe someone is at immediate risk of suicide, you should not leave the person alone.**

    True. It's much less likely that a person will attempt suicide when someone else is present, so it's important to stay with the care receiver at least until professional help arrives. A Stephen Minister's presence can be a critical factor in preventing a suicide.

19. **Due to confidentiality, you should not tell anyone when you believe a care receiver might be considering suicide.**

    False. If a Stephen Minister thinks a care receiver may harm him- or herself, safety supersedes strict confidentiality, and the Stephen Minister needs to widen the circle of confidentiality (as described in module 9) in order to get the person the help he or she needs.

20. **A mental health professional's care is essential for helping a person who is having suicidal thoughts or exhibiting suicidal behavior.**

   True. Because of the complex factors and risks involved, a person thinking about suicide needs professional care.

21. **A Stephen Minister must always refer a care receiver to a mental health professional if the care receiver is struggling with suicidal thoughts.**

   True. Because a Stephen Minister is not equipped to be the primary caregiver for a person who may be at risk for suicide, he or she needs to work with the Stephen Ministry Crisis Contacts to connect the care receiver with a trained professional. If the situation seems urgent, the Stephen Minister needs to contact emergency services first, followed by the Stephen Ministry Crisis Contacts.

22. **Stephen Ministers should be 100-percent certain that a care receiver is suicidal before acting to get him or her professional help.**

   False. Stephen Ministers should connect care receivers with the appropriate professional caregivers if they believe there may be any risk of suicide, even if they aren't certain.

How to Help Persons Considering Suicide Get Help

The best way Stephen Ministers can help those considering suicide is by being aware of the realities of suicide, knowing how to recognize thoughts and behaviors that may indicate someone is considering suicide, and then helping connect the care receiver with professional help.

Understanding the Realities of Suicide

Over one million people attempt suicide every year in the U.S.[2] Although different risk factors and life situations can make some individuals more likely to die by suicide, suicide is by no means limited to particular demographics.

Suicide is one of the top ten causes of death in most age groups, as well as across nearly every ethnicity.[3] The highest suicide rate for men is among those over the age of 65, while for women it's between the ages of 45 and 64.[4] Firearms are the most common means of suicide, followed by suffocation and poisoning, which may include drug overdose or ingesting harmful substances.

Although statistics like these can help us understand general risks, a Stephen Minister's responsibility is to care for a specific individual, and everyone's situation is unique.

---

2 "Suicide," National Institute of Mental Health, accessed December 11, 2017, https://www.nimh.nih.gov/health/statistics/suicide.

3 "Deaths, percent of total deaths, and death rates for the 15 leading causes of death in 5-year age groups, by race and Hispanic origin, and sex: United States, 2016," Centers for Disease Control and Prevention, accessed November 9, 2018, https://www.cdc.gov/nchs/data/dvs/LCWK/LCWK1_hr_2016.pdf.

4 "Suicide," National Institute of Mental Health, accessed December 11, 2017, https://www.nimh.nih.gov/health/statistics/suicide.

You'll need to be alert to any signs suggesting your care receiver is thinking about suicide, regardless of his or her demographic groups.

How to Recognize Suicide Risk Factors and Signs of Suicidal Ideation

Recognizing when a care receiver may be at risk for suicide is the critical first step in getting him or her the necessary help. To facilitate this recognition, there are two key areas to be knowledgeable about: *suicide risk factors* and signs of *suicidal ideation.*

Focus Notes B and C provide definitions for these two important terms.

FOCUS NOTE B

Definition of Suicide Risk Factors

Suicide risk factors are circumstances that increase the possibility that a person may become suicidal.

FOCUS NOTE C

Definition of Suicidal Ideation

Suicidal ideation is defined as "thoughts of engaging in suicide-related behavior."[5] It can refer to a wide range of suicidal thoughts, from fleeting consideration to active preparation for suicide. Signs of suicidal ideation may include verbal statements as well as certain behaviors, activities, or actions.

Being aware of risk factors and signs of suicidal ideation will help you to recognize when your care receiver is at risk of suicide and respond effectively.

Risk Factors That Make Suicide More Likely

Several risk factors indicate when people are more likely than the general population to become suicidal. Although no risk factor can predict with absolute certainty that someone will attempt suicide, a Stephen Minister caring for a person with one or more of these factors should be alert for signs that the care receiver may be having suicidal thoughts.

Risk Factor: Depression

Depression, particularly severe depression, is one of the biggest risk factors for suicide. Review pages 287 to 315 from "Caring for Those with Depression: The Stephen Minister's Role" in your *Stephen Minister Training Manual* for signs of depression.

Risk Factor: Mental Disorders

Some mental disorders, such as bipolar disorder and schizophrenia, substantially increase the risk of suicide. This is one reason why Stephen Ministers are not assigned to people known to have a mental disorder—and why, when a care receiver is identified as having a mental disorder and referred to a mental health professional, the Stephen Minister needs to receive approval from that professional in order to continue providing care.[6]

---

5 Alex E. Crosby, LaVonne Ortega, and Cindi Melanson, *Self-Directed Violence Surveillance: Uniform Definitions and Recommended Data Elements,* Version 1.0 (Atlanta: Centers for Disease Control and Prevention, National Center for Injury Prevention and Control, 2011), p. 90, accessed November 14, 2019, https://www.cdc.gov/violenceprevention/pdf/Self-Directed-Violence-a.pdf.

6 For more on referring Stephen Ministry care receivers to mental health professionals, see *When and How to Use Mental Health Resources: A Stephen Ministry Guide.*

Risk Factor: Substance Use

People who use alcohol or other substances are at increased risk of suicide for a number of reasons.

- Those under the influence of alcohol or other substances have lowered inhibitions and are thus more likely to attempt suicide. Suicide is the leading cause of death for people who struggle with substance use disorders, and alcohol is present in 30 to 40 percent of attempts.[7]

- People often turn to alcohol or other substances to avoid facing painful realities. If this defensive measure stops working, the additional stress and feelings such as helplessness and hopelessness can increase the risk of suicide.

- Substance use disorders can have a destructive impact on a person's relationships, livelihood, and self-esteem. A person may be at increased risk of suicide if he or she comes to believe that, as a result of substance use, he or she has nothing left to live for.

As with severe depression and mental disorders, Stephen Ministers are not equipped to handle issues related to substance use. If you learn that your care receiver is struggling with substance use, consult with your Community Resource Contacts about connecting your care receiver with professional help.

Risk Factor: Few or No Significant Relationships

People who have few or no significant relationships are at a higher risk for suicide. Strong relationships can serve as an emotional anchor that gives a hurting person a reason to stay alive. When someone feels alone and doesn't have others to serve as an outlet for painful feelings or to offer a positive reason to live, he or she is less likely to cope effectively with emotional or physical pain. A lack of close relationships also increases the risk that signs of suicidal ideation will go unnoticed.

Risk Factor: Intense Emotional Pain

Dr. Edwin S. Shneidman, a pioneer in the field of suicide prevention and the founder of the American Association of Suicidology, described the pain that drives people to suicide as *psychache*, "the hurt, anguish, or ache that takes hold in the mind. . . . the pain of excessively felt shame, guilt, fear, anxiety, loneliness, angst, dread of growing old or of dying badly."[8] For those who have become suicidal, their emotional pain has become so intensely felt that it harms their mental state, leaving them unable to perceive any way out other than death.

Risk Factor: Intense Physical Pain

A person experiencing great physical pain, such as chronic pain or a condition where pain management methods are not working, may be at increased risk of suicide. As with emotional pain, when someone cannot see an end to physical pain or perceives that there's no hope for improvement, death may seem like the only solution.

---

7 Craig Love, Laurie Davidson, and Maria Valenti, "Understanding the Connection Between Suicide and Substance Abuse: What the Research Tells Us," Substance Abuse and Mental Health Services Administration, accessed December 11, 2017, https://www.samhsa.gov/capt/sites/default/files/resources/suicide-substance-abuse-research.pdf.

8 Edwin S. Shneidman, *The Suicidal Mind* (Oxford: Oxford University Press, 1996), p. 13.

Risk Factor: Previous Suicide Attempts

People who have previously attempted suicide are at a higher risk to try again—the more recent the attempt and the larger the number of previous attempts, the greater the risk. Even if a person attempted suicide many years ago, that previous attempt is still a risk factor.

Risk Factor: Family History of Suicide

People with family members who have died by suicide are at greater risk of dying by suicide themselves. In combination with other risk factors, a loved one's suicide can open the door to suicide for other family members as a way of dealing with pain.

Risk Factor: Recent Major Loss

Usually, a major loss—such as the death of a loved one or close friend, a divorce, job loss, diagnosis of a terminal illness, or some other major negative life event—does not in itself lead people to consider suicide. When combined with other risk factors, however, such a loss may put a person at greater risk. When caring for a person who has suffered a major loss, Stephen Ministers should be alert for other risk factors that may compound a care receiver's grief and increase the chances of suicidal thoughts.

Risk Factor: Extreme Stress

As with a recent major loss, extreme stress may not lead to suicidal thoughts on its own. Because it often reduces people's ability to cope with life difficulties, however, it can increase the risk of suicide when other risk factors are present.

STEPHEN MINISTER INSIGHT

"Before training, my biggest concern about being a Stephen Minister was the possibility that my care receiver would have suicidal thoughts. Now, having been through training and served as a Stephen Minister, I'm reassured that I'm equipped to spot the signs and know what to do."

Signs That May Indicate Suicidal Ideation

There are a number of common signs of suicidal ideation—thoughts of engaging in suicide-related behavior. Even one of these signs is cause for concern, so Stephen Ministers should take it seriously if a care receiver shows any sign of suicidal ideation.

Sign: Clear Expression of Suicidal Thoughts or Intentions

A care receiver who clearly expresses suicidal thoughts is at risk for suicide. This includes someone explicitly talking about killing him- or herself, "ending it all," or making similar statements. Even if the care receiver later downplays such statements as sarcasm or jokes, those original comments should be taken very seriously.

Sign: Feelings of Hopelessness, Helplessness, or Worthlessness

Rather than talk about suicide directly, a care receiver may make statements about feeling hopeless, possibly implying that he or she is despairing over personal circumstances or no longer has a reason to live. Statements of helplessness, such as talking about being unable to affect a situation or make changes, are another sign. In addition, a person considering suicide may share feelings of worthlessness, being a burden on others, extremely low self-esteem, or self-hatred.

Sign: Statements about Death

A care receiver who is contemplating suicide might share thoughts and feelings about death. If your care receiver talks about death often or makes statements like "I wish I could just die," or "The pain would go away if I was dead," it's important to ask directly whether he or she is contemplating suicide. Statements like these can be strong clues that a person is thinking about suicide but is reluctant to openly say so.

Sign: Sudden Improvement of Mood

A care receiver who is considering suicide may suddenly become calm and happy when he or she was previously depressed, extremely anxious, or stressed. When the change of mood occurs abruptly or without any clear reason, rather than after a gradual healing process, it's a critical warning sign that may indicate that the person has made up his or her mind to die by suicide. Having made the decision, the care receiver's emotional struggles and internal conflict may lessen in anticipation of an end to the pain.

Sign: Decreased Coping Ability

If a care receiver previously was able to deal with problems in healthy ways but begins to display signs of reduced coping ability—such as anxiety, disorganized functioning, withdrawal, or turning to self-destructive behaviors like excessive substance use—he or she may be at risk for suicide. As a person's capacity to cope in constructive, healthy ways decreases, the possibility increases that he or she may consider suicide as an alternative coping mechanism.

Sign: Putting Affairs in Order

Care receivers getting ready to take their own life may make efforts to get their affairs in order. They might create or update their will, pay off debts, inform others about the location of important papers, tell loved ones what they want to happen after they die, make arrangements with a funeral home, or write their own funeral service. They may also visit loved ones to say goodbye and attempt to repair relationships with others or with God. Of course, there are good reasons anyone might put affairs in order, but in combination with other signs and risk factors, these efforts may indicate an increased risk of suicide.

Sign: Giving Away Prized Possessions

Although not as frequent as other signs, giving away important possessions can be a very strong indication that a care receiver is considering suicide. This sign is especially serious when coupled with statements that imply the person doesn't need the items anymore or won't be around to appreciate them for much longer.

Steps to Take If You Believe Your Care Receiver May Be Considering Suicide

If you believe your care receiver may be thinking about suicide, your role as a Stephen Minister is to bring up the topic of suicide with your care receiver and determine, to the best of your ability, the immediate danger to the person.

Focus Note D shows the process to identify how high the risk is for your care receiver and how you should respond. Rely on these steps as a guide until the care receiver is safe.

FOCUS NOTE D

Six Steps for Responding to a Care Receiver Who May Be Considering Suicide

1. Take any sign of suicidal ideation seriously.

2. Ask, "Are you considering suicide?"

3. Ask about a plan.

4. Determine the level of suicide risk.

5. Convey that you want the person to stay alive.

6. Help connect the person to the care he or she needs.

Step 1: Take Any Sign of Suicidal Ideation Seriously

It's essential that you respond quickly, assertively, and seriously if your care receiver displays any of the signs described in this Pre-Class Reading. Focus Note E lists some reasons people might be tempted to dismiss signs they notice or not respond to them.

FOCUS NOTE E

Why People Might Miss Signs of Suicidal Ideation

1. Personal anxiety or fear about the topic of suicide or dealing with a person who is suicidal

2. Denial that the individual could really be considering suicide

3. Fear of offending the individual by asking about suicide

4. Previous signs, in the individual or others, that turned out to be false alarms

5. Lack of familiarity with the signs of suicidal ideation

Because suicide is a life-and-death matter, it's essential not to allow these reasons or any other to prevent you from taking any possible signs seriously. If a care receiver is not thinking about suicide, no harm is done by exploring the topic to make sure. But if a care receiver is thinking about suicide, bringing it up may very well save his or her life.

Step 2: Ask, "Are You Considering Suicide?"

If you see a sign of suicidal ideation in your care receiver, assertively ask whether he or she is considering suicide. The best way is to ask simply and gently, *"Are you considering suicide?"* or *"Have you been thinking about suicide?"*

When you ask a direct, closed-ended question like this, the care receiver can respond with either a *yes* or *no*. Your assertiveness makes it less likely that the care receiver will give an ambiguous or evasive answer. You don't need to feel bad about your directness;

being very clear with your question expresses great care for the care receiver's well-being.

If the answer turns out to be no, there's no need to apologize. Instead, simply let your care receiver know that you asked because you care for and are concerned about him or her. You may want to confirm again that the answer really is no, especially if the care receiver's answer seems unconvincing or uncertain. Focus Note F gives an example of what you might say.

FOCUS NOTE F

Responding When a Care Receiver Says He or She Is Not Considering Suicide

"That's good to hear. The reason I asked is that I care about you and want to make sure you're safe. When you said [what the person said], I wondered whether you'd been thinking about suicide, and if you have been, I thought it would be good for us to talk about it. Since I care about you, I want to be very sure—are you thinking at all about suicide?"

If the answer is still no, then resume your conversation. Continue, however, to be alert for any signs of suicidal ideation, and ask about them as necessary in the future.

If your care receiver's answer is yes or maybe, move to the next step.

Step 3: Ask About a Plan

Ask your care receiver whether he or she has a plan for suicide, and then learn as many details about it as you can. In most cases, the care receiver will be willing to talk, but with some people you may need to be persistent in asking questions.

As you ask questions, consider three factors: *specificity, lethality,* and *availability.* The more specific the plan, the more lethal the method, and the more readily available the means or opportunity for carrying the plan out, the higher the level of risk. For example, someone who has only thought about "possibly getting some pills" is at a lower level of risk than someone who has a firearm in the house and has decided to shoot him- or herself in a nearby wooded area while a spouse is out of town in the next week.

Focus Note G lists a number of details to learn about a suicide plan in order to determine the risk level of a care receiver.

FOCUS NOTE G

Details to Learn about a Suicide Plan

1. Does the person have a plan?

Ask something like, **"How have you been thinking you would end your life?"** to gauge how serious the person is. If the answer is something like, "I don't know; I haven't really thought that much about it," then the immediate risk of suicide is lower. On the other hand, if the person answers with a concrete plan, he or she is most likely at moderate or high risk.

2. How specific is the plan?

If the person may have a plan but hasn't shared many details, say something like, **"Tell me more about your plan."** Ask follow-up questions as needed to find out more. The more a person knows about how, when, and where he or she will attempt suicide, the higher the suicide risk.

3. How available are the planned means of suicide?

If you don't already know at this point in the conversation, it's critical to ask, *"Do you have what you would need to carry out your plan?"* A person who has both a plan and available means (pills, a gun, a noose, the ability to drive to a bridge) is at moderate or high risk.

4. Has the person taken any suicide-oriented actions?

Ask something like, *"What kind of preparations have you made for your plan?"* If a person has taken any specific steps toward suicide—for example, buying a gun, saving up sleeping pills, or visiting or mapping out the specific planned location—he or she is at very high risk. In a sense, he or she has already begun the act of suicide.

5. How lethal and fast-acting is the method the person is planning on using?

It's important to ask something like, *"What are you planning to use?"* if you don't already know. Suicide methods vary widely in how lethal they are—how likely they are to result in death. Some methods may also have a period of time between the suicidal act and death, during which the person may be found and helped. The more lethal and the faster-acting the person's planned means are, the higher the suicide risk.

6. Has the person rehearsed the suicide?

Ask, *"Have you practiced your plan?"* The person may tell you, for instance, about driving past the bridge abutment where the planned car crash will take place, or about walking around the top of the building he or she intends to jump from. Someone who has rehearsed a suicide plan has begun the suicidal act and is at extremely high risk.

7. Does the person seem likely to attempt suicide soon?

Find out from the person, *"When are you thinking you might do this?"* Even if the person doesn't share a specific time, pay attention to the language he or she uses when talking about the plan. If the person implies he or she is going to act soon or has picked a time, consider the person to be at high risk. You can also ask how likely the care receiver thinks it is that he or she will take action.

At any point, if you have *any* doubt about a person's level of suicide risk—or even about whether he or she is considering suicide at all—*always err on the side of caution.* Your role as a Stephen Minister is to do what you can to protect and preserve life by helping connect your care receiver with the necessary professional care. From there, the professional caregivers will provide the necessary help and support for the care receiver.

If your care receiver turns out not to be at a high risk, your efforts have still shown great care for him or her, and you can connect him or her with additional help. If, however, your care receiver is indeed at risk of suicide, you very well may have saved a life.

Step 4: Determine the Level of Suicide Risk

Based on the information gathered in the previous step, determine, to the best of your ability, your care receiver's level of suicide risk to help you identify what kind of help you need to connect him or her with. Focus Note H shows three levels of suicide risk. If you are in doubt, consider the person to be at a higher level of risk.

FOCUS NOTE H

Levels of Suicide Risk

Low Risk. The person has had some thoughts about suicide but doesn't appear to have a concrete plan or any intention to attempt suicide.

Moderate Risk. The person is actively considering suicide and has an idea of how he or she might make a suicide attempt, but he or she doesn't have the means to carry out the plan or seem to have any intention to do so in the immediate future.

High Risk. The person has a specific and potentially lethal suicide plan, has the means to do it readily at hand, and seems likely to act on his or her plan soon.

In general, those considering suicide are not constantly on the verge of acting on their suicidal thoughts. Rather, suicidal impulses come in waves, which Edwin Shneidman describes as a process of introspection: "Suicide is the result of an interior dialogue. The mind scans its options; the topic of suicide comes up, the mind rejects it, scans again; there is suicide, it is rejected again, and then finally the mind accepts suicide as a solution, then plans it, and fixes it as the only answer."[9]

Most of the time, the suicidal impulse will fade and the person will be safe for a time until it surfaces again. Someone who is at high risk for attempting suicide has reached the end of this introspection process and is prepared to go through with the act. The role of the caregiver in following these steps is to intervene in the introspection process: to

recognize signs of suicidal ideation and connect the person with professional help.

Step 5: Convey That You Want the Person to Stay Alive

Once you've determined the level of suicide risk to the best of your ability, take some time to communicate to your care receiver that you care and want him or her to stay alive. Even if you believe the risk of suicide is low, caring words like those in Focus Note I can be extremely valuable for the person to hear.

FOCUS NOTE I

Examples of Ways to Say You Want the Care Receiver to Stay Alive

- "I'm here with you, and I care about you."
- "Please know that I want you to live."
- "I want you to know you're not alone. I want to help you through this difficult time."
- "You matter to me. I don't want you to die."

For people contemplating suicide, hearing you say you want them to live can help reduce their immediate suicidal impulses, giving you time to connect them with help.

Step 6: Help Connect the Person to the Care He or She Needs

Finally, help connect your care receiver with the appropriate kind of care for his or her level of immediate risk.

- A person at *high risk* requires help as soon as possible, which involves calling emergency services, followed by your Stephen

---

9 Shneidman, p. 15.

Ministry Crisis Contacts. Stay with the care receiver until the necessary help arrives.

- When a person is at *moderate risk,* the need for care is serious but somewhat less urgent, so it's important to refer him or her to a mental health professional. Ask the care receiver to commit to receiving professional care, and then immediately follow up with your Crisis Contacts to begin the referral process.

- If a care receiver is at *low risk,* you can best help by having him or her promise to call someone—such as you, a trusted family member, or a suicide hotline—if he or she begins to feel suicidal. Also talk with your care receiver about getting professional help. Then, consult with your Crisis Contacts to talk about making a referral. You and your Stephen Leaders can also get consultation from a mental health professional.

During the In-Class Session, you'll learn more about connecting care receivers who are thinking about suicide with the necessary care, and you'll have an opportunity to practice some of these skills.

Helping Those outside Stephen Ministry Who May Be Considering Suicide

Although this module focuses on helping Stephen Ministry care receivers, the concepts and skills you're learning can also be applied when relating to others considering suicide. Over the years, Stephen Ministers have shared how they've used their training to recognize the signs of suicidal ideation in others they know in their personal lives and other ministries—and then how they've connected those people with professional

care. Even if you never need to help a care receiver who is thinking about suicide, you'll be equipped to help any person who may be struggling with suicidal thoughts.

STEPHEN MINISTER INSIGHT

"One day, my son came home from school upset because a friend of his had told him some very disturbing thoughts and feelings. From my Stephen Minister training, I recognized the friend's thoughts as signs that he was suicidal. We immediately went to see his parents, and we were able to get him the help he needed. My Stephen Minister training helped save that boy's life."

Getting Ready for the In-Class Session

Before the In-Class Session, review "How to Recognize Suicide Risk Factors and Signs of Suicidal Ideation" on pages 323–326 of this Pre-Class Reading and become familiar with keys to determining suicide risk.

stephenministries.org/library

See the ***Stephen Minister Online Library*** for additional resources and downloads related to this Stephen Minister training topic.

Understanding Suicide: How to Help People Get the Care They Need

Module 14 | Presentation Outline

For I am convinced that neither death nor life, neither angels nor demons, neither the present nor the future, nor any powers, neither height nor depth, nor anything else in all creation, will be able to separate us from the love of God that is in Christ Jesus our Lord.
Romans 8:38–39

 Devotion: Nothing Can Separate Us

I. Determining the Risk of Suicide

FOCUS NOTE 1

Levels of Suicide Risk

Low Risk. The person has had some thoughts about suicide but doesn't appear to have a concrete plan or any intention to attempt suicide.

Moderate Risk. The person is actively considering suicide and has an idea of how he or she might make a suicide attempt, but he or she doesn't have the means to carry out the plan or seem to have any intention to do so in the immediate future.

High Risk. The person has a specific and potentially lethal suicide plan, has the means to do it readily at hand, and seems likely to act on his or her plan soon.

FOCUS NOTE 2

Summary of Pre-Class Reading on Determining Suicide Risk

Suicide Risk Factors:

- Depression
- Mental disorders
- Substance use
- Few or no significant relationships
- Intense emotional pain
- Intense physical pain
- Previous suicide attempts
- Family history of suicide
- Recent major loss
- Extreme stress

Signs of Possible Suicidal Ideation:

- Clear expression of suicidal thoughts or intentions
- Feelings of hopelessness, helplessness, or worthlessness
- Statements about death
- Sudden improvement of mood
- Decreased coping ability
- Putting affairs in order
- Giving away prized possessions

Three Factors to Consider about a Person's Suicide Plan in Order to Help Determine Risk:

- Specificity of the person's plan
- Lethality of the planned method of suicide
- Availability of the means or opportunity for the planned method of suicide

FOCUS NOTE 3

Care Receiver Situation A

For the last three months, you've been caring for Ms. A, a 35-year-old woman who has been divorced for about two years. At your most recent visit, she shared that she's been feeling very alone lately. She has some close friends she talks with, but they haven't been able to spend much time with her in the past few months. Ms. A suffers from a chronic spinal condition that interferes with her movement and causes her severe physical pain. Because of this condition, she is in frequent contact with her physician, with whom she has a good relationship.

One day, Ms. A calls you on the phone and tells you that she's considering suicide. She confides that after her husband left her, she had made a suicide attempt. Ms. A now says she's planning to cut her wrists and has a knife beside her. She has written a suicide note.

What factors point to a lower suicide risk?

FEW RELATIONSHIP
RECENT MAJOR loss
DECREASED coping ability

What factors point to a higher suicide risk?

INTENSE physical pain — Attempting suicide
Ch INTENSE EMOTIONAL pain
Clear expression of suicide thoughts or intentions

IMMEDIATE HELP NEEDED
— WHERE ARE YOU AT?

Your determination (circle a word): (High) Moderate Low

FOCUS NOTE 4

Care Receiver Situation B

Mrs. B is 32 years old and sounds very tired and hopeless today. Born and raised in another country, she moved here with her spouse six years ago and has been adjusting ever since. She says that her spouse recently started a new job and has had very little time to spend with her. She feels worthless and abandoned but has been unable to talk with her spouse about the problems. She has been able to open up to a few close friends about her struggles.

During this caring visit, Mrs. B confides in you that about three weeks ago she took an overdose of tranquilizers, but the dose was not lethal. Her spouse discovered the empty bottle and has since removed every pill from the house. When you ask Mrs. B whether she has plans for another attempt, she says she doesn't know how she would do it.

What factors point to a lower suicide risk?

Worthness, depressed, few relationship

What factors point to a higher suicide risk?

Decreased increased emotional pain
Clear expression of suicidal thoughts or intenses.
Attampting suicide

Your determination (circle a word): (High)   Moderate   Low

FOCUS NOTE 5

Care Receiver Situation C

Mr. C is 66 years old and suffers from heart disease. He's lived alone since his wife took her own life about a year and a half ago. Thanks to the comfort and support of his family and friends, Mr. C was able to cope in the months after her funeral. But, as time went on, and as family and friends seemed to be going on with their normal lives, Mr. C began to feel depressed. In the last six months, he has only had occasional contact with any of them. He says that he's feeling increasingly isolated and growing more and more depressed.

During your caring visit last week, Mr. C shared that he thinks often of the release of death. He believes his life is absolutely hopeless—he expects to be dead soon anyway with his heart condition, and he's convinced that continuing to live will only prolong the agony. At the time, you strongly encouraged him to meet with a mental health professional, and he agreed to do that. You then called him the next day to provide a few contacts, which he thanked you for.

During your visit this week, Mr. C shares that he's been stockpiling painkillers and is sure he has a lethal dose available in his medicine cabinet. Every other time you have visited him, he's seemed sad and dejected, but at this visit he seems calm and even hopeful, even though he hasn't met with the mental health professional yet.

What factors point to a lower suicide risk?

Depression
Few Relationship
Isolation

What factors point to a higher suicide risk?

Suicide by spouse
Thought of Death because of heart condition
Immediate things in house to use to commit suicide (pain pills)
Sad, then Better mood

Your determination (circle a word): (High) Moderate Low

FOCUS NOTE 6

Care Receiver Situation D

After working for the same company for 35 years, Mrs. D was forced to retire at 62, which is why she began seeing a Stephen Minister. She lost her husband about ten years ago. During your caring visits, she's talked about feeling like she's no longer needed. The circumstances and inactivity of her retirement have really bothered her; she's uncertain what to do with her life.

During today's visit, Mrs. D mentions that the idea of suicide has briefly crossed her mind once or twice in the past week. When you ask more about it, she says she has no plans and has never seriously considered suicide. She adds that she's talked to her physician and her pastor about her emotional struggles, although her suicidal thoughts are more recent so she hasn't mentioned them yet. Both her physician and pastor have made helpful suggestions and comments, but she just can't seem to act on their ideas. Her children want to help too, but they have no idea how because they've never seen their mother struggle like this before.

What factors point to a lower suicide risk?

WORTHINESS, Etc.
Forced to retire
Depressed

What factors point to a higher suicide risk?

Suicidal indetions

Your determination (circle a word):   High   Moderate   Low

FOCUS NOTE 7

Care Receiver Situation E

Mr. E hasn't been feeling like himself lately. For several months, he's been telling you he's had increased difficulty sleeping, often waking up in the middle of the night and being unable to get back to sleep. His appetite isn't what it used to be, and he has lost about 20 pounds. At work, he puts off making important decisions because he struggles to make up his mind. When he gets home, he's so tired that he just sits and watches TV.

Lately, Mr. E has begun to consider himself a failure and wonder whether life is worth living. Although his wife and best friend have been supportive, he can't stop thinking about mistakes he made in his past and about how little he has accomplished. During your visit, he casually mentions to you that the thought of suicide has popped into his mind recently. When you ask whether he's planning suicide, Mr. E says he hasn't gotten beyond just thinking about the possibility.

What factors point to a lower suicide risk?

DEPRESSED worthless, etc.

What factors point to a higher suicide risk?

Suicidal Indention

Your determination (circle a word):   High   Moderate   (Low)

II. Steps to Take If You Believe Your Care Receiver May Be Considering Suicide

Six Steps for Responding to a Care Receiver Who May Be Considering Suicide

1. Take any sign of suicidal ideation seriously.
2. Ask, "Are you considering suicide?"
3. Ask about a plan.
4. Determine the level of suicide risk.
5. Convey that you want the person to stay alive.
6. Help connect the person to the care he or she needs.

Step 1: Take Any Sign of Suicidal Ideation Seriously

Expressions of Possible Suicidal Ideation

- "I'm going to kill myself."
- "All my problems will be over soon."
- "My family will be better off without me."
- "Life has lost all meaning for me."
- "I've decided it's time to update my will."
- "I hate to face each day more and more."
- "What does God think of people who take their own life?"
- "I'm no good to anyone."
- "I keep thinking about how much easier it would be if I were dead."
- "I just can't go on like this anymore."

Step 2: Ask, "Are You Considering Suicide?"

FOCUS NOTE 10

Asking Whether a Care Receiver Is Considering Suicide

- "I'm worried about what you said. Are you considering suicide?"
- "Have you been thinking about suicide?"

Step 3: Ask about a Plan

FOCUS NOTE 11

Asking about a Plan

"How have you been thinking you would end your life?"

Step 4: Determine the Level of Suicide Risk

Step 5: Convey That You Want the Person to Stay Alive

FOCUS NOTE 12

Examples of Ways to Say You Want the Care Receiver to Stay Alive

- "I'm here with you, and I care about you."
- "Please know that I want you to live."
- "I want you to know you're not alone. I want to help you through this difficult time."
- "You matter to me. I don't want you to die."

Step 6: Help Connect the Person to the Care He or She Needs

FOCUS NOTE 13

Flowchart from Confidentiality Module

1 **Encourage** the care receiver to make the contact. ✓ - Care Receiver **AGREES** ┈┈┈┐

✗

Care Receiver ┊ **DECLINES**

2 **Suggest that _you_** make the contact for the care receiver. ✓ ┈ Care Receiver **AGREES** ┈┈→ Confidentiality remains intact as the care receiver agrees to contact those who can provide the necessary help.

✗

Care Receiver ┊ **DECLINES**

3 **Say you _will_ make the contact** out of care and concern for the care receiver. ✓ - Care Receiver **AGREES** ┈┈┈┘

✗

Care Receiver ┊ **DECLINES**

4 **Make the contact** without the care receiver's permission. Confidentiality remains intact— the circle of confidentiality has been widened slightly to include others who can provide the necessary help.

(See the Pre-Class Reading for module 9, "Confidentiality," for more detailed information on these steps.)

III. Skill Practice: Helping Persons Considering Suicide Get the Help They Need

Skill Practice 1

FOCUS NOTE 18

Stephen Minister's Situation Description for Skill Practice 1

You have been caring for your care receiver for several months as he or she recovers from hip surgery. Your care receiver has just found out that he or she is in the early stages of Alzheimer's. You are visiting a couple of days after he or she received the diagnosis.

The care receiver will begin the skill practice.

Review Focus Note 8 on page 340, "Six Steps for Responding to a Care Receiver Who May Be Considering Suicide," while the others in your group finish reading their Focus Notes.

FOCUS NOTE 19

Care Receiver's Situation Description for Skill Practice 1

You have been meeting with your Stephen Minister for several months while you recover from hip surgery. You've been recovering well, but a few days ago you learned that you are in the early stages of Alzheimer's. Your physician has told you that some medications can lessen symptoms for a time—but indicated that it's time for you and your family to begin making plans for the future.

The diagnosis has left you shocked, frightened, and overwhelmed. You've found yourself thinking it might be better to just go ahead and kill yourself and not put yourself and your family through years of dealing with your Alzheimer's. You don't want your family to have to bear the burden of caring for you and watching you degenerate over the coming years, and you don't want to have to endure the humiliation of experiencing it. Although you aren't sure you have the courage to kill yourself, you aren't sure you have the courage to go through this disease either.

The thought of suicide frightens you almost as much as Alzheimer's does. You don't have any plans to end your life at this time, but you've been surprised and scared by how much thoughts of suicide have occupied your mind since you received the diagnosis. You want to talk to your Stephen Minister about these thoughts and feelings. You are meeting with your Stephen Minister a couple of days after receiving the news about your diagnosis.

Begin the skill practice by saying, "I'm so scared that I can't think straight." Then tell your Stephen Minister about your Alzheimer's diagnosis, your worries about your family having to take care of you, and finally your thoughts about suicide. If your Stephen Minister suggests that you get help for your suicidal thoughts, resist the suggestion at first by saying it is unnecessary, but eventually give in and agree.

FOCUS NOTE 20

Discussion Questions for the Skill Practices

• What level of suicide risk did the Stephen Minister determine the care receiver as having? Does everyone else in your group agree?

• Was the Stephen Minister's response appropriate to the level of risk?

• How did the care receiver feel about the care the Stephen Minister provided?

• What might the Stephen Minister do differently next time?

Skill Practice 2

Stephen Minister's Situation Description for Skill Practice 2

Your care receiver's spouse died about two and a half years ago. You've been concerned because he or she seems to be stuck in grief and unable to adjust.

When you begin this caring visit, you notice that your care receiver looks much more tired and unhappy than usual. You're wondering what has happened since the last time you met.

Your care receiver will begin the skill practice.

Review Focus Note 8 on page 340, "Six Steps for Responding to a Care Receiver Who May Be Considering Suicide," while the others in your group finish reading their Focus Notes.

Care Receiver's Situation Description for Skill Practice 2

You've been under extreme stress recently. You're a single parent and the sole provider for your three children. Your spouse died two and a half years ago, leaving you to care for yourself and your family without any outside means of help or support.

Yesterday, your oldest child was suspended for getting into a fight and injuring another student. Up until now, you weren't aware of any aggressive behavior on your child's part, and you wonder how you missed that.

You've been feeling very sad for months and have only been able to sleep a few hours a night, which leaves you feeling exhausted. You thought you were putting up with as much unhappiness as you could handle before this latest crisis.

You've been thinking that one way out would be to end your life. You've thought about methods that would look like an accident, since you don't want your children to live with the stigma of having a parent who died by suicide. You rationalize that your children would be better off being raised by your sister and her husband, who have a stable home and are financially well off.

Begin the skill practice by telling your Stephen Minister what has happened recently in your life. Say you don't know what you are going to do. After talking for a minute or two, hint at suicide by saying something like, "The only time I feel any peace is when I imagine moving on to the next life, where my trouble will be behind me." If your Stephen Minister asks you if you've thought of suicide, say yes, but indicate that you haven't been able to come up with a definite plan yet. If your Stephen Minister suggests that you get help, resist at first, saying it won't do any good and you can't afford it. Eventually, however, give in and agree.

Skill Practice 3

FOCUS NOTE 23

Stephen Minister's Situation Description for Skill Practice 3

Your care receiver is an older person who has suffered very painful arthritis for 30 years. The care receiver is unable to care for him- or herself completely, but his or her daughter lives a couple of blocks away and comes over to help every day. Your care receiver has told you about his or her grandchildren at least a hundred times, saying they make life worthwhile.

You're sitting at home watching TV with your spouse when your phone rings. You see that the call is from your care receiver, so you move to another room and answer the phone.

Your care receiver will begin the skill practice.

Review Focus Note 8 on page 340, "Six Steps for Responding to a Care Receiver Who May Be Considering Suicide," while the others in your group finish reading their Focus Notes.

FOCUS NOTE 24

Care Receiver's Situation Description for Skill Practice 3

You've suffered from arthritis for the past 30 years, which has made it difficult and painful to use your hands. The medication you've taken for years has left you with ulcers, so you also suffer regular heartburn and stomach pain and cannot eat the foods you used to enjoy.

Your daughter has helped you stay in your own home. She lives two blocks away, and you spend time with her every day. Her two children are your greatest pleasure. They come over to see you most afternoons after school. You've said that they keep you going and keep you young.

An hour ago, you found out that your daughter and her children were killed in a car accident. You're distraught, unable to imagine life without your daughter and grandchildren.

You have a bottle of sleeping pills on the nightstand. You're calling your Stephen Minister to say goodbye before you kill yourself.

Begin the skill practice by telling your Stephen Minister what has happened to your daughter and grandchildren. Then say something like, "I can't imagine living without them. I just called to thank you for all your care and say goodbye." If your Stephen Minister asks about your plans, be very forthcoming. If your Stephen Minister asks you to change your plans and get help, say you appreciate his or her concern but you can't imagine anything that could help you at this point.

IV. Caregiver's Compass Review

Write your ideas around the compass.

COMPASSIONATE · FULL OF FAITH · SKILLED · TRUSTWORTHY ·
℗
®

V. Looking Ahead